I0528450

www.ingramcontent.com/pod-product-compliance
Lightning Source LLC
Chambersburg PA
CBHW051326120626
46547CB00015B/2410

עזרה ונחמיה

THE
ISRAEL
BIBLE

EZRA AND NEHEMIAH

EDITED BY

Rabbi Tuly Weisz

ISRAEL
365

The Israel Bible: Ezra and Nehemiah

First Edition, 2021

The Israel Bible was produced by Israel365 in cooperation with Teach for Israel and is used with permission from Teach for Israel. All rights reserved. The English translation was adapted by Israel365 from the JPS Tanakh. Copyright © 1985 by the Jewish Publication Society. All rights reserved.

Cover image used under license from Shutterstock.com

ISBN 978-1-957109-44-2

A CIP catalogue record for this title is available from the British Library

The Israel Bible: Ezra and Nehemiah is a holy book that contains the name of God and should be treated with respect.

Table of Contents

Introduction

The Hebrew Bible is commonly known as the *Tanakh* which stands for *Torah* (the Five Books of Moses), *Neviim* (the Prophets) and *Ketuvim* (the Writings). The *Tanakh* consists of 24 books that are considered by Jews to be the word of God. While these books have been referred to as the "Old Testament," many Jews reject this label since it implies the replacement of the Hebrew Bible with something newer and prefer the more authentic Jewish name.

The *Tanakh* is not only the most important book known to man, it is God's word that is perfect and absolute. It is therefore a daunting undertaking to publish an edition of the *Tanakh*, and the responsibilities are awesome. There is no room for error or carelessness in dealing with the eternal word of God. Further, upon embarking on such a serious initiative, we ask ourselves if our efforts are gratuitous. Considering the many editions of the Bible in print, is there truly a need for yet another one?

While there are numerous Bibles in circulation today, its most central aspect – the Land of Israel – has often been overlooked. References to Israel appear on nearly every page, and the city of Jerusalem is specifically referred to hundreds of times throughout the Bible. The essential link between Israel and *Torah* is emphasized repeatedly in verses such as, "For instruction (*Torah*) shall come forth from *Tzion*, the word of *Hashem* from *Yerushalayim*" (Micah 4:2).

The miraculous return of the People of Israel to the Land of Israel in our own generation provides the perfect moment for a new volume to fill this void in biblical literature. *The Israel Bible* includes many special features elucidating God's focus on Israel throughout *Tanakh* and there are many additional, multimedia features available on our website **www.theisraelbible.com**.

Ordering and Presentation – In presenting *The Israel Bible*, our goal is to spread awareness of the biblical significance of the Land of Israel as well as the Jewish people's eternal connection to the land, based on the text of the *Tanakh*, the Hebrew Bible. We aim to honor "the God, the People and the Land of Israel" from an Orthodox Jewish perspective. To that end, *The Israel Bible* follows the traditional Jewish ordering of the books and the customary Hebrew division of chapters. Therefore, for example, we count 24 books of *Tanakh* with *Sefer Divrei Hayamim* (Chronicles) appearing last. It is our hope that our rich content will speak to all Jews and non-Jews who appreciate Israel as the God given land of the Jewish people.

English Translation – Throughout history, Jews have studied the Bible in Hebrew, as any form of translation would miss much of the nuance of the original holy tongue in which *Torah* has been transmitted since the days of Moses. However, as many Jews settled in America in the 19th Century, the need for an English translation became necessary. To be sure, there were already English translations prepared over the centuries by Christians, but in the words of the original editors of the Jewish Publication Society (JPS), "The Jew cannot afford to have his Bible translation prepared for him by others. He cannot have it as a gift, even as he cannot borrow his soul from others."

JPS set out in the late 1800s to publish an authoritative English translation "in the spirit of Jewish tradition." It was compiled over decades by some of the leading Jewish scholars of the time. They formed committees and subcommittees to compare existing English versions, considering medieval and modern Jewish commentators. The monumental JPS translation, originally published in 1917, has been updated in recent years, and *The Israel Bible* is proud to utilize the 1984 New Jewish Publication Society (NJPS) version with its modern, clear language, as well as its wide-ranging acceptance as an accurate and high-quality translation. We applied the NJPS translation verbatim, except for a select list of nouns which we replaced with their traditional Hebrew names. This is true even when we found the NJPS translation to be different than the popular translation of a word or phrase and when the NJPS switched the order of the text for the sake of clarity (see, for example, Ezekiel 24:22–24).

Hebrew Transliteration – To give our readers an authentic *Tanakh* experience, every verse that has commentary is transliterated from Hebrew into English. The Hebrew alphabet chart includes our standards for transliteration and pronunciation of Hebrew verses, enabling readers of *The Israel Bible* to decipher key biblical passages in the holy language. Readers can hear the entire Bible read in Hebrew on our website **www.theisraelbible.com**.

There are various standards when it comes to transliterating Hebrew words into English letters. While we have relied primarily on the classical Hebrew transliteration, we have occasionally deviated for the sake of simplicity, clarity and to reflect common usage.

In addition to whole verses, we have also transliterated many proper nouns in the English translation so that our readers can learn the names of key biblical figures and locations in their Hebrew form. As a rule, we chose to transliterate names of people that were central in the establishment and functioning of the nation of Israel, as well as significant places in the Holy Land. Therefore, regarding Adam's sons, for example, only *Shet* (Seth) is transliterated since it was from him that *Noach* (Noah), and ultimately *Avraham* (Abraham), descended. For this reason, there might be verses or sections of *The Israel Bible* that contains multiple names and only some of them are transliterated.

For the same reason, we have transliterated the names of the books of *Tanakh* when referring to them in our introductions and commentary. When referencing a specific chapter or verse, however, we use the English names of the books in our citations for clarity. We also transliterated ideas and concepts that are central to Judaism such as *Shabbat* (Sabbath), the names of the Jewish holidays and the *Beit Hamikdash* (Temple), as well as biblical measurements. Finally, the name of God is transliterated. Out of respect, Orthodox Jews generally refer to the Lord as *Hashem*, which literally means 'the Name.' Referring to God as *Hashem* reminds us that we feel close to Him but also recognize our distance at the same time. To stress this moniker, we transliterated both the Tetragrammaton as well as the name *Elohim* as *Hashem*.

Study Notes – Our unique commentary was compiled by Orthodox Jewish scholars who live in Israel. It is an anthology in the sense that most of the commentary is not original, but draws from traditional teachings of early Jewish Sages and modern rabbinic commentators. We also include quotations from individuals who have played a significant part in the past century of modern Israeli history including Israeli prime ministers, poets and military leaders.

Our commentary can be broken into four categories, three of which are identified by an icon at the beginning of the study note:

 Israel lessons are indicated with an icon bearing the map of Israel and focus on the Land of Israel and the modern State of Israel.

 Jewish lessons are indicated with a *Torah* scroll and teach a concept in Judaism or a classic idea from rabbinic thought.

 Hebrew lessons are represented by an icon bearing the letter *aleph* and focus on the meaning of a Hebrew word or phrase.

All other comments are considered general comments and are not assigned an icon.

Supplemental Material – In addition to our unique translation and original commentary, *The Israel Bible* offers supplementary material to enrich the learning experience of our readers. Before every book of *Tanakh,* we provide an introduction, as well as information, generally in the form of a map, a chart or a list, which is central to the specific book.

Maps – As the purpose of *The Israel Bible* is to highlight the biblical significance of the Land of Israel, significant time was spent researching and preparing maps to bring the physical contours of the holy land to life with great accuracy. However, since there is a lack of information regarding the precise locations of certain ancient cities, some of the places on our maps are approximate or subject to debate. In these cases, we followed the opinion that we are most comfortable with, but acknowledge that there is room for disagreement. We continue to produce new maps, which are available on our website **www.theisraelbible.com/maps**.

***Torah* Readings** – The *Torah* is not just a work that is studied privately, it is also read out loud in synagogue. Every *Shabbat* and holiday a portion of the *Torah* is read, as well as a related section from *Neviim,* the prophets, called the *haftarah.* We included the blessings recited before and after the reading of the *Torah,* a list of the weekly *Torah* portions and their corresponding *haftarot,* and a chart of the *Torah* readings for special days with their corresponding *haftarot.* Readers can always find the current week's *Torah* portion by visiting **www.theisraelbible.com/weekly-torah-portion**. In this volume, we indicate where a new *Torah* portion begins by highlighting the Hebrew verse number with a gray box so readers can follow along with the communal *Torah* readings. Furthermore, we have included prayers for the State of Israel and the soldiers of the Israel Defense Forces (IDF) that are generally recited following the *Torah* reading in synagogue. It is our constant prayer that God watch over the State of Israel and the members of the IDF, who defend Israel every hour of every day.

In 1948, the State of Israel was created providing a modern answer to Isaiah's ancient question, "Is a nation born all at once?" (Isaiah 66:8). *The Israel Bible* was first published in the 70th year of God's miraculous restoration of the People of Israel to the Land of Israel. Jewish wisdom teaches that 70 is a significant number: *Moshe* (Moses) translated the *Torah* into 70 languages for all 70 nations of the world. From our very origins, the Jewish people were meant to be a light unto the 70 nations, spreading God's truth to the masses.

In the seven decades since the modern rebirth of the State of Israel, God's plan has been unfolding with unprecedented speed, dramatic highs and heartbreaking lows. Never has Israel been at the forefront of the world's attention as it is in our generation. Efforts to vilify the Jewish State seem to spread every day across the globe. At the same time, so does the growing movement of millions of non-Jewish biblical Zionists who stand with the nation of Israel as an expression of their commitment to God's word. As we seek to understand the clash of these two conflicting worldviews, the need for *The Israel Bible* has never been so important.

Standing on the great shoulders of those who came before us and emanating from the land that has always served as the birthplace for the Bible, we conclude with a heartfelt prayer: May the Almighty bless our efforts in offering this *Tanakh* to influence the hearts, minds and actions of its readers. In this way, it is our hope to spread God's name so that the publication of *The Israel Bible* brings us one step closer to the final redemption of Israel and the entire world.

Rabbi Tuly Weisz
Editor, *The Israel Bible*

Foreword

The mandate to study God's word daily is interestingly not found in the Five Books of Moses (Pentateuch), but rather in the first book of our prophetic writings: "Let not this Book of the Teaching cease from your lips, but recite it day and night, so that you may observe faithfully all that is written in it. Only then will you prosper in your undertakings and only then will you be successful" (Joshua 1:8). Charged with bringing the Israelites into the land covenantally promised to Abraham, Isaac and Jacob, God ensures Joshua of His protection if the nation observes His ways as dictated in the Divine constitution known as the *Torah*.

In Jewish tradition, Joshua (1:8) is directly linked with Deuteronomy (11:14), "You shall gather in your new grain and wine, and oil."[1] Our Sages deduced from this scriptural combination the importance of merging *Torah* study with a profession. Completely dedicating oneself to the study of *Torah* without having the financial means to sustain this lifestyle can lead one to eventually straying from observance of God's will. Poverty and crime can have an intimate relationship.

We must also be careful that our work does not affect our daily study of Scripture. The addiction of becoming a workaholic and not making *Torah* study a priority can also lead one into temptations that can violate our personal relationship with Him as well as our fellow human beings. The goal is to achieve a healthy balance between our study of God's word and our daily work.

The Deuteronomic verse quoted above is part of the second section of the Shema[2] that discusses the concept of reward and punishment. Sanctifying God by fulfilling His commandments results in the Land of Israel practically benefitting from rains that occur in the right season and reaping the abundance from the fields. However, if the nation follows pagan gods and practices, the consequences are devastating – famine and death. The Land of Israel is intrinsically linked with the keeping of the *Torah*. Covenant Land comes with covenant responsibility.

---

1   Talmud Bavli Berachot 35b
2   Consisting of three sections within the Five Books of Moses (Deut. 6:4–8; 11:13–22 and Numbers 15:37–42), the *Shema* is proclamation of accepting God's Kingdom in our lives, loyalty to His commandments and remembering His redemptive act of liberating us from Egypt. Jews recite the *Shema* twice a day as stated in Deut. 6:7.

Born into slavery, Joshua is now leading His people into the Promised Land. More than 500 years separates him from his ancestral forefather Abraham. The historical narratives that took place between Abraham leaving everything behind to follow God in Genesis 12 and the death of Moses in the last chapter of Deuteronomy are filled with intrigue, suspense, joy, sorrow and hope. What began as a family is now a nation actualizing its mission to be a kingdom of priests to the world. However, for the Israelites to succeed in the Land of Israel, they must see the *Torah* as the only compass to direct their lives.

The biblical episodes after our first entry into the land are well known. Our ancestors' triumphs and sins are all on public record. We learned the harsh reality of Leviticus (18:28) "So let not the land spew you out for defiling it as it spewed out the nation that came before you." Twice, we lost the privilege to be stewards of the Land of Israel and to fulfill our nation state mandate to be a light to the world. However, when the annals of history were ready to archive the Jewish people after the Holocaust, God kept His covenantal promise and gathered us from the four corners of the globe to come home. The year 1948 was a game changer. Biblical prophecies were and are being realized. We are now living in the birth pangs of the messianic era.

In our morning prayers, we recite a series of blessings over the *Torah* that include petitioning God to have a sweet tooth for His word, to study it without any ulterior motive and to have Him to teach it to us. They are some congregations that invoke the following liturgical prayer after the completion of these blessings: *May the Torah be my faith and El Shaddai my help. Blessed be the name of His glorious kingdom forever and all time.*

According to Jewish tradition, the neglect of not blessing the *Torah* before engaging in its study was one of the reasons for the destruction of the Temple.[3] This is deduced from the redundancy of words in Jeremiah (9:12) that talks about Israel not following God: "... Because they forsook the teaching I had set before them. They did not obey Me and they did not follow it [did not make a blessing before studying it]." Our inability to properly cherish God's greatest gift to the world, the *Torah*, led to our eventual exile from our land.

On Israel's Independence Day, Jews around the world recite Psalms 113–118 to express our gratitude to God for His Divine hand in helping establish the State of Israel. We have learned from our past and realize the privilege to see firsthand the land, people and *Torah* operating all together in our generation.

---

3   Babylonian Talmud Nedarim 81a

When Rabbi Tuly Weisz approached me about his intent to publish *The Israel Bible* that would highlight commentary about the special relationship between the land and people, I saw this project as another way to publicly demonstrate our appreciation to God for having the State of Israel. In addition, it is another educational tool to ensure biblical literacy. If we are to truly enjoy the Land of Israel, it is incumbent upon us to continually study the *Torah*. Isaiah once prophesied that the Jewish people would return to Zion with songs, "crowned with everlasting joy" (35:10). *The Israel Bible* provides us the lyrical content to express our joy in living in the land that God calls holy.

Rabbi Shlomo Riskin
Chief Rabbi of Efrat
Founder of the Center for Jewish-Christian
Understanding & Cooperation (CJCUC)

Sefer Ezra v'Nechemya
The Book of Ezra and Nehemiah

Introduction and commentary by Josh Even-Chen

Sefer Ezra v'Nechemya (Ezra and Nehemiah) is the penultimate book of the Hebrew Bible. Though comprised of two smaller books, *Sefer Ezra* and *Sefer Nechemya* were joined, as they concisely discuss the same general era, the final period included in the *Tanakh*. While some of the recorded events occur in faraway Persia, the focus of the book is the realization of the yearning of the Jewish exiles to return to *Eretz Yisrael*.

Many people associate the term "Zionism" only with the movement that began in the late nineteenth century, with the Jewish émigrés who returned to the Land of Israel in what became known as the "First *Aliya*." In truth, however, the first returnees to Zion were those who returned from the Babylonian exile in the time of *Ezra* and *Nechemya* some 2500 years ago, in what is referred to as *Shivat Tzion* (the return to Zion). Scholars have pointed out that the two events share similar characteristics. In both cases, the majority of exiles did not opt to return, and most of those who did come were young, driven by idealism and without strong ties to their host countries. Indeed, history, especially Jewish history, tends to repeat itself.

Seventy years before the reign of the Persian king Cyrus, Nebuchadnezzar and the Babylonians took control of the Land of Israel, exiling the inhabitants of *Yehuda* and destroying *Yerushalayim* and the *Beit Hamikdash*. One might have expected the Judean people to disappear in the Babylonian exile, as had happen to their brothers from the northern kingdom following the earlier exile at the hands of Assyria, but incredibly, as the prophet *Yirmiyahu* had predicted, they persisted. To assure their survival, they adopted a three-step approach: remember the past, live in the present, and hope for the future. And within that projected future, *Eretz Yisrael* was always central.

Sefer Ezra v'Nechemya begins with Cyrus's proclamation allowing the Jews to return to Israel and rebuild the *Beit Hamikdash*. While some Jews did heed the call, many chose to remain in Persia, where, over the years of Babylonian rule, they had become comfortable and had built a life for themselves. The returnees are met with resistance and hardship, and the construction of the Temple is halted until the second year of the reign of King Darius. In response to the encouragement of the prophets *Chagai* and *Zecharya*, construction of the *Beit Hamikdash* resumes and is finally completed in Darius's sixth year.

A short time later, in the seventh year of King Artaxerxes, *Ezra*, "a scribe expert in the Teaching of *Moshe*" (Ezra 7:6), brings a second wave of returnees to the Land of Israel, with *Nechemya* following thirteen years later. *Ezra* and *Nechemya* were both reformers, but while *Ezra* implemented spiritual reforms, *Nechemya* focused on pragmatic matters involving the country's material infrastructure. *Ezra's* attention turns to combating assimilation, promoting Jewish education and reestablishing a proper system of justice. *Nechemya* concentrates on physically reestablishing Jewish communities and reconstructing the fortifications of *Yerushalayim*. Both aspects were essential for the survival of the nation. Like *Nechemya*, the early twentieth-century Zionists were mostly responsible for building the country physically. However, as modern-day Israel's first Chief Rabbi, Abraham Isaac Kook, commented, even the most mundane tasks like plowing a field or building a home, if performed in Israel, constitute a fulfillment of the word of God.

All twenty-four books of the Hebrew Bible relate to *Eretz Yisrael*, but this is the only one that is dedicated to the rejuvenation of the land and its people, and the *Torah* laws. Our generation has merited seeing these words come to life before our eyes. It is therefore our privilege and obligation to study this book, in order to learn and benefit from the successes and failures, core messages, and divinely inspired wisdom that relates to the Jewish people's *first* attempt at resettling the Land of Israel, in the days of *Ezra* and *Nechemya*.

Chart of Important Milestones in the Settlement of the Land of Israel

Sefer Ezra v'Nechemya discusses the return of the Jews to the Land of Israel following 70 years of Babylonian exile. The return happened in stages and, to a certain degree, was incomplete. Over the years, small retorations of the Jewish people have taken place, each bringing us a little closer to the ultimate redemption. The following is a partial list of milestones in the settlement of the Jewish people in the Land of Israel:

Event	Description	Year	Relevant verses
Exodus from Egypt and entry into the Land of Israel	Under the leadership of *Moshe*, *Hashem* redeemed the Children of Israel from Egyptian slavery. After spending 40 years in the desert they reached their final destination – the Land of Israel.	Exodus – 2448 (Hebrew date) Entry into the land – 2488 (Hebrew date)	Exodus 6:6–8
Return to *Tzion*	Following Cyrus' proclamation allowing the Jews to return to Israel and rebuild the *Beit Hamikdash*, *Zerubavel*, along with *Yehoshua* the High Priest, led the first group of 42,360 returnees to the Land of Israel from the Babylonian exile. They re-settled the land and rebuilt the *Beit Hamikdash*. A number of years later, *Ezra* followed with a second wave of about 5,000 returnees. He worked hard to bring about religious reform among the Jews in Israel. Finally, *Nechemya* travelled to the Land of Israel to rebuild Jerusalem and repair its walls.	*Zerubavel* – 538 BCE *Ezra* – 458 BCE *Nechemya* – 445 BCE	Ezra 1–2, 7 Nehemiah 2, 13:6–7
Jewish independence – Hasmonean dynasty	The priestly Hasmonean family led a revolt against the Syrian-Greek rulers who had forbade the practice of Judaism and defiled the *Beit Hamikdash*. They won the battle for *Yerushalayim*, purified the *Beit Hamikdash*, and continued to fight their Seleucid oppressors. Eventually, the Hasmoneans were victorious, and, with the collapse of the Seleucid kingdom, Jewish independence was restored in the Land of Israel until its capture by the Romans in 63 BCE.	165 BCE – *Beit Hamikdash* is restored 142 BCE – Jews granted autonomy	
Aliyot	*Aliyah*, return to Israel, was always a national aspiration of the Jewish people but was not fulfilled on a large-scale until the rise of Zionism. From 1882 until the establishment of the State of Israel in 1948, over 550,000 Jews immigrated to the Land of Israel through several waves of *aliyah*.	1882–1948	
Declaration of the State of Israel	The State of Israel was officially declared by David Ben-Gurion on May, 14th 1948 (the 5th of *Iyar* 5708), and the Jews again have a national homeland in the Land of Israel. Many refer to this as the beginning of the final redemption.	1948	
Rescue Operations	Since the establishment of the State of Israel, there have been a number of rescue operations carried out by the Israel, bringing Jews all over the world to freedom in the Jewish State. Some of these operations include: Operation Magic Carpet, which brought approximately 50,000 Yemenite Jews to Israel, Operation Ezra and Nehemiah, which airlifted more than 120,000 Iraqi Jews to Israel, and Operation Moses, which brought approximately 8,000 Ethiopian Jews to the Jewish state.	Operation Magic Carpet – 1949–1950, Operation Ezra and Nehemiah – 1950–1951, Operation Moses – 1984	
Re-unification of *Yerushalayim*	The Six-Day war resulted in Israel's acquisition of the Sinai Peninsula and the Gaza Strip (both eventually given back), the West Bank, the Golan Heights, and East Jerusalem. For the first time since 1948, Jerusalem was reunited and Jews were able to pray at the Western Wall, the remaining outer wall of the Second *Beit Hamikdash*.	1967	
Jewish Immigration	Since 1948, more than 3 million Jews from all over the world have made *aliyah* to the Land of Israel. This is seen by many as a partial fulfillment of the prophecies of the ingathering of the exiles.	1948–present	

1 ¹ In the first year of King Cyrus of Persia, when the word of *Hashem* spoken by *Yirmiyahu* was fulfilled, *Hashem* roused the spirit of King Cyrus of Persia to issue a proclamation throughout his realm by word of mouth and in writing as follows:

² "Thus said King Cyrus of Persia: God of Heaven has given me all the kingdoms of the earth and has charged me with building Him a house in *Yerushalayim*, which is in *Yehuda*.

³ Anyone of you of all His people – may his God be with him, and let him go up to *Yerushalayim* that is in *Yehuda* and build the House of God of *Yisrael*, the God that is in *Yerushalayim*;

⁴ and all who stay behind, wherever he may be living, let the people of his place assist him with silver, gold, goods, and livestock, besides the freewill offering to the House of *Hashem* that is in *Yerushalayim*."

⁵ So the chiefs of the clans of *Yehuda* and *Binyamin*, and the *Kohanim* and *Leviim*, all whose spirit had been roused by *Hashem*, got ready to go up to build the House of *Hashem* that is in *Yerushalayim*.

⁶ All their neighbors supported them with silver vessels, with gold, with goods, with livestock, and with precious objects, besides what had been given as a freewill offering.

⁷ King Cyrus of Persia released the vessels of *Hashem*'s house which Nebuchadnezzar had taken away from *Yerushalayim* and had put in the house of his god.

⁸ These King Cyrus of Persia released through the office of Mithredath the treasurer, who gave an inventory of them to *Sheshbatzar* the prince of *Yehuda*.

⁹ This is the inventory: 30 gold basins, 1,000 silver basins, 29 knives,

¹⁰ 30 gold bowls, 410 silver double bowls, 1,000 other vessels;

א וּבִשְׁנַת אַחַת לְכוֹרֶשׁ מֶלֶךְ פָּרַס לִכְלוֹת דְּבַר־יְהֹוָה מִפִּי יִרְמְיָה הֵעִיר יְהֹוָה אֶת־רוּחַ כֹּרֶשׁ מֶלֶךְ־פָּרַס וַיַּעֲבֶר־קוֹל בְּכָל־מַלְכוּתוֹ וְגַם־בְּמִכְתָּב לֵאמֹר:

ב כֹּה אָמַר כֹּרֶשׁ מֶלֶךְ פָּרַס כֹּל מַמְלְכוֹת הָאָרֶץ נָתַן לִי יְהֹוָה אֱלֹהֵי הַשָּׁמָיִם וְהוּא־פָקַד עָלַי לִבְנוֹת־לוֹ בַיִת בִּירוּשָׁלַם אֲשֶׁר בִּיהוּדָה:

ג מִי־בָכֶם מִכָּל־עַמּוֹ יְהִי אֱלֹהָיו עִמּוֹ וְיַעַל לִירוּשָׁלַם אֲשֶׁר בִּיהוּדָה וְיִבֶן אֶת־בֵּית יְהֹוָה אֱלֹהֵי יִשְׂרָאֵל הוּא הָאֱלֹהִים אֲשֶׁר בִּירוּשָׁלָם:

ד וְכָל־הַנִּשְׁאָר מִכָּל־הַמְּקֹמוֹת אֲשֶׁר הוּא גָר־שָׁם יְנַשְּׂאוּהוּ אַנְשֵׁי מְקֹמוֹ בְּכֶסֶף וּבְזָהָב וּבִרְכוּשׁ וּבִבְהֵמָה עִם־הַנְּדָבָה לְבֵית הָאֱלֹהִים אֲשֶׁר בִּירוּשָׁלָם:

ה וַיָּקוּמוּ רָאשֵׁי הָאָבוֹת לִיהוּדָה וּבִנְיָמִן וְהַכֹּהֲנִים וְהַלְוִיִּם לְכֹל הֵעִיר הָאֱלֹהִים אֶת־רוּחוֹ לַעֲלוֹת לִבְנוֹת אֶת־בֵּית יְהֹוָה אֲשֶׁר בִּירוּשָׁלָם:

ו וְכָל־סְבִיבֹתֵיהֶם חִזְּקוּ בִידֵיהֶם בִּכְלֵי־כֶסֶף בַּזָּהָב בָּרְכוּשׁ וּבַבְּהֵמָה וּבַמִּגְדָּנוֹת לְבַד עַל־כָּל־הִתְנַדֵּב:

ז וְהַמֶּלֶךְ כּוֹרֶשׁ הוֹצִיא אֶת־כְּלֵי בֵית־יְהֹוָה אֲשֶׁר הוֹצִיא נְבוּכַדְנֶצַּר מִירוּשָׁלַם וַיִּתְּנֵם בְּבֵית אֱלֹהָיו:

ח וַיּוֹצִיאֵם כּוֹרֶשׁ מֶלֶךְ פָּרַס עַל־יַד מִתְרְדָת הַגִּזְבָּר וַיִּסְפְּרֵם לְשֵׁשְׁבַּצַּר הַנָּשִׂיא לִיהוּדָה:

ט וְאֵלֶּה מִסְפָּרָם אֲגַרְטְלֵי זָהָב שְׁלֹשִׁים אֲגַרְטְלֵי־כֶסֶף אָלֶף מַחֲלָפִים תִּשְׁעָה וְעֶשְׂרִים:

י כְּפוֹרֵי זָהָב שְׁלֹשִׁים כְּפוֹרֵי כֶסֶף מִשְׁנִים אַרְבַּע מֵאוֹת וַעֲשָׂרָה כֵּלִים אֲחֵרִים אָלֶף:

11 in all, 5,400 gold and silver vessels. *Sheshbatzar* brought all these back when the exiles came back from Babylon to *Yerushalayim*.

יא כָּל־כֵּלִים לַזָּהָב וְלַכֶּסֶף חֲמֵשֶׁת אֲלָפִים וְאַרְבַּע מֵאוֹת הַכֹּל הֶעֱלָה שֵׁשְׁבַּצַּר עִם הֵעָלוֹת הַגּוֹלָה מִבָּבֶל לִירוּשָׁלָ͏ִם:

kol kay-LEEM la-za-HAV v'-la-KE-sef kha-MAY-shet a-la-FEEM v'-ar-BA may-OT ha-KOL he-e-LAH shaysh-ba-TZAR IM hay-a-LOT ha-go-LAH mi-ba-VEL lee-ru-sha-LA-im

ב 2 ¹ These are the people of the province who came up from among the captive exiles whom King Nebuchadnezzar of Babylon had carried into exile to Babylon, who returned to *Yerushalayim* and *Yehuda*, each to his own city,

א וְאֵלֶּה בְּנֵי הַמְּדִינָה הָעֹלִים מִשְּׁבִי הַגּוֹלָה אֲשֶׁר הֶגְלָה נבוכדנצור [נְבוּכַדְנֶצַּר] מֶלֶךְ־בָּבֶל לְבָבֶל וַיָּשׁוּבוּ לִירוּשָׁלַ͏ִם וִיהוּדָה אִישׁ לְעִירוֹ:

² who came with *Zerubavel*, *Yeshua*, *Nechemya*, *Seraya*, *Reelaiah*, *Mordechai*, Bilshan, Mispar, Bigvai, Rehum, Baanah: The list of the men of the people of *Yisrael*:

ב אֲשֶׁר־בָּאוּ עִם־זְרֻבָּבֶל יֵשׁוּעַ נְחֶמְיָה שְׂרָיָה רְעֵלָיָה מָרְדֳּכַי בִּלְשָׁן מִסְפָּר בִּגְוַי רְחוּם בַּעֲנָה מִסְפַּר אַנְשֵׁי עַם יִשְׂרָאֵל:

³ the sons of Parosh – 2,172;

ג בְּנֵי פַרְעֹשׁ אַלְפַּיִם מֵאָה שִׁבְעִים וּשְׁנָיִם:

⁴ the sons of Shephatiah – 372;

ד בְּנֵי שְׁפַטְיָה שְׁלֹשׁ מֵאוֹת שִׁבְעִים וּשְׁנָיִם:

⁵ the sons of Arah – 775;

ה בְּנֵי אָרַח שְׁבַע מֵאוֹת חֲמִשָּׁה וְשִׁבְעִים:

⁶ the sons of Pahath-moab: the sons of *Yeshua* and *Yoav* – 2,812;

ו בְּנֵי־פַחַת מוֹאָב לִבְנֵי יֵשׁוּעַ יוֹאָב אַלְפַּיִם שְׁמֹנֶה מֵאוֹת וּשְׁנֵים עָשָׂר:

⁷ the sons of Elam – 1,254;

ז בְּנֵי עֵילָם אֶלֶף מָאתַיִם חֲמִשִּׁים וְאַרְבָּעָה:

⁸ the sons of Zattu – 945;

ח בְּנֵי זַתּוּא תְּשַׁע מֵאוֹת וְאַרְבָּעִים וַחֲמִשָּׁה:

⁹ the sons of Zaccai – 760;

ט בְּנֵי זַכָּי שְׁבַע מֵאוֹת וְשִׁשִּׁים:

¹⁰ the sons of Bani – 642;

י בְּנֵי בָנִי שֵׁשׁ מֵאוֹת אַרְבָּעִים וּשְׁנָיִם:

¹¹ the sons of Bebai – 623;

יא בְּנֵי בֵבָי שֵׁשׁ מֵאוֹת עֶשְׂרִים וּשְׁלֹשָׁה:

¹² the sons of Azgad – 1,222;

יב בְּנֵי עַזְגָּד אֶלֶף מָאתַיִם עֶשְׂרִים וּשְׁנָיִם:

¹³ the sons of Adonikam – 666;

יג בְּנֵי אֲדֹנִיקָם שֵׁשׁ מֵאוֹת שִׁשִּׁים וְשִׁשָּׁה:

Yerushalayim

1:11 When the exiles came back from *Bavel* to *Yerushalayim*. The beloved Rabbi Shlomo Carlebach would quip, "Did you know that Jerusalem is the highest city in the world?" Many were skeptical, but he was correct – in the spiritual, if not topographical, sense. The Bible states that "*Avram* went *down* to Egypt" from Canaan (Genesis 12:10), and when the people returned to the Land of Israel from the Babylonian exile, although translated here as "the exiles *came back*," the more exacting translation is "the exiles *ascended*." Ever since the magnetic north has dictated the directional illustration of maps, people have said things like, "I'm going *down* south," or "I'm heading *up* north." However, this verse teaches that no matter where a person is in the world, his "spiritual compass" should always indicate that *Yerushalayim* is "up."

14 the sons of Bigvai – 2,056;	יד בְּנֵי בִגְוָי אַלְפַּיִם חֲמִשִּׁים וְשִׁשָּׁה:
15 the sons of Adin – 454;	טו בְּנֵי עָדִין אַרְבַּע מֵאוֹת חֲמִשִּׁים וְאַרְבָּעָה:
16 the sons of Ater: *Chizkiyahu* – 98;	טז בְּנֵי־אָטֵר לִיחִזְקִיָּה תִּשְׁעִים וּשְׁמֹנָה:
17 the sons of Bezai – 323;	יז בְּנֵי בֵצָי שְׁלֹשׁ מֵאוֹת עֶשְׂרִים וּשְׁלֹשָׁה:
18 the sons of Jorah – 112;	יח בְּנֵי יוֹרָה מֵאָה וּשְׁנֵים עָשָׂר:
19 the sons of Hashum – 223;	יט בְּנֵי חָשֻׁם מָאתַיִם עֶשְׂרִים וּשְׁלֹשָׁה:
20 the sons of Gibbar – 95;	כ בְּנֵי גִבָּר תִּשְׁעִים וַחֲמִשָּׁה:
21 the sons of *Beit Lechem* – 123;	כא בְּנֵי בֵית־לָחֶם מֵאָה עֶשְׂרִים וּשְׁלֹשָׁה:
22 the sons of Netophah – 56;	כב אַנְשֵׁי נְטֹפָה חֲמִשִּׁים וְשִׁשָּׁה:
23 the sons of *Anatot* – 128;	כג אַנְשֵׁי עֲנָתוֹת מֵאָה עֶשְׂרִים וּשְׁמֹנָה:
24 the sons of Azmaveth – 42;	כד בְּנֵי עַזְמָוֶת אַרְבָּעִים וּשְׁנָיִם:
25 the sons of Kiriath-arim: Chephirah and Beeroth – 743;	כה בְּנֵי קִרְיַת עָרִים כְּפִירָה וּבְאֵרוֹת שְׁבַע מֵאוֹת וְאַרְבָּעִים וּשְׁלֹשָׁה:
26 the sons of *Rama* and Geba – 621;	כו בְּנֵי הָרָמָה וָגָבַע שֵׁשׁ מֵאוֹת עֶשְׂרִים וְאֶחָד:
27 the men of Michmas – 122;	כז אַנְשֵׁי מִכְמָס מֵאָה עֶשְׂרִים וּשְׁנָיִם:
28 the men of *Beit El* and Ai – 223;	כח אַנְשֵׁי בֵית־אֵל וְהָעָי מָאתַיִם עֶשְׂרִים וּשְׁלֹשָׁה:
29 the men of Nebo – 52;	כט בְּנֵי נְבוֹ חֲמִשִּׁים וּשְׁנָיִם:
30 the sons of Magbish – 156;	ל בְּנֵי מַגְבִּישׁ מֵאָה חֲמִשִּׁים וְשִׁשָּׁה:
31 the sons of the other Elam – 1,254;	לא בְּנֵי עֵילָם אַחֵר אֶלֶף מָאתַיִם חֲמִשִּׁים וְאַרְבָּעָה:
32 the sons of Harim – 320;	לב בְּנֵי חָרִם שְׁלֹשׁ מֵאוֹת וְעֶשְׂרִים:
33 the sons of Lod, Hadid, and Ono – 725;	לג בְּנֵי־לֹד חָדִיד וְאוֹנוֹ שְׁבַע מֵאוֹת עֶשְׂרִים וַחֲמִשָּׁה:
34 the sons of *Yericho* – 345;	לד בְּנֵי יְרֵחוֹ שְׁלֹשׁ מֵאוֹת אַרְבָּעִים וַחֲמִשָּׁה:
35 the sons of Senaah – 3,630.	לה בְּנֵי סְנָאָה שְׁלֹשֶׁת אֲלָפִים וְשֵׁשׁ מֵאוֹת וּשְׁלֹשִׁים:
36 The *Kohanim*: the sons of Jedaiah: the house of Yeshua – 973;	לו הַכֹּהֲנִים בְּנֵי יְדַעְיָה לְבֵית יֵשׁוּעַ תְּשַׁע מֵאוֹת שִׁבְעִים וּשְׁלֹשָׁה:
37 the sons of Immer – 1,052;	לז בְּנֵי אִמֵּר אֶלֶף חֲמִשִּׁים וּשְׁנָיִם:
38 the sons of Pashhur – 1,247;	לח בְּנֵי פַשְׁחוּר אֶלֶף מָאתַיִם אַרְבָּעִים וְשִׁבְעָה:
39 the sons of Harim – 1,017.	לט בְּנֵי חָרִם אֶלֶף וְשִׁבְעָה עָשָׂר:

40 The *Leviim*: the sons of *Yeshua* and *Kadmiel*: the sons of Hodaviah – 74.

מ הַלְוִיִּם בְּנֵי־יֵשׁוּעַ וְקַדְמִיאֵל לִבְנֵי הוֹדַוְיָה שִׁבְעִים וְאַרְבָּעָה:

41 The singers: the sons of *Asaf* – 128.

מא הַמְשֹׁרְרִים בְּנֵי אָסָף מֵאָה עֶשְׂרִים וּשְׁמֹנָה:

42 The gatekeepers: the sons of *Shalum*, the sons of Ater, the sons of Talmon, the sons of Akkub, the sons of Hatita, the sons of Shobai, all told – 139.

מב בְּנֵי הַשֹּׁעֲרִים בְּנֵי־שַׁלּוּם בְּנֵי־אָטֵר בְּנֵי־טַלְמוֹן בְּנֵי־עַקּוּב בְּנֵי חֲטִיטָא בְּנֵי שֹׁבָי הַכֹּל מֵאָה שְׁלֹשִׁים וְתִשְׁעָה:

43 The temple servants: the sons of Ziha, the sons of Hasupha, the sons of Tabbaoth,

מג הַנְּתִינִים בְּנֵי־צִיחָא בְנֵי־חֲשׂוּפָא בְּנֵי טַבָּעוֹת:

44 the sons of Keros, the sons of Siaha, the sons of Padon,

מד בְּנֵי־קֵרֹס בְּנֵי־סִיעֲהָא בְּנֵי פָדוֹן:

45 the sons of Lebanah, the sons of Hagabah, the sons of Akkub,

מה בְּנֵי־לְבָנָה בְנֵי־חֲגָבָה בְּנֵי עַקּוּב:

46 the sons of Hagab, the sons of Salmai, the sons of Hanan,

מו בְּנֵי־חָגָב בְּנֵי־שמלי [שַׁלְמַי] בְּנֵי חָנָן:

47 the sons of Giddel, the sons of Gahar, the sons of Reaiah,

מז בְּנֵי־גִדֵּל בְּנֵי־גַחַר בְּנֵי רְאָיָה:

48 the sons of Rezin, the sons of Nekoda, the sons of Gazzam,

מח בְּנֵי־רְצִין בְּנֵי־נְקוֹדָא בְּנֵי גַזָּם:

49 the sons of Uzza, the sons of Paseah, the sons of Besai,

מט בְּנֵי־עֻזָּא בְנֵי־פָסֵחַ בְּנֵי בֵסָי:

50 the sons of Asnah, the sons of Meunim, the sons of Nephusim,

נ בְּנֵי־אַסְנָה בְנֵי־מעינים [מְעוּנִים] בְּנֵי נפיסים [נְפוּסִים:]

51 the sons of Bakbuk, the sons of Hakupha, the sons of Harhur,

נא בְּנֵי־בַקְבּוּק בְּנֵי־חֲקוּפָא בְּנֵי חַרְחוּר:

52 the sons of Bazluth, the sons of Mehida, the sons of Harsha,

נב בְּנֵי־בַצְלוּת בְּנֵי־מְחִידָא בְּנֵי חַרְשָׁא:

53 the sons of Barkos, the sons of Sisera, the sons of Temah,

נג בְּנֵי־בַרְקוֹס בְּנֵי־סִיסְרָא בְּנֵי־תָמַח:

54 the sons of Neziah, the sons of Hatipha.

נד בְּנֵי נְצִיחַ בְּנֵי חֲטִיפָא:

55 The sons of *Shlomo*'s servants: the sons of Sotai, the sons of Hassophereth, the sons of Peruda,

נה בְּנֵי עַבְדֵי שְׁלֹמֹה בְּנֵי־סֹטַי בְּנֵי־הַסֹּפֶרֶת בְּנֵי פְרוּדָא:

56 the sons of Jaalah, the sons of Darkon, the sons of Giddel,

נו בְּנֵי־יַעֲלָה בְנֵי־דַרְקוֹן בְּנֵי גִדֵּל:

57 the sons of Shephatiah, the sons of Hattil, the sons of Pochereth-hazzebaim, the sons of Ami.

נז בְּנֵי שְׁפַטְיָה בְנֵי־חַטִּיל בְּנֵי פֹּכֶרֶת הַצְּבָיִים בְּנֵי אָמִי:

58 The total of temple servants and the sons of *Shlomo*'s servants – 392.

נח כָּל־הַנְּתִינִים וּבְנֵי עַבְדֵי שְׁלֹמֹה שְׁלֹשׁ מֵאוֹת תִּשְׁעִים וּשְׁנָיִם:

59 The following were those who came up from Tel-melah, Tel-harsha, Cherub, Addan, and Immer – they were unable to tell whether their father's house and descent were Israelite:

נט וְאֵלֶּה הָעֹלִים מִתֵּל מֶלַח תֵּל חַרְשָׁא כְּרוּב אַדָּן אִמֵּר וְלֹא יָכְלוּ לְהַגִּיד בֵּית־אֲבוֹתָם וְזַרְעָם אִם מִיִּשְׂרָאֵל הֵם:

60 the sons of Delaiah, the sons of Tobiah, the sons of Nekoda – 652.

ס בְּנֵי־דְלָיָה בְנֵי־טוֹבִיָּה בְּנֵי נְקוֹדָא שֵׁשׁ מֵאוֹת חֲמִשִּׁים וּשְׁנָיִם:

61 Of the sons of the *Kohanim,* the sons of Habaiah, the sons of Hakkoz, the sons of *Barzilai* who had married a daughter of *Barzilai* and had taken his name –

סא וּמִבְּנֵי הַכֹּהֲנִים בְּנֵי חֳבַיָּה בְּנֵי הַקּוֹץ בְּנֵי בַרְזִלַּי אֲשֶׁר לָקַח מִבְּנוֹת בַּרְזִלַּי הַגִּלְעָדִי אִשָּׁה וַיִּקָּרֵא עַל־שְׁמָם:

62 these searched for their genealogical records, but they could not be found, so they were disqualified for the priesthood.

סב אֵלֶּה בִּקְשׁוּ כְתָבָם הַמִּתְיַחְשִׂים וְלֹא נִמְצָאוּ וַיְגֹאֲלוּ מִן־הַכְּהֻנָּה:

63 The Tirshatha ordered them not to eat of the most holy things until a *Kohen* with Urim and Thummim should appear.

סג וַיֹּאמֶר הַתִּרְשָׁתָא לָהֶם אֲשֶׁר לֹא־יֹאכְלוּ מִקֹּדֶשׁ הַקֳּדָשִׁים עַד עֲמֹד כֹּהֵן לְאוּרִים וּלְתֻמִּים:

64 The sum of the entire community was 42,360,

סד כָּל־הַקָּהָל כְּאֶחָד אַרְבַּע רִבּוֹא אַלְפַּיִם שְׁלֹשׁ־מֵאוֹת שִׁשִּׁים:

65 not counting their male and female servants, those being 7,337; they also had 200 male and female singers.

סה מִלְּבַד עַבְדֵיהֶם וְאַמְהֹתֵיהֶם אֵלֶּה שִׁבְעַת אֲלָפִים שְׁלֹשׁ מֵאוֹת שְׁלֹשִׁים וְשִׁבְעָה וְלָהֶם מְשֹׁרְרִים וּמְשֹׁרְרוֹת מָאתָיִם:

66 Their horses – 736; their mules – 245;

סו סוּסֵיהֶם שְׁבַע מֵאוֹת שְׁלֹשִׁים וְשִׁשָּׁה פִּרְדֵיהֶם מָאתַיִם אַרְבָּעִים וַחֲמִשָּׁה:

67 their camels – 435; their asses – 6,720.

סז גְּמַלֵּיהֶם אַרְבַּע מֵאוֹת שְׁלֹשִׁים וַחֲמִשָּׁה חֲמֹרִים שֵׁשֶׁת אֲלָפִים שְׁבַע מֵאוֹת וְעֶשְׂרִים:

68 Some of the chiefs of the clans, on arriving at the House of *Hashem* in *Yerushalayim,* gave a freewill offering to erect the House of *Hashem* on its site.

סח וּמֵרָאשֵׁי הָאָבוֹת בְּבוֹאָם לְבֵית יְהֹוָה אֲשֶׁר בִּירוּשָׁלָ͏ִם הִתְנַדְּבוּ לְבֵית הָאֱלֹהִים לְהַעֲמִידוֹ עַל־מְכוֹנוֹ:

69 In accord with their means, they donated to the treasury of the work: gold – 6,100 drachmas, silver – 5,000 *manim,* and priestly robes – 100.

סט כְּכֹחָם נָתְנוּ לְאוֹצַר הַמְּלָאכָה זָהָב דַּרְכְּמוֹנִים שֵׁשׁ־רִבֹּאות וָאֶלֶף וְכֶסֶף מָנִים חֲמֵשֶׁת אֲלָפִים וְכָתְנֹת כֹּהֲנִים מֵאָה:

70 The *Kohanim,* the *Leviim* and some of the people, and the singers, gatekeepers, and the temple servants took up residence in their towns and all *Yisrael* in their towns.

ע וַיֵּשְׁבוּ הַכֹּהֲנִים וְהַלְוִיִּם וּמִן־הָעָם וְהַמְשֹׁרְרִים וְהַשּׁוֹעֲרִים וְהַנְּתִינִים בְּעָרֵיהֶם וְכָל־יִשְׂרָאֵל בְּעָרֵיהֶם:

va-yay-sh'-VU ha-ko-ha-NEEM v'-hal-vi-YIM u-min ha-AM
v'-ham-sho-r'-REEM v'-ha-sho-a-REEM v'-ha-n'-tee-NEEM
b'-a-ray-HEM v'-khol yis-ra-AYL b'-a-ray-HEM

2:70 And all *Yisrael* in their towns In this chapter we learn of the many Jewish families who return to their ancestral lands and villages, es- tablishing new communities on the deserted and ruined old sites of the Land of Israel. As one travels across the landscape of the contemporary State of Israel, it is amaz-

3 ¹ When the seventh month arrived – the Israelites being settled in their towns – the entire people assembled as one man in *Yerushalayim*.

א וַיִּגַּע הַחֹדֶשׁ הַשְּׁבִיעִי וּבְנֵי יִשְׂרָאֵל בֶּעָרִים וַיֵּאָסְפוּ הָעָם כְּאִישׁ אֶחָד אֶל־יְרוּשָׁלָ͏ִם:

va-yi-GA ha-KHO-desh ha-sh'-vee-EE uv-NAY yis-ra-AYL be-a-REEM
va-yay-a-s'-FU ha-AM k'-EESH e-KHAD el y'-ru-sha-LA-im

² Then *Yeshua* son of *Yotzadak* and his brother *Kohanim*, and *Zerubavel* son of *Shealtiel* and his brothers set to and built the *Mizbayach* of the God of *Yisrael* to offer burnt offerings upon it as is written in the Teaching of *Moshe*, the man of *Hashem*.

ב וַיָּקָם יֵשׁוּעַ בֶּן־יוֹצָדָק וְאֶחָיו הַכֹּהֲנִים וּזְרֻבָּבֶל בֶּן־שְׁאַלְתִּיאֵל וְאֶחָיו וַיִּבְנוּ אֶת־מִזְבַּח אֱלֹהֵי יִשְׂרָאֵל לְהַעֲלוֹת עָלָיו עֹלוֹת כַּכָּתוּב בְּתוֹרַת מֹשֶׁה אִישׁ־הָאֱלֹהִים:

³ They set up the *Mizbayach* on its site because they were in fear of the peoples of the land, and they offered burnt offerings on it to *Hashem*, burnt offerings each morning and evening.

ג וַיָּכִינוּ הַמִּזְבֵּחַ עַל־מְכוֹנֹתָיו כִּי בְּאֵימָה עֲלֵיהֶם מֵעַמֵּי הָאֲרָצוֹת וַיַּעַל [וַיַּעֲלוּ] עָלָיו עֹלוֹת לַיהוָה עֹלוֹת לַבֹּקֶר וְלָעָרֶב:

⁴ Then they celebrated the festival of *Sukkot* as is written, with its daily burnt offerings in the proper quantities, on each day as is prescribed for it,

ד וַיַּעֲשׂוּ אֶת־חַג הַסֻּכּוֹת כַּכָּתוּב וְעֹלַת יוֹם בְּיוֹם בְּמִסְפָּר כְּמִשְׁפַּט דְּבַר־יוֹם בְּיוֹמוֹ:

⁵ followed by the regular burnt offering and the offerings for the new moons and for all the sacred fixed times of *Hashem*, and whatever freewill offerings were made to *Hashem*.

ה וְאַחֲרֵיכֵן עֹלַת תָּמִיד וְלֶחֳדָשִׁים וּלְכָל־מוֹעֲדֵי יְהוָה הַמְקֻדָּשִׁים וּלְכֹל מִתְנַדֵּב נְדָבָה לַיהוָה:

⁶ From the first day of the seventh month they began to make burnt offerings to *Hashem*, though the foundation of the Temple of *Hashem* had not been laid.

ו מִיּוֹם אֶחָד לַחֹדֶשׁ הַשְּׁבִיעִי הֵחֵלּוּ לְהַעֲלוֹת עֹלוֹת לַיהוָה וְהֵיכַל יְהוָה לֹא יֻסָּד:

Modern *Beer Sheva*

ing to see this very process reoccurring. The communities of *Beersheva*, *Kibbutz Dan*, *Givon* and dozens of others were all constructed on the very same locations as their original, biblical namesakes. It is indeed wondrous to witness the fulfillment of the prophecy "... children shall return to *their* country" (Jeremiah 31:16), and to see "all *Yisrael* in their towns."

3:1 The entire people assembled as one man in *Yerushalayim* This particular wording recalls the Revelation at Mount Sinai, in reference to which it says: "They [plural] encamped in the wilderness; and there Israel [singular] encamped before the mount." (Exodus 19:2). The great medieval commentator, *Rashi*,

points out that the transition from the plural to the singular form of the verb indicates that at Sinai, the Israelites were "as one person, with one heart." Just as the magnitude of the Sinai experience had the power to unite the multitudes of people from twelve independent tribes into one nation, such is the power of *Yerushalayim*. The Talmudic sage Rabbi Yehoshua ben Levi homiletically explains the verse "*Yerushalayim* built up, a city knit together," (Psalms 122:3), to mean that Jerusalem is a city "that makes all of Israel friends" (*Yerushalmi Chagiga* 3:6). As it did in the time of the return from Babylonia, today as well *Yerushalayim* has the power to bring Israel together as one, and to serve as a source of unity for all humanity.

Israel comes together for a holiday prayer at the Western Wall in *Yerushalayim*

7 They paid the hewers and craftsmen with money, and the Sidonians and Tyrians with food, drink, and oil to bring cedarwood from Lebanon by sea to *Yaffo*, in accord with the authorization granted them by King Cyrus of Persia.

ז וַיִּתְּנוּ־כֶסֶף לַחֹצְבִים וְלֶחָרָשִׁים וּמַאֲכָל וּמִשְׁתֶּה וָשֶׁמֶן לַצִּדֹנִים וְלַצֹּרִים לְהָבִיא עֲצֵי אֲרָזִים מִן־הַלְּבָנוֹן אֶל־יָם יָפוֹא כְּרִשְׁיוֹן כּוֹרֶשׁ מֶלֶךְ־פָּרַס עֲלֵיהֶם:

8 In the second year after their arrival at the House of *Hashem*, at *Yerushalayim*, in the second month, *Zerubavel* son of *Shealtiel* and *Yeshua* son of *Yotzadak*, and the rest of their brother *Kohanim* and *Leviim*, and all who had come from the captivity to *Yerushalayim*, as their first step appointed *Leviim* from the age of twenty and upward to supervise the work of the House of *Hashem*.

ח וּבַשָּׁנָה הַשֵּׁנִית לְבוֹאָם אֶל־בֵּית הָאֱלֹהִים לִירוּשָׁלַם בַּחֹדֶשׁ הַשֵּׁנִי הֵחֵלּוּ זְרֻבָּבֶל בֶּן־שְׁאַלְתִּיאֵל וְיֵשׁוּעַ בֶּן־יוֹצָדָק וּשְׁאָר אֲחֵיהֶם הַכֹּהֲנִים וְהַלְוִיִּם וְכָל־הַבָּאִים מֵהַשְּׁבִי יְרוּשָׁלַם וַיַּעֲמִידוּ אֶת־הַלְוִיִּם מִבֶּן עֶשְׂרִים שָׁנָה וָמַעְלָה לְנַצֵּחַ עַל־מְלֶאכֶת בֵּית־יְהוָה:

9 *Yeshua*, his sons and brothers, *Kadmiel* and his sons, the sons of *Yehuda*, together were appointed in charge of those who did the work in the House of *Hashem*; also the sons of Henadad, their sons and brother *Leviim*.

ט וַיַּעֲמֹד יֵשׁוּעַ בָּנָיו וְאֶחָיו קַדְמִיאֵל וּבָנָיו בְּנֵי־יְהוּדָה כְּאֶחָד לְנַצֵּחַ עַל־עֹשֵׂה הַמְּלָאכָה בְּבֵית הָאֱלֹהִים בְּנֵי חֵנָדָד בְּנֵיהֶם וַאֲחֵיהֶם הַלְוִיִּם:

10 When the builders had laid the foundation of the Temple of *Hashem*, *Kohanim* in their vestments with trumpets, and *Leviim* sons of *Asaf* with cymbals were stationed to give praise to *Hashem*, as King *David* of *Yisrael* had ordained.

י וְיִסְּדוּ הַבֹּנִים אֶת־הֵיכַל יְהוָה וַיַּעֲמִידוּ הַכֹּהֲנִים מְלֻבָּשִׁים בַּחֲצֹצְרוֹת וְהַלְוִיִּם בְּנֵי־אָסָף בַּמְצִלְתַּיִם לְהַלֵּל אֶת־יְהוָה עַל־יְדֵי דָּוִיד מֶלֶךְ־יִשְׂרָאֵל:

11 They sang songs extolling and praising *Hashem*, "For He is good, His steadfast love for *Yisrael* is eternal." All the people raised a great shout extolling *Hashem* because the foundation of the House of *Hashem* had been laid.

יא וַיַּעֲנוּ בְּהַלֵּל וּבְהוֹדֹת לַיהוָה כִּי טוֹב כִּי־לְעוֹלָם חַסְדּוֹ עַל־יִשְׂרָאֵל וְכָל־הָעָם הֵרִיעוּ תְרוּעָה גְדוֹלָה בְהַלֵּל לַיהוָה עַל הוּסַד בֵּית־יְהוָה:

12 Many of the *Kohanim* and *Leviim* and the chiefs of the clans, the old men who had seen the first house, wept loudly at the sight of the founding of this house. Many others shouted joyously at the top of their voices.

יב וְרַבִּים מֵהַכֹּהֲנִים וְהַלְוִיִּם וְרָאשֵׁי הָאָבוֹת הַזְּקֵנִים אֲשֶׁר רָאוּ אֶת־הַבַּיִת הָרִאשׁוֹן בְּיָסְדוֹ זֶה הַבַּיִת בְּעֵינֵיהֶם בֹּכִים בְּקוֹל גָּדוֹל וְרַבִּים בִּתְרוּעָה בְשִׂמְחָה לְהָרִים קוֹל:

13 The people could not distinguish the shouts of joy from the people's weeping, for the people raised a great shout, the sound of which could be heard from afar.

יג וְאֵין הָעָם מַכִּירִים קוֹל תְּרוּעַת הַשִּׂמְחָה לְקוֹל בְּכִי הָעָם כִּי הָעָם מְרִיעִים תְּרוּעָה גְדוֹלָה וְהַקּוֹל נִשְׁמַע עַד־לְמֵרָחוֹק:

4 1 When the adversaries of *Yehuda* and *Binyamin* heard that the returned exiles were building a temple to God of *Yisrael*,

ד א וַיִּשְׁמְעוּ צָרֵי יְהוּדָה וּבִנְיָמִן כִּי־בְנֵי הַגּוֹלָה בּוֹנִים הֵיכָל לַיהוָה אֱלֹהֵי יִשְׂרָאֵל:

2 they approached *Zerubavel* and the chiefs of the clans and said to them, "Let us build with you, since we too worship your God, having offered sacrifices to Him since the time of King Esarhaddon of Assyria, who brought us here."

ב וַיִּגְּשׁוּ אֶל־זְרֻבָּבֶל וְאֶל־רָאשֵׁי הָאָבוֹת וַיֹּאמְרוּ לָהֶם נִבְנֶה עִמָּכֶם כִּי כָכֶם נִדְרוֹשׁ לֵאלֹהֵיכֶם וְלֹא [וְלוֹ] אֲנַחְנוּ זֹבְחִים מִימֵי אֵסַר חַדֹּן מֶלֶךְ אַשּׁוּר הַמַּעֲלֶה אֹתָנוּ פֹּה:

3 *Zerubavel, Yeshua,* and the rest of the chiefs of the clans of *Yisrael* answered them, "It is not for you and us to build a House to our God, but we alone will build it to God of *Yisrael,* in accord with the charge that the king, King Cyrus of Persia, laid upon us."

4 Thereupon the people of the land undermined the resolve of the people of *Yehuda,* and made them afraid to build.

5 They bribed ministers in order to thwart their plans all the years of King Cyrus of Persia and until the reign of King Darius of Persia.

6 And in the reign of Ahasuerus, at the start of his reign, they drew up an accusation against the inhabitants of *Yehuda* and *Yerushalayim.*

7 And in the time of Artaxerxes, Bishlam, Mithredath, Tabeel, and the rest of their colleagues wrote to King Artaxerxes of Persia, a letter written in Aramaic and translated. Aramaic:

8 Rehum the commissioner and Shimshai the scribe wrote a letter concerning *Yerushalayim* to King Artaxerxes as follows:

9 (Then Rehum the commissioner and Shimshai the scribe, and the rest of their colleagues, the judges, officials, officers, and overseers, the men of Erech, and of Babylon, and of Susa – that is the Elamites –

10 and other peoples whom the great and glorious Osnappar deported and settled in the city of *Shomron* and the rest of the province Beyond the River [wrote] – and now

11 this is the text of the letter which they sent to him:) – "To King Artaxerxes [from] your servants, men of the province Beyond the River. And now

12 be it known to the king that the *Yehudim* who came up from you to us have reached *Yerushalayim* and are rebuilding that rebellious and wicked city; they are completing the walls and repairing the foundation.

ג וַיֹּאמֶר לָהֶם זְרֻבָּבֶל וְיֵשׁוּעַ וּשְׁאָר רָאשֵׁי הָאָבוֹת לְיִשְׂרָאֵל לֹא־לָכֶם וָלָנוּ לִבְנוֹת בַּיִת לֵאלֹהֵינוּ כִּי אֲנַחְנוּ יַחַד נִבְנֶה לַיהוָה אֱלֹהֵי יִשְׂרָאֵל כַּאֲשֶׁר צִוָּנוּ הַמֶּלֶךְ כּוֹרֶשׁ מֶלֶךְ־פָּרָס:

ד וַיְהִי עַם־הָאָרֶץ מְרַפִּים יְדֵי עַם־יְהוּדָה וּמְבַלְהִים [וּמְבַהֲלִים] אוֹתָם לִבְנוֹת:

ה וְסֹכְרִים עֲלֵיהֶם יוֹעֲצִים לְהָפֵר עֲצָתָם כָּל־יְמֵי כּוֹרֶשׁ מֶלֶךְ פָּרַס וְעַד־מַלְכוּת דָּרְיָוֶשׁ מֶלֶךְ־פָּרָס:

ו וּבְמַלְכוּת אֲחַשְׁוֵרוֹשׁ בִּתְחִלַּת מַלְכוּתוֹ כָּתְבוּ שִׂטְנָה עַל־יֹשְׁבֵי יְהוּדָה וִירוּשָׁלָ͏ִם:

ז וּבִימֵי אַרְתַּחְשַׁשְׂתָּא כָּתַב בִּשְׁלָם מִתְרְדָת טָבְאֵל וּשְׁאָר כְּנָוֹתו [כְּנָוֹתָיו] עַל־ארתחששתא [אַרְתַּחְשַׁשְׂתְּ] מֶלֶךְ פָּרָס וּכְתָב הַנִּשְׁתְּוָן כָּתוּב אֲרָמִית וּמְתֻרְגָּם אֲרָמִית:

ח רְחוּם בְּעֵל־טְעֵם וְשִׁמְשַׁי סָפְרָא כְּתַבוּ אִגְּרָה חֲדָה עַל־יְרוּשְׁלֶם לְאַרְתַּחְשַׁשְׂתְּא מַלְכָּא כְּנֵמָא:

ט אֱדַיִן רְחוּם בְּעֵל־טְעֵם וְשִׁמְשַׁי סָפְרָא וּשְׁאָר כְּנָוָתְהוֹן דִּינָיֵא וַאֲפַרְסַתְכָיֵא טַרְפְּלָיֵא אֲפָרְסָיֵא ארכוי [אַרְכְּוָיֵא] בָּבְלָיֵא שׁוּשַׁנְכָיֵא דהוא [דֶּהָיֵא] עֵלְמָיֵא:

י וּשְׁאָר אֻמַּיָּא דִּי הַגְלִי אָסְנַפַּר רַבָּא וְיַקִּירָא וְהוֹתֵב הִמּוֹ בְּקִרְיָה דִּי שָׁמְרָיִן וּשְׁאָר עֲבַר־נַהֲרָה וּכְעֶנֶת:

יא דְּנָה פַּרְשֶׁגֶן אִגַּרְתָּא דִּי שְׁלַחוּ עֲלוֹהִי עַל־אַרְתַּחְשַׁשְׂתְּא מַלְכָּא עַבְדָיךְ אֱנָשׁ עֲבַר־נַהֲרָה וּכְעֶנֶת:

יב יְדִיעַ לֶהֱוֵא לְמַלְכָּא דִּי יְהוּדָיֵא דִּי סְלִקוּ מִן־לְוָתָךְ עֲלֶינָא אֲתוֹ לִירוּשְׁלֶם קִרְיְתָא מָרָדְתָּא ובאישתא [וּבִישְׁתָּא] בָּנַיִן ושורי [וְשׁוּרַיָּא] אשכללו [שַׁכְלִלוּ] וְאֻשַּׁיָּא יַחִיטוּ:

Ezra/Nehemiah

4:12 The *Yehudim* The chosen people have many biblical titles: Hebrews, children of *Yaakov,* and Israelites, to name a few. What is the origin of the branding 'Jew', in Hebrew *Yehudi* (יהודי)? The term is first employed as a specific ethnic title during the Babylonian exile, as can be seen in this verse and also in

יהודים

*y'-DEE-a le-he-VAY l'-mal-KA DEE y'-hu-da-YAY DEE s'-LI-ku min
l'-va-TAKH a-LE-na a-TO lee-ru-sh'-LEM kir-y'-TA ma-ra-d'-TA u-veesh-TA
ba-NA-yin v'-shu-ra-YA shakh-LEE-lu v'-u-sha-YA ya-KHEE-tu*

13 Now be it known to the king that if this city is rebuilt and the walls completed, they will not pay tribute, poll-tax, or land-tax, and in the end it will harm the kingdom.

כְּעַן יְדִיעַ לֶהֱוֵא לְמַלְכָּא דִּי הֵן קִרְיְתָא דָךְ תִּתְבְּנֵא וְשׁוּרַיָּה יִשְׁתַּכְלְלוּן מִנְדָּה־בְלוֹ וַהֲלָךְ לָא יִנְתְּנוּן וְאַפְּתֹם מַלְכִים תְּהַנְזִק:

14 Now since we eat the salt of the palace, and it is not right that we should see the king dishonored, we have written to advise the king [of this]

כְּעַן כָּל־קֳבֵל דִּי־מְלַח הֵיכְלָא מְלַחְנָא וְעַרְוַת מַלְכָּא לָא אֲרִיךְ לָנָא לְמֶחֱזֵא עַל־דְּנָה שְׁלַחְנָא וְהוֹדַעְנָא לְמַלְכָּא:

15 so that you may search the records of your fathers and find in the records and know that this city is a rebellious city, harmful to kings and states. Sedition has been rife in it from early times; on that account this city was destroyed.

דִּי יְבַקַּר בִּסְפַר־דָּכְרָנַיָּא דִּי אֲבָהָתָךְ וּתְהַשְׁכַּח בִּסְפַר דָּכְרָנַיָּא וְתִנְדַּע דִּי קִרְיְתָא דָךְ קִרְיָא מָרָדָא וּמְהַנְזְקַת מַלְכִין וּמְדִנָן וְאֶשְׁתַּדּוּר עָבְדִין בְּגַוַּהּ מִן־יוֹמָת עָלְמָא עַל־דְּנָה קִרְיְתָא דָךְ הָחָרְבַת:

16 We advise the king that if this city is rebuilt and its walls are completed, you will no longer have any portion in the province Beyond the River."

מְהוֹדְעִין אֲנַחְנָה לְמַלְכָּא דִּי הֵן קִרְיְתָא דָךְ תִּתְבְּנֵא וְשׁוּרַיָּה יִשְׁתַּכְלְלוּן לָקֳבֵל דְּנָה חֲלָק בַּעֲבַר נַהֲרָא לָא אִיתַי לָךְ:

17 The king sent back the following message: "To Rehum the commissioner and Shimshai the scribe, and the rest of their colleagues, who dwell in *Shomron* and in the rest of the province of Beyond the River, greetings.

פִּתְגָמָא שְׁלַח מַלְכָּא עַל־רְחוּם בְּעֵל־טְעֵם וְשִׁמְשַׁי סָפְרָא וּשְׁאָר כְּנָוָתְהוֹן דִּי יָתְבִין בְּשָׁמְרָיִן וּשְׁאָר עֲבַר־נַהֲרָה שְׁלָם וּכְעֶת:

18 Now the letter that you wrote me has been read to me in translation.

נִשְׁתְּוָנָא דִּי שְׁלַחְתּוּן עֲלֶינָא מְפָרַשׁ קֱרִי קֳדָמָי:

19 At my order a search has been made, and it has been found that this city has from earliest times risen against kings, and that rebellion and sedition have been rife in it.

וּמִנִּי שִׂים טְעֵם וּבַקַּרוּ וְהַשְׁכַּחוּ דִּי קִרְיְתָא דָךְ מִן־יוֹמָת עָלְמָא עַל־מַלְכִין מִתְנַשְּׂאָה וּמְרַד וְאֶשְׁתַּדּוּר מִתְעֲבֶד־בַּהּ:

20 Powerful kings have ruled over *Yerushalayim* and exercised authority over the whole province of Beyond the River, and tribute, poll-tax, and land-tax were paid to them.

וּמַלְכִין תַּקִּיפִין הֲווֹ עַל־יְרוּשְׁלֶם וְשַׁלִּיטִין בְּכֹל עֲבַר נַהֲרָה וּמִדָּה בְלוֹ וַהֲלָךְ מִתְיְהֵב לְהוֹן:

IDF soldier praying in a field

the books of *Daniel* and *Esther*. Historically, this name indicated an association with the tribe of *Yehuda* (יהודה), from which most of the Babylonian exiles descended. However, the name ultimately derives from the Hebrew root which means to 'praise' or 'give thanks', as it says "She [Leah] conceived again and bore a son, and declared, 'This time I will praise *Hashem*.' Therefore she named him *Yehudah*" (Genesis 29:35). The name thus highlights the inherent Jewish value of gratitude to God. The fact that this collective name was given in exile shows that sometimes one has to travel far away to discover who he really is.

²¹ Now issue an order to stop these men; this city is not to be rebuilt until I so order.

²² Take care not to be lax in this matter or there will be much damage and harm to the kingdom."

²³ When the text of the letter of King Artaxerxes was read before Rehum and Shimshai the scribe and their colleagues, they hurried to *Yerushalayim*, to the *Yehudim*, and stopped them by main force.

²⁴ At that time, work on the House of *Hashem* in *Yerushalayim* stopped and remained in abeyance until the second year of the reign of King Darius of Persia.

5 ¹ Then the *Neviim*, *Chagai* the *Navi* and *Zecharya* son of *Ido*, prophesied to the *Yehudim* in *Yehuda* and *Yerushalayim*, inspired by the God of *Yisrael*.

² Thereupon *Zerubavel* son of *Shealtiel* and *Yeshua* son of *Yotzadak* began rebuilding the House of *Hashem* in *Yerushalayim*, with the full support of the *Neviim* of *Hashem*.

bay-DA-yin KA-mu z'-ru-ba-VEL bar sh'-al-tee-AYL v'-yay-SHU-a bar yo-tza-DAK v'-sha-REEV l'-miv-NAY BAYT e-la-HA DEE vee-ru-sh'-LEM v'-i-m'-HON n'-vi-ya-YA dee e-la-HA m'-sa-a-DEEN l'-HON

³ At once Tattenai, governor of the province of Beyond the River, Shethar-bozenai, and their colleagues descended upon them and said this to them, "Who issued orders to you to rebuild this house and complete its furnishing?"

⁴ Then we said to them, "What are the names of the men who are engaged in the building?"

כא כְּעַן שִׂימוּ טְּעֵם לְבַטָּלָא גֻּבְרַיָּא אִלֵּךְ וְקִרְיְתָא דָךְ לָא תִתְבְּנֵא עַד־מִנִּי טַעְמָא יִתְּשָׂם:

כב וּזְהִירִין הֱווֹ שָׁלוּ לְמֶעְבַּד עַל־דְּנָה לְמָה יִשְׂגֵּא חֲבָלָא לְהַנְזָקַת מַלְכִין:

כג אֱדַיִן מִן־דִּי פַּרְשֶׁגֶן נִשְׁתְּוָנָא דִּי ארתחשׁשתא [אַרְתַּחְשַׁשְׂתְּ] מַלְכָּא קֱרִי קֳדָם־רְחוּם וְשִׁמְשַׁי סָפְרָא וּכְנָוָתְהוֹן אֲזַלוּ בִבְהִילוּ לִירוּשְׁלֶם עַל־יְהוּדָיֵא וּבַטִּלוּ הִמּוֹ בְּאֶדְרָע וְחָיִל:

כד בֵּאדַיִן בְּטֵלַת עֲבִידַת בֵּית־אֱלָהָא דִּי בִּירוּשְׁלֶם וַהֲוָת בָּטְלָא עַד שְׁנַת תַּרְתֵּין לְמַלְכוּת דָּרְיָוֶשׁ מֶלֶךְ־פָּרָס:

ה א וְהִתְנַבִּי חַגַּי נביאה [נְבִיָּא] וּזְכַרְיָה בַר־עִדּוֹא נְבִיאַיָּא [נְבִיַּיָּא] עַל־יְהוּדָיֵא דִּי בִיהוּד וּבִירוּשְׁלֶם בְּשֻׁם אֱלָהּ יִשְׂרָאֵל עֲלֵיהוֹן:

ב בֵּאדַיִן קָמוּ זְרֻבָּבֶל בַּר־שְׁאַלְתִּיאֵל וְיֵשׁוּעַ בַּר־יוֹצָדָק וְשָׁרִיו לְמִבְנֵא בֵּית אֱלָהָא דִּי בִירוּשְׁלֶם וְעִמְּהוֹן נְבִיאַיָּא [נְבִיַּיָּא] דִּי־אֱלָהָא מְסָעֲדִין לְהוֹן:

ג בֵּהּ־זִמְנָא אֲתָא עֲלֵיהוֹן תַּתְּנַי פַּחַת עֲבַר־נַהֲרָה וּשְׁתַר בּוֹזְנַי וּכְנָוָתְהוֹן וְכֵן אָמְרִין לְהֹם מַן־שָׂם לְכֹם טְעֵם בַּיְתָא דְנָה לִבְּנֵא וְאֻשַּׁרְנָא דְנָה לְשַׁכְלָלָה:

ד אֱדַיִן כְּנֵמָא אֲמַרְנָא לְהֹם מַן־אִנּוּן שְׁמָהָת גֻּבְרַיָּא דִּי־דְנָה בִנְיָנָא בָּנַיִן:

Ezra/Nehemiah

5:2 With the full support of the *Neviim* of *Hashem*
Starting with chapter 4, verse 8, the language of *Sefer Ezra* switches from Hebrew to Aramaic. However, the *Neviim* of the time, *Chagai*, *Zecharya* and *Malachi*, address the nation exclusively in Hebrew. The Jewish people have been exiled to every corner of the world and, in the process, have learned many different languages. This is as true in the modern Diaspora as it was during the Babylonian and Persian eras. And yet, with the minor exceptions of the Aramaic sections of *Daniel* and *Ezra*, the *Tanakh* was written entirely in Hebrew. Although the Jews spoke other languages, Hebrew remained their essential language. Even if they did not speak it for every-day matter, it continued to be the language used for prayer and study, connecting to Hashem. The fact that Hebrew is again the vibrant and dynamic language of communication in contemporary Israel should not be underestimated. The revival of He-brew as a spoken language in the 19th century, due largely to the ef-forts of Eliezer Ben-Yehuda, is as miraculous as the survival of the Hebrew people them-selves. As Shimon Peres, former president of Israel, pointed out, "None in the Middle East speak their original language, except for Israel."

Hebrew Bible opened to Ecclesiastes

5 But *Hashem* watched over the elders of the *Yehudim* and they were not stopped while a report went to Darius and a letter was sent back in reply to it.

ה וְעֵין אֱלָהֲהֹם הֲוָת עַל־שָׂבֵי יְהוּדָיֵא וְלָא־בַטִּלוּ הִמּוֹ עַד־טַעְמָא לְדָרְיָוֶשׁ יְהָךְ וֶאֱדַיִן יְתִיבוּן נִשְׁתְּוָנָא עַל־דְּנָה:

6 This is the text of the letter that Tattenai, governor of the province of Beyond the River, and Shethar-bozenai and his colleagues, the officials of Beyond the River, sent to King Darius.

ו פַּרְשֶׁגֶן אִגַּרְתָּא דִּי־שְׁלַח תַּתְּנַי פַּחַת עֲבַר־נַהֲרָה וּשְׁתַר בּוֹזְנַי וּכְנָוָתֵהּ אֲפַרְסְכָיֵא דִּי בַּעֲבַר נַהֲרָה עַל־דָּרְיָוֶשׁ מַלְכָּא:

7 They sent a message to him and this is what was written in it: "To King Darius, greetings, and so forth.

ז פִּתְגָמָא שְׁלַחוּ עֲלוֹהִי וְכִדְנָה כְּתִיב בְּגַוֵּהּ לְדָרְיָוֶשׁ מַלְכָּא שְׁלָמָא כֹלָּא:

8 Be it known to the king, that we went to the province of *Yehuda*, to the house of the great *Hashem*. It is being rebuilt of hewn stone, and wood is being laid in the walls. The work is being done with dispatch and is going well.

ח יְדִיעַ לֶהֱוֵא לְמַלְכָּא דִּי־אֲזַלְנָא לִיהוּד מְדִינְתָּא לְבֵית אֱלָהָא רַבָּא וְהוּא מִתְבְּנֵא אֶבֶן גְּלָל וְאָע מִתְּשָׂם בְּכֻתְלַיָּא וַעֲבִידְתָּא דָךְ אָסְפַּרְנָא מִתְעַבְדָא וּמַצְלַח בְּיֶדְהֹם:

9 Thereupon we directed this question to these elders, 'Who issued orders to you to rebuild this house and to complete its furnishings?'

ט אֱדַיִן שְׁאֵלְנָא לְשָׂבַיָּא אִלֵּךְ כְּנֵמָא אֲמַרְנָא לְהֹם מַן־שָׂם לְכֹם טְעֵם בַּיְתָא דְנָה לְמִבְנְיָה וְאֻשַּׁרְנָא דְנָה לְשַׁכְלָלָה:

10 We also asked their names so that we could write down the names of their leaders for your information.

י וְאַף שְׁמָהָתְהֹם שְׁאֵלְנָא לְּהֹם לְהוֹדָעוּתָךְ דִּי נִכְתֻּב שֻׁם־גֻּבְרַיָּא דִּי בְרָאשֵׁיהֹם:

11 This is what they answered us: 'We are the servants of the God of heaven and earth; we are rebuilding the house that was originally built many years ago; a great king of *Yisrael* built it and completed it.

יא וּכְנֵמָא פִתְגָמָא הֲתִיבוּנָא לְמֵמַר אֲנַחְנָא הִמּוֹ עַבְדוֹהִי דִּי־אֱלָהּ שְׁמַיָּא וְאַרְעָא וּבָנַיִן בַּיְתָא דִּי־הֲוָא בְנֵה מִקַּדְמַת דְּנָה שְׁנִין שַׂגִּיאָן וּמֶלֶךְ לְיִשְׂרָאֵל רַב בְּנָהִי וְשַׁכְלְלֵהּ:

12 But because our fathers angered the God of Heaven, He handed them over to Nebuchadnezzar the Chaldean, king of Babylon, who demolished this house and exiled the people to Babylon.

יב לָהֵן מִן־דִּי הַרְגִּזוּ אֲבָהֲתַנָא לֶאֱלָהּ שְׁמַיָּא יְהַב הִמּוֹ בְּיַד נְבוּכַדְנֶצַּר מֶלֶךְ־בָּבֶל כַּסְדָּיָא [כַּסְדָּאָה] וּבַיְתָה דְנָה סַתְרֵהּ וְעַמָּה הַגְלִי לְבָבֶל:

13 But in the first year of King Cyrus of Babylon, King Cyrus issued an order to rebuild this House of *Hashem*.

יג בְּרַם בִּשְׁנַת חֲדָה לְכוֹרֶשׁ מַלְכָּא דִּי בָבֶל כּוֹרֶשׁ מַלְכָּא שָׂם טְעֵם בֵּית־אֱלָהָא דְנָה לִבְּנֵא:

14 Also the silver and gold vessels of the House of *Hashem* that Nebuchadnezzar had taken away from the temple in *Yerushalayim* and brought to the temple in Babylon – King Cyrus released them from the temple in Babylon to be given to the one called *Sheshbatzar* whom he had appointed governor.

יד וְאַף מָאנַיָּא דִי־בֵית־אֱלָהָא דִּי דַהֲבָה וְכַסְפָּא דִּי נְבוּכַדְנֶצַּר הַנְפֵּק מִן־הֵיכְלָא דִּי בִירוּשְׁלֶם וְהֵיבֵל הִמּוֹ לְהֵיכְלָא דִּי בָבֶל הַנְפֵּק הִמּוֹ כּוֹרֶשׁ מַלְכָּא מִן־הֵיכְלָא דִּי בָבֶל וִיהִיבוּ לְשֵׁשְׁבַּצַּר שְׁמֵהּ דִּי פֶחָה שָׂמֵהּ:

15 He said to him, "Take these vessels, go, deposit them in the temple in *Yerushalayim*, and let the House of *Hashem* be rebuilt on its original site."

טו וַאֲמַר־לֵהּ אלה [אֵל] מָאנַיָּא שֵׂא אֵזֶל־אֲחֵת הִמּוֹ בְּהֵיכְלָא דִּי בִירוּשְׁלֶם וּבֵית אֱלָהָא יִתְבְּנֵא עַל־אַתְרֵהּ:

16 That same *Sheshbatzar* then came and laid the foundations for the House of *Hashem* in *Yerushalayim*; and ever since then it has been under construction, but is not yet finished.'

טו אֱדַיִן שֵׁשְׁבַּצַּר דֵּךְ אֲתָא יְהַב אֻשַּׁיָּא דִּי־בֵית אֱלָהָא דִּי בִּירוּשְׁלֶם וּמִן־אֱדַיִן וְעַד־כְּעַן מִתְבְּנֵא וְלָא שְׁלִם:

17 And now, if it please the king, let the royal archives there in Babylon be searched to see whether indeed an order had been issued by King Cyrus to rebuild this House of *Hashem* in *Yerushalayim*. May the king convey to us his pleasure in this matter."

יז וּכְעַן הֵן עַל־מַלְכָּא טָב יִתְבַּקַּר בְּבֵית גִּנְזַיָּא דִּי־מַלְכָּא תַמָּה דִּי בְּבָבֶל הֵן אִיתַי דִּי־מִן־כּוֹרֶשׁ מַלְכָּא שִׂים טְעֵם לְמִבְנֵא בֵּית־אֱלָהָא דֵךְ בִּירוּשְׁלֶם וּרְעוּת מַלְכָּא עַל־דְּנָה יִשְׁלַח עֲלֶינָא:

6 1 Thereupon, at the order of King Darius, they searched the archives where the treasures were stored in Babylon.

א בֵּאדַיִן דָּרְיָוֶשׁ מַלְכָּא שָׂם טְעֵם וּבַקַּרוּ בְּבֵית סִפְרַיָּא דִּי גִנְזַיָּא מְהַחֲתִין תַּמָּה בְּבָבֶל:

2 But it was in the citadel of Ecbatana, in the province of Media, that a scroll was found in which the following was written: "Memorandum:

ב וְהִשְׁתְּכַח בְּאַחְמְתָא בְּבִירְתָא דִּי בְמָדַי מְדִינְתָּה מְגִלָּה חֲדָה וְכֵן־כְּתִיב בְּגַוַּהּ דִּכְרוֹנָה:

3 In the first year of King Cyrus, King Cyrus issued an order concerning the House of *Hashem* in *Yerushalayim*: 'Let the house be rebuilt, a place for offering sacrifices, with a base built up high. Let it be sixty *amot* high and sixty *amot* wide,

ג בִּשְׁנַת חֲדָה לְכוֹרֶשׁ מַלְכָּא כּוֹרֶשׁ מַלְכָּא שָׂם טְעֵם בֵּית־אֱלָהָא בִירוּשְׁלֶם בַּיְתָא יִתְבְּנֵא אֲתַר דִּי־דָבְחִין דִּבְחִין וְאֻשּׁוֹהִי מְסוֹבְלִין רוּמֵהּ אַמִּין שִׁתִּין פְּתָיֵהּ אַמִּין שִׁתִּין:

4 with a course of unused timber for each three courses of hewn stone. The expenses shall be paid by the palace.

ד נִדְבָּכִין דִּי־אֶבֶן גְּלָל תְּלָתָא וְנִדְבָּךְ דִּי־אָע חֲדַת וְנִפְקְתָא מִן־בֵּית מַלְכָּא תִּתְיְהִב:

5 And the gold and silver vessels of the House of *Hashem* which Nebuchadnezzar had taken away from the temple in *Yerushalayim* and transported to Babylon shall be returned, and let each go back to the temple in *Yerushalayim* where it belongs; you shall deposit it in the House of *Hashem*.'

ה וְאַף מָאנֵי בֵית־אֱלָהָא דִּי דַהֲבָה וְכַסְפָּא דִּי נְבוּכַדְנֶצַּר הַנְפֵּק מִן־הֵיכְלָא דִּי־בִירוּשְׁלֶם וְהֵיבֵל לְבָבֶל יַהֲתִיבוּן וִיהָךְ לְהֵיכְלָא דִי־בִירוּשְׁלֶם לְאַתְרֵהּ וְתַחֵת בְּבֵית אֱלָהָא:

6 "Now you, Tattenai, governor of the province of Beyond the River, Shethar-bozenai and colleagues, the officials of the province of Beyond the River, stay away from that place.

ו כְּעַן תַּתְּנַי פַּחַת עֲבַר־נַהֲרָה שְׁתַר בּוֹזְנַי וּכְנָוָתְהוֹן אֲפַרְסְכָיֵא דִּי בַּעֲבַר נַהֲרָה רַחִיקִין הֲווֹ מִן־תַּמָּה:

7 Allow the work of this House of *Hashem* to go on; let the governor of the *Yehudim* and the elders of the *Yehudim* rebuild this House of *Hashem* on its site.

ז שְׁבֻקוּ לַעֲבִידַת בֵּית־אֱלָהָא דֵךְ פַּחַת יְהוּדָיֵא וּלְשָׂבֵי יְהוּדָיֵא בֵּית־אֱלָהָא דֵךְ יִבְנוֹן עַל־אַתְרֵהּ:

8 And I hereby issue an order concerning what you must do to help these elders of the *Yehudim* rebuild this House of *Hashem*: the expenses are to be paid to these men with dispatch out of the resources of the king, derived from the taxes of the province of Beyond the River, so that the work not be stopped.

ח וּמִנִּי שִׂים טְעֵם לְמָא דִי־תַעַבְדוּן עִם־שָׂבֵי יְהוּדָיֵא אִלֵּךְ לְמִבְנֵא בֵּית־אֱלָהָא דֵךְ וּמִנִּכְסֵי מַלְכָּא דִּי מִדַּת עֲבַר נַהֲרָה אָסְפַּרְנָא נִפְקְתָא תֶּהֱוֵא מִתְיַהֲבָא לְגֻבְרַיָּא אִלֵּךְ דִּי־לָא לְבַטָּלָא:

9 They are to be given daily, without fail, whatever they need of young bulls, rams, or lambs as burnt offerings for the God of Heaven, and wheat, salt, wine, and oil, at the order of the *Kohanim* in *Yerushalayim,*

ט וּמָה חַשְׁחָן וּבְנֵי תוֹרִין וְדִכְרִין וְאִמְּרִין לַעֲלָוָן לֶאֱלָהּ שְׁמַיָּא חִנְטִין מְלַח חֲמַר וּמְשַׁח כְּמֵאמַר כָּהֲנַיָּא דִי־בִירוּשְׁלֶם לֶהֱוֵא מִתְיְהֵב לְהֹם יוֹם בְּיוֹם דִּי־לָא שָׁלוּ:

10 so that they may offer pleasing sacrifices to the God of Heaven and pray for the life of the king and his sons.

י דִּי־לֶהֱוֹן מְהַקְרְבִין נִיחוֹחִין לֶאֱלָהּ שְׁמַיָּא וּמְצַלַּיִן לְחַיֵּי מַלְכָּא וּבְנוֹהִי:

11 I also issue an order that whoever alters this decree shall have a beam removed from his house, and he shall be impaled on it and his house confiscated.

יא וּמִנִּי שִׂים טְעֵם דִּי כָל־אֱנָשׁ דִּי יְהַשְׁנֵא פִּתְגָמָא דְנָה יִתְנְסַח אָע מִן־בַּיְתֵהּ וּזְקִיף יִתְמְחֵא עֲלֹהִי וּבַיְתֵהּ נְוָלוּ יִתְעֲבֵד עַל־דְּנָה:

12 And may the God who established His name there cause the downfall of any king or nation that undertakes to alter or damage that House of *Hashem* in *Yerushalayim.* I, Darius, have issued the decree; let it be carried out with dispatch."

יב וֵאלָהָא דִּי שַׁכִּן שְׁמֵהּ תַּמָּה יְמַגַּר כָּל־מֶלֶךְ וְעַם דִּי יִשְׁלַח יְדֵהּ לְהַשְׁנָיָה לְחַבָּלָה בֵּית־אֱלָהָא דֵךְ דִּי בִירוּשְׁלֶם אֲנָה דָרְיָוֶשׁ שָׂמֵת טְעֵם אָסְפַּרְנָא יִתְעֲבִד:

13 Then Tattenai, governor of the province of Beyond the River, Shethar-bozenai, and their colleagues carried out with dispatch what King Darius had written.

יג אֱדַיִן תַּתְּנַי פַּחַת עֲבַר־נַהֲרָה שְׁתַר בּוֹזְנַי וּכְנָוָתְהוֹן לָקֳבֵל דִּי־שְׁלַח דָּרְיָוֶשׁ מַלְכָּא כְּנֵמָא אָסְפַּרְנָא עֲבַדוּ:

14 So the elders of the *Yehudim* progressed in the building, urged on by the prophesying of *Chagai* the *Navi* and *Zecharya* son of *Ido,* and they brought the building to completion under the aegis of the God of *Yisrael* and by the order of Cyrus and Darius and King Artaxerxes of Persia.

יד וְשָׂבֵי יְהוּדָיֵא בָּנַיִן וּמַצְלְחִין בִּנְבוּאַת חַגַּי נְבִיאָה [נְבִיָּא] וּזְכַרְיָה בַּר־עִדּוֹא וּבְנוֹ וְשַׁכְלִלוּ מִן־טַעַם אֱלָהּ יִשְׂרָאֵל וּמִטְּעֵם כּוֹרֶשׁ וְדָרְיָוֶשׁ וְאַרְתַּחְשַׁשְׂתְּא מֶלֶךְ פָּרָס:

v'-sha-VAY y'-hu-da-YAY ba-NA-yin u-matz-l'-KHEEN
bin-vu-AT kha-GAI n'-vi-YAH uz-khar-YAH bar i-DO uv-NO
v'-shakh-LI-lu min TA-am e-LAH yis-ra-AYL u-mi-t'-AYM KO-resh
v'-dar-YA-vesh v'-ar-takh-SHAS-t' ME-lekh pa-RAS

6:14 By the order of Cyrus and Darius and King Artaxerxes The autonomy of the Jewish people has often been subject to the blessings or restraints of foreigners. Cyrus's edict to allow the People of Israel to return to the Land of Israel and rebuild the *Beit Hamikdash* was a ray of hope in a bleak time. Persian approval of Jewish authority constituted a remarkable turning of the tide for the exiled Jews. Though construction of the Temple was temporarily halted, it was eventually completed in the sixth year of the reign of Darius, with his permission. The British Government's 1917 Balfour Declaration possessed similar promise when it declared: "His Majesty's government view with favour the establishment in Palestine of a national home for the Jewish people, and will use their best endeavours to facilitate the achievement of this object." In fact, Harry Truman said of his May 1948 recognition of the State of Israel as president of the United States: "I am Cyrus." In all these cases, it was non-Jews serving as God's agents who facilitated the return of the Jewish people to *Eretz Yisrael.*

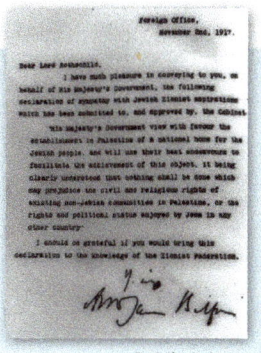

The Balfour Declaration

15 The house was finished on the third of the month of *Adar* in the sixth year of the reign of King Darius.

טו וְשֵׁיצִיא בַּיְתָה דְנָה עַד יוֹם תְּלָתָה לִירַח אֲדָר דִּי־הִיא שְׁנַת־שֵׁת לְמַלְכוּת דָּרְיָוֶשׁ מַלְכָּא:

16 The Israelites, the *Kohanim*, and the *Leviim*, and all the other exiles celebrated the dedication of the House of *Hashem* with joy.

טז וַעֲבַדוּ בְנֵי־יִשְׂרָאֵל כָּהֲנַיָּא וְלֵוָיֵא וּשְׁאָר בְּנֵי־גָלוּתָא חֲנֻכַּת בֵּית־אֱלָהָא דְנָה בְּחֶדְוָה:

17 And they sacrificed for the dedication of this House of *Hashem* one hundred bulls, two hundred rams, four hundred lambs, and twelve goats as a purification offering for all of *Yisrael*, according to the number of the tribes of *Yisrael*.

יז וְהַקְרִבוּ לַחֲנֻכַּת בֵּית־אֱלָהָא דְנָה תּוֹרִין מְאָה דִּכְרִין מָאתַיִן אִמְּרִין אַרְבַּע מְאָה וּצְפִירֵי עִזִּין לְחַטָּיָא [לְחַטָּאָה] עַל־כָּל־יִשְׂרָאֵל תְּרֵי־עֲשַׂר לְמִנְיָן שִׁבְטֵי יִשְׂרָאֵל:

18 They appointed the *Kohanim* in their courses and the *Leviim* in their divisions for the service of *Hashem* in *Yerushalayim*, according to the prescription in the Book of *Moshe*.

יח וַהֲקִימוּ כָהֲנַיָּא בִּפְלֻגָּתְהוֹן וְלֵוָיֵא בְּמַחְלְקָתְהוֹן עַל־עֲבִידַת אֱלָהָא דִּי בִירוּשְׁלֶם כִּכְתָב סְפַר מֹשֶׁה:

19 The returned exiles celebrated the *Pesach* on the fourteenth day of the first month,

יט וַיַּעֲשׂוּ בְנֵי־הַגּוֹלָה אֶת־הַפָּסַח בְּאַרְבָּעָה עָשָׂר לַחֹדֶשׁ הָרִאשׁוֹן:

20 for the *Kohanim* and *Leviim* had purified themselves to a man; they were all pure. They slaughtered the *Pesach* offering for all the returned exiles, and for their brother *Kohanim* and for themselves.

כ כִּי הִטַּהֲרוּ הַכֹּהֲנִים וְהַלְוִיִּם כְּאֶחָד כֻּלָּם טְהוֹרִים וַיִּשְׁחֲטוּ הַפֶּסַח לְכָל־בְּנֵי הַגּוֹלָה וְלַאֲחֵיהֶם הַכֹּהֲנִים וְלָהֶם:

21 The children of *Yisrael* who had returned from the exile, together with all who joined them in separating themselves from the uncleanliness of the nations of the lands to worship God of *Yisrael*, ate of it.

כא וַיֹּאכְלוּ בְנֵי־יִשְׂרָאֵל הַשָּׁבִים מֵהַגּוֹלָה וְכֹל הַנִּבְדָּל מִטֻּמְאַת גּוֹיֵ־הָאָרֶץ אֲלֵהֶם לִדְרֹשׁ לַיהוָה אֱלֹהֵי יִשְׂרָאֵל:

22 They joyfully celebrated the festival of *Pesach* for seven days, for *Hashem* had given them cause for joy by inclining the heart of the Assyrian king toward them so as to give them support in the work of the House of *Hashem*, the God of *Yisrael*.

כב וַיַּעֲשׂוּ חַג־מַצּוֹת שִׁבְעַת יָמִים בְּשִׂמְחָה כִּי שִׂמְּחָם יְהוָה וְהֵסַב לֵב מֶלֶךְ־אַשּׁוּר עֲלֵיהֶם לְחַזֵּק יְדֵיהֶם בִּמְלֶאכֶת בֵּית־הָאֱלֹהִים אֱלֹהֵי יִשְׂרָאֵל:

7 1 After these events, during the reign of King Artaxerxes of Persia, *Ezra* son of *Seraya* son of *Azarya* son of *Chilkiya*

ז א וְאַחַר הַדְּבָרִים הָאֵלֶּה בְּמַלְכוּת אַרְתַּחְשַׁסְתְּא מֶלֶךְ־פָּרָס עֶזְרָא בֶּן־שְׂרָיָה בֶּן־עֲזַרְיָה בֶּן־חִלְקִיָּה:

2 son of *Shalum* son of *Tzadok* son of *Achituv*

ב בֶּן־שַׁלּוּם בֶּן־צָדוֹק בֶּן־אֲחִיטוּב:

3 son of Amariah son of *Azarya* son of Meraioth

ג בֶּן־אֲמַרְיָה בֶן־עֲזַרְיָה בֶּן־מְרָיוֹת:

4 son of Zerahiah son of Uzzi son of Bukki

ד בֶּן־זְרַחְיָה בֶן־עֻזִּי בֶּן־בֻּקִּי:

5 son of Abishua son of *Pinchas* son of *Elazar* son of *Aharon* the chief *Kohen* –

ה בֶּן־אֲבִישׁוּעַ בֶּן־פִּינְחָס בֶּן־אֶלְעָזָר בֶּן־אַהֲרֹן הַכֹּהֵן הָרֹאשׁ:

6 that *Ezra* came up from Babylon, a scribe expert in the Teaching of *Moshe* which God of *Yisrael* had given, whose request the king had granted in its entirety, thanks to the benevolence of *Hashem* toward him.

ו הוּא עֶזְרָא עָלָה מִבָּבֶל וְהוּא־סֹפֵר מָהִיר בְּתוֹרַת מֹשֶׁה אֲשֶׁר־נָתַן יְהוָה אֱלֹהֵי יִשְׂרָאֵל וַיִּתֶּן־לוֹ הַמֶּלֶךְ כְּיַד־יְהוָה אֱלֹהָיו עָלָיו כֹּל בַּקָּשָׁתוֹ׃

> HU ez-RA a-LAH mi-ba-VEL v'-hu so-FAYR ma-HEER b'-to-RAT
> mo-SHEH a-sher na-TAN a-do-NAI e-lo-HAY yis-ra-AYL va-yi-ten LO
> ha-ME-lekh k'-yad a-do-NAI e-lo-HAV a-LAV KOL ba-ka-sha-TO

7 Some of the Israelites, the *Kohanim* and *Leviim*, the singers, the gatekeepers, and the temple servants set out for *Yerushalayim* in the seventh year of King Artaxerxes,

ז וַיַּעֲלוּ מִבְּנֵי־יִשְׂרָאֵל וּמִן־הַכֹּהֲנִים וְהַלְוִיִּם וְהַמְשֹׁרְרִים וְהַשֹּׁעֲרִים וְהַנְּתִינִים אֶל־יְרוּשָׁלִַם בִּשְׁנַת־שֶׁבַע לְאַרְתַּחְשַׁסְתְּא הַמֶּלֶךְ׃

8 arriving in *Yerushalayim* in the fifth month in the seventh year of the king.)

ח וַיָּבֹא יְרוּשָׁלִַם בַּחֹדֶשׁ הַחֲמִישִׁי הִיא שְׁנַת הַשְּׁבִיעִית לַמֶּלֶךְ׃

9 On the first day of the first month the journey up from Babylon was started, and on the first day of the fifth month he arrived in *Yerushalayim*, thanks to the benevolent care of his God for him.

ט כִּי בְּאֶחָד לַחֹדֶשׁ הָרִאשׁוֹן הוּא יְסֻד הַמַּעֲלָה מִבָּבֶל וּבְאֶחָד לַחֹדֶשׁ הַחֲמִישִׁי בָּא אֶל־יְרוּשָׁלִַם כְּיַד־אֱלֹהָיו הַטּוֹבָה עָלָיו׃

> KEE b'-e-KHAD la-KHO-desh ha-ri-SHON HU y'-SUD ha-ma-a-LAH
> mi-ba-VEL uv-e-KHAD la-KHO-desh ha-kha-mee-SHEE BA
> el y'-ru-sha-LA-im k'-yad e-lo-HAV ha-to-VAH a-LAV

Ezra 7:6 A scribe expert in the Teaching of *Moshe*
Ezra was known as a *sofer* (סופר), a 'scribe' who reintroduced the *Torah* to public life in Jerusalem following the Babylonian exile. According the Talmud (*Bava Kama* 82a), he instituted public reading of the *Torah* on *Shabbat* in order to make it more dear to the People of Israel. In modern times, another "scribe" made a great contribution to Israel's love for the *Torah*. Eliyahu Koren (1907–2001) was a master typographer who emigrated from Germany to Israel in 1933. He opened Koren Publishers Jerusalem in 1961, and the following year published the "Koren *Tanakh*," the first Bible edited, designed, produced and bound by Jews in nearly 500 years. David Ben Gurion responded to the publication of the *Tanakh*, "Israel is redeemed from shame." Koren, along with his team of experts, considered the precision of every letter, the placement of every word on every page and designed a new font to ensure maximum clarity and to signify the renewal of ancient Hebrew in modern times. The Koren *Tanakh's* textual accuracy, innovative design and superior quality won it worldwide acclaim. After its publication, it became the Bible that IDF soldiers received, along with a gun, upon their induction into the Israel Defense Forces, and it is the Bible upon which Knesset members are sworn into office. As then Speaker of the Knesset Mr. Kadish Luz declared, "From this day forth, all of Israel's presidents shall take their oaths of office upon this Bible. We have been governed by a Provisional State Council, a Provisional Government and even now sit in the temporary Knesset building. To date, Israeli presidents have been sworn in using a temporary edition of the Bible. This occasion symbolizes our overcoming of foreign heritage and return to our origins".

7:9 The journey up from Babylon was started
The late nineteenth and twentieth centuries witnessed a series of massive waves of Jewish immigration to Israel, known as *aliyot*, literally, 'ascents.' Each *aliyah* had a specific demographic character. The nature of the returning Babylonian Jews was similar to the immigrants who came during the years 1882–1904 on what is known as the "First *Aliyah*". In both cases, the groups were mostly comprised of poor religious families. But to call these modern Zionists immigrants "first" is not entirely correct. Not only have there

Yesud Hamaala

10 For *Ezra* had dedicated himself to study the Teaching of *Hashem* so as to observe it, and to teach laws and rules to *Yisrael*.

י" כִּי עֶזְרָא הֵכִין לְבָבוֹ לִדְרוֹשׁ אֶת־תּוֹרַת יְהֹוָה וְלַעֲשֹׂת וּלְלַמֵּד בְּיִשְׂרָאֵל חֹק וּמִשְׁפָּט:

11 The following is the text of the letter which King Artaxerxes gave *Ezra* the *Kohen*-scribe, a scholar in matters concerning the commandments of *Hashem* and His laws to *Yisrael*:

יא וְזֶה פַּרְשֶׁגֶן הַנִּשְׁתְּוָן אֲשֶׁר נָתַן הַמֶּלֶךְ אַרְתַּחְשַׁסְתְּא לְעֶזְרָא הַכֹּהֵן הַסֹּפֵר סֹפֵר דִּבְרֵי מִצְוֹת־יְהֹוָה וְחֻקָּיו עַל־יִשְׂרָאֵל:

12 "Artaxerxes king of kings, to *Ezra* the *Kohen*, scholar in the law of the God of heaven, and so forth. And now,

יב אַרְתַּחְשַׁסְתְּא מֶלֶךְ מַלְכַיָּא לְעֶזְרָא כָהֲנָא סָפַר דָּתָא דִּי־אֱלָהּ שְׁמַיָּא גְּמִיר וּכְעֶנֶת:

13 I hereby issue an order that anyone in my kingdom who is of the people of *Yisrael* and its *Kohanim* and *Leviim* who feels impelled to go to *Yerushalayim* may go with you.

יג מִנִּי שִׂים טְעֵם דִּי כָל־מִתְנַדַּב בְּמַלְכוּתִי מִן־עַמָּא יִשְׂרָאֵל וְכָהֲנוֹהִי וְלֵוָיֵא לִמְהָךְ לִירוּשְׁלֶם עִמָּךְ יְהָךְ:

14 For you are commissioned by the king and his seven advisers to regulate *Yehuda* and *Yerushalayim* according to the law of your God, which is in your care,

יד כָּל־קֳבֵל דִּי מִן־קֳדָם מַלְכָּא וְשִׁבְעַת יָעֲטֹהִי שְׁלִיחַ לְבַקָּרָא עַל־יְהוּד וְלִירוּשְׁלֶם בְּדָת אֱלָהָךְ דִּי בִידָךְ:

15 and to bring the freewill offering of silver and gold, which the king and his advisers made to the God of *Yisrael*, whose dwelling is in *Yerushalayim*,

טו וּלְהֵיבָלָה כְּסַף וּדְהַב דִּי־מַלְכָּא וְיָעֲטוֹהִי הִתְנַדַּבוּ לֶאֱלָהּ יִשְׂרָאֵל דִּי בִירוּשְׁלֶם מִשְׁכְּנֵהּ:

16 and whatever silver and gold that you find throughout the province of Babylon, together with the freewill offerings that the people and the *Kohanim* will give for the House of their God, which is in *Yerushalayim*.

טז וְכֹל כְּסַף וּדְהַב דִּי תְהַשְׁכַּח בְּכֹל מְדִינַת בָּבֶל עִם הִתְנַדָּבוּת עַמָּא וְכָהֲנַיָּא מִתְנַדְּבִין לְבֵית אֱלָהֲהֹם דִּי בִירוּשְׁלֶם:

17 You shall, therefore, with dispatch acquire with this money bulls, rams, and lambs, with their meal offerings and libations, and offer them on the *Mizbayach* of the House of your God in *Yerushalayim*.

יז כָּל־קֳבֵל דְּנָה אָסְפַּרְנָא תִקְנֵא בְּכַסְפָּא דְנָה תּוֹרִין דִּכְרִין אִמְּרִין וּמִנְחָתְהוֹן וְנִסְכֵּיהוֹן וּתְקָרֵב הִמּוֹ עַל־מַדְבְּחָה דִּי בֵּית אֱלָהֲכֹם דִּי בִירוּשְׁלֶם:

18 And whatever you wish to do with the leftover silver and gold, you and your kinsmen may do, in accord with the will of your God.

יח וּמָה דִי עֲלָיִךְ [עֲלָךְ] וְעַל־אֶחָיִךְ [אֶחָךְ] יֵיטַב בִּשְׁאָר כַּסְפָּא וְדַהֲבָה לְמֶעְבַּד כִּרְעוּת אֱלָהֲכֹם תַּעַבְדוּן:

19 The vessels for the service of the House of your God that are given to you, deliver to *Hashem* in *Yerushalayim*,

יט וּמָאנַיָּא דִּי־מִתְיַהֲבִין לָךְ לְפָלְחָן בֵּית אֱלָהָךְ הַשְׁלֵם קֳדָם אֱלָהּ יְרוּשְׁלֶם:

been waves of immigration to Israel throughout the centuries, but their forefathers returning from Babylon preceded them by two-thousand five-hundred years. In 1883, the first modern Jewish community in the northern Hula Valley was established by members of the "First aliyah." Inspired by this verse in *Ezra* describing the return of the Babylonian Jews, its founders named it *Yesud 'Ha'Ma'ala*, translated here as 'the journey up was started.'

20 and any other needs of the House of your God that it falls to you to supply, do so from the royal treasury.

כ וּשְׁאָר חַשְׁחוּת בֵּית אֱלָהָךְ דִּי יִפֶּל־לָךְ לְמִנְתַּן תִּנְתֵּן מִן־בֵּית גִּנְזֵי מַלְכָּא:

21 I, King Artaxerxes, for my part, hereby issue an order to all the treasurers in the province of Beyond the River that whatever request *Ezra* the *Kohen*, scholar in the law of the God of Heaven, makes of you is to be fulfilled with dispatch

כא וּמִנִּי אֲנָה אַרְתַּחְשַׁסְתְּא מַלְכָּא שִׂים טְעֵם לְכֹל גִּזַּבְרַיָּא דִּי בַּעֲבַר נַהֲרָה דִּי כָל־דִּי יִשְׁאֲלֶנְכוֹן עֶזְרָא כָהֲנָא סָפַר דָּתָא דִּי־אֱלָהּ שְׁמַיָּא אָסְפַּרְנָא יִתְעֲבִד:

22 up to the sum of one hundred *kikarot* of silver, one hundred *kor* of wheat, one hundred *batim* of wine, one hundred *batim* of oil, and salt without limit.

כב עַד־כְּסַף כַּכְּרִין מְאָה וְעַד־חִנְטִין כֹּרִין מְאָה וְעַד־חֲמַר בַּתִּין מְאָה וְעַד־בַּתִּין מְשַׁח מְאָה וּמְלַח דִּי־לָא כְתָב:

23 Whatever is by order of the God of Heaven must be carried out diligently for the House of the God of Heaven, else wrath will come upon the king and his sons.

כג כָּל־דִּי מִן־טַעַם אֱלָהּ שְׁמַיָּא יִתְעֲבֵד אַדְרַזְדָּא לְבֵית אֱלָהּ שְׁמַיָּא דִּי־לְמָה לֶהֱוֵא קְצַף עַל־מַלְכוּת מַלְכָּא וּבְנוֹהִי:

24 We further advise you that it is not permissible to impose tribute, poll tax, or land tax on any *Kohen*, *Levi*, singer, gatekeeper, temple servant, or other servant of this House of *Hashem*.

כד וּלְכֹם מְהוֹדְעִין דִּי כָל־כָּהֲנַיָּא וְלֵוָיֵא זַמָּרַיָּא תָרָעַיָּא נְתִינַיָּא וּפָלְחֵי בֵּית אֱלָהָא דְנָה מִנְדָּה בְלוֹ וַהֲלָךְ לָא שַׁלִּיט לְמִרְמֵא עֲלֵיהֹם:

25 And you, *Ezra*, by the divine wisdom you possess, appoint magistrates and judges to judge all the people in the province of Beyond the River who know the laws of your God, and to teach those who do not know them.

כה וְאַנְתְּ עֶזְרָא כְּחָכְמַת אֱלָהָךְ דִּי־בִידָךְ מֶנִּי שָׁפְטִין וְדַיָּנִין דִּי־לֶהֱוֹן דָּאֲנִין [דָּאיְנִין] לְכָל־עַמָּה דִּי בַּעֲבַר נַהֲרָה לְכָל־יָדְעֵי דָּתֵי אֱלָהָךְ וְדִי לָא יָדַע תְּהוֹדְעוּן:

26 Let anyone who does not obey the law of your God and the law of the king be punished with dispatch, whether by death, corporal punishment, confiscation of possessions, or imprisonment."

כו וְכָל־דִּי־לָא לֶהֱוֵא עָבֵד דָּתָא דִי־אֱלָהָךְ וְדָתָא דִּי מַלְכָּא אָסְפַּרְנָא דִּינָה לֶהֱוֵא מִתְעֲבֵד מִנֵּהּ הֵן לְמוֹת הֵן לִשְׁרֹשׁוּ [לִשְׁרֹשִׁי] הֵן־לַעֲנָשׁ נִכְסִין וְלֶאֱסוּרִין:

27 Blessed is God of our fathers, who put it into the mind of the king to glorify the House of *Hashem* in *Yerushalayim*,

כז בָּרוּךְ יְהֹוָה אֱלֹהֵי אֲבוֹתֵינוּ אֲשֶׁר נָתַן כָּזֹאת בְּלֵב הַמֶּלֶךְ לְפָאֵר אֶת־בֵּית יְהֹוָה אֲשֶׁר בִּירוּשָׁלָםִ:

28 and who inclined the king and his counselors and the king's military officers to be favorably disposed toward me. For my part, thanks to the care of *Hashem* for me, I summoned up courage and assembled leading men in *Yisrael* to go with me.

כח וְעָלַי הִטָּה־חֶסֶד לִפְנֵי הַמֶּלֶךְ וְיוֹעֲצָיו וּלְכָל־שָׂרֵי הַמֶּלֶךְ הַגִּבֹּרִים וַאֲנִי הִתְחַזַּקְתִּי כְּיַד־יְהֹוָה אֱלֹהַי עָלַי וָאֶקְבְּצָה מִיִּשְׂרָאֵל רָאשִׁים לַעֲלוֹת עִמִּי:

8 1 These are the chiefs of the clans and the register of the genealogy of those who came up with me from Babylon in the reign of King Artaxerxes:

ח א וְאֵלֶּה רָאשֵׁי אֲבֹתֵיהֶם וְהִתְיַחְשָׂם הָעֹלִים עִמִּי בְּמַלְכוּת אַרְתַּחְשַׁסְתְּא הַמֶּלֶךְ מִבָּבֶל:

2 Of the sons of *Pinchas*, *Gershom*; of the sons of *Itamar*, *Daniel*; of the sons of *David*, Hattush.

ב מִבְּנֵי פִינְחָס גֵּרְשֹׁם מִבְּנֵי אִיתָמָר דָּנִיֵּאל מִבְּנֵי דָוִיד חַטּוּשׁ:

3   Of the sons of *Shechanya*: of the sons of Parosh, *Zecharya*; through him the genealogy of 150 males was registered.

ג   מִבְּנֵי שְׁכַנְיָה מִבְּנֵי פַרְעֹשׁ זְכַרְיָה וְעִמּוֹ הִתְיַחֵשׂ לִזְכָרִים מֵאָה וַחֲמִשִּׁים:

4   Eliehoenai son of Zerahiah, of the sons of Pahathmoab, and with him 200 males.

ד   מִבְּנֵי פַּחַת מוֹאָב אֶלְיְהוֹעֵינַי בֶּן־זְרַחְיָה וְעִמּוֹ מָאתַיִם הַזְּכָרִים:

5   Of the sons of *Shechanya* son of *Yachaziel*; and with him 300 males.

ה   מִבְּנֵי שְׁכַנְיָה בֶּן־יַחֲזִיאֵל וְעִמּוֹ שְׁלֹשׁ מֵאוֹת הַזְּכָרִים:

6   And of the sons of Adin, Ebed son of *Yonatan*; and with him 50 males.

ו   וּמִבְּנֵי עָדִין עֶבֶד בֶּן־יוֹנָתָן וְעִמּוֹ חֲמִשִּׁים הַזְּכָרִים:

7   And of the sons of Elam, Jeshaiah son of *Atalya*; and with him 70 males.

ז   וּמִבְּנֵי עֵילָם יְשַׁעְיָה בֶּן־עֲתַלְיָה וְעִמּוֹ שִׁבְעִים הַזְּכָרִים:

8   And of the sons of Shephatiah, Zebadiah son of *Michael*; and with him 80 males.

ח   וּמִבְּנֵי שְׁפַטְיָה זְבַדְיָה בֶּן־מִיכָאֵל וְעִמּוֹ שְׁמֹנִים הַזְּכָרִים:

9   Of the sons of *Yoav*, *Ovadya* son of *Yechiel*; and with him 218 males.

ט   מִבְּנֵי יוֹאָב עֹבַדְיָה בֶּן־יְחִיאֵל וְעִמּוֹ מָאתַיִם וּשְׁמֹנָה עָשָׂר הַזְּכָרִים:

10   And of the sons of Shelomith, the son of Josiphiah; and with him 160 males.

י   וּמִבְּנֵי שְׁלוֹמִית בֶּן־יוֹסִפְיָה וְעִמּוֹ מֵאָה וְשִׁשִּׁים הַזְּכָרִים:

11   And of the sons of Bebai, *Zecharya* son of Bebai; and with him 28 males.

יא   וּמִבְּנֵי בֵבַי זְכַרְיָה בֶּן־בֵּבָי וְעִמּוֹ עֶשְׂרִים וּשְׁמֹנָה הַזְּכָרִים:

12   And of the sons of Azgad, *Yochanan* son of Hakkatan; and with him 110 males.

יב   וּמִבְּנֵי עַזְגָּד יוֹחָנָן בֶּן־הַקָּטָן וְעִמּוֹ מֵאָה וַעֲשָׂרָה הַזְּכָרִים:

13   And of the sons of Adonikam, who were the last; and these are their names: Eliphelet, Jeiel, and *Shemaya*; and with them 60 males.

יג   וּמִבְּנֵי אֲדֹנִיקָם אַחֲרֹנִים וְאֵלֶּה שְׁמוֹתָם אֱלִיפֶלֶט יְעִיאֵל וּשְׁמַעְיָה וְעִמָּהֶם שִׁשִּׁים הַזְּכָרִים:

14   And of the sons of Bigvai, Uthai and Zaccur; and with them 70 males.

יד   וּמִבְּנֵי בִגְוַי עוּתַי וזבוד [וְזַכּוּר] וְעִמּוֹ שִׁבְעִים הַזְּכָרִים:

15   These I assembled by the river that enters Ahava, and we encamped there for three days. I reviewed the people and the *Kohanim*, but I did not find any *Leviim* there.

טו   וָאֶקְבְּצֵם אֶל־הַנָּהָר הַבָּא אֶל־אַהֲוָא וַנַּחֲנֶה שָׁם יָמִים שְׁלֹשָׁה וָאָבִינָה בָעָם וּבַכֹּהֲנִים וּמִבְּנֵי לֵוִי לֹא־מָצָאתִי שָׁם:

16   I sent for *Eliezer*, Ariel, *Shemaya*, Elnathan, Jarib, Elnathan, *Natan*, *Zecharya*, and Meshullam, the leading men, and also for Joiarib and Elnathan, the instructors,

טז   וָאֶשְׁלְחָה לֶאֱלִיעֶזֶר לַאֲרִיאֵל לִשְׁמַעְיָה וּלְאֶלְנָתָן וּלְיָרִיב וּלְאֶלְנָתָן וּלְנָתָן וְלִזְכַרְיָה וְלִמְשֻׁלָּם רָאשִׁים וּלְיוֹיָרִיב וּלְאֶלְנָתָן מְבִינִים:

17   and I gave them an order for *Ido*, the leader at the place [called] Casiphia. I gave them a message to convey to *Ido* [and] his brother, temple-servants at the place [called] Casiphia, that they should bring us attendants for the House of our God.

יז   ואוצאה [וָאֲצַוֶּה] אוֹתָם עַל־אִדּוֹ הָרֹאשׁ בְּכָסִפְיָא הַמָּקוֹם וָאָשִׂימָה בְּפִיהֶם דְּבָרִים לְדַבֵּר אֶל־אִדּוֹ אָחִיו הנתונים [הַנְּתִינִים] בְּכָסִפְיָא הַמָּקוֹם לְהָבִיא־לָנוּ מְשָׁרְתִים לְבֵית אֱלֹהֵינוּ:

18

18 Thanks to the benevolent care of our God for us, they brought us a capable man of the family of Mahli son of *Levi* son of *Yisrael*, and Sherebiah and his sons and brothers, 18 in all,

יח וַיָּבִיאוּ לָנוּ כְּיַד־אֱלֹהֵינוּ הַטּוֹבָה עָלֵינוּ אִישׁ שֶׂכֶל מִבְּנֵי מַחְלִי בֶּן־לֵוִי בֶּן־יִשְׂרָאֵל וְשֵׁרֵבְיָה וּבָנָיו וְאֶחָיו שְׁמֹנָה עָשָׂר:

19 and Hashabiah, and with him Jeshaiah of the family of *Merari*, his brothers and their sons, 20 in all;

יט וְאֶת־חֲשַׁבְיָה וְאִתּוֹ יְשַׁעְיָה מִבְּנֵי מְרָרִי אֶחָיו וּבְנֵיהֶם עֶשְׂרִים:

20 and of the temple servants whom *David* and the officers had appointed for the service of the *Leviim* – 220 temple servants, all of them listed by name.

כ וּמִן־הַנְּתִינִים שֶׁנָּתַן דָּוִיד וְהַשָּׂרִים לַעֲבֹדַת הַלְוִיִּם נְתִינִים מָאתַיִם וְעֶשְׂרִים כֻּלָּם נִקְּבוּ בְשֵׁמוֹת:

21 I proclaimed a fast there by the Ahava River to afflict ourselves before our God to beseech Him for a smooth journey for us and for our children and for all our possessions;

כא וָאֶקְרָא שָׁם צוֹם עַל־הַנָּהָר אַהֲוָא לְהִתְעַנּוֹת לִפְנֵי אֱלֹהֵינוּ לְבַקֵּשׁ מִמֶּנּוּ דֶּרֶךְ יְשָׁרָה לָנוּ וּלְטַפֵּנוּ וּלְכָל־רְכוּשֵׁנוּ:

22 for I was ashamed to ask the king for soldiers and horsemen to protect us against any enemy on the way, since we had told the king, "The benevolent care of our God is for all who seek Him, while His fierce anger is against all who forsake Him."

כב כִּי בֹשְׁתִּי לִשְׁאוֹל מִן־הַמֶּלֶךְ חַיִל וּפָרָשִׁים לְעָזְרֵנוּ מֵאוֹיֵב בַּדָּרֶךְ כִּי־אָמַרְנוּ לַמֶּלֶךְ לֵאמֹר יַד־אֱלֹהֵינוּ עַל־כָּל־מְבַקְשָׁיו לְטוֹבָה וְעֻזּוֹ וְאַפּוֹ עַל כָּל־עֹזְבָיו:

23 So we fasted and besought our God for this, and He responded to our plea.

כג וַנָּצוּמָה וַנְּבַקְשָׁה מֵאֱלֹהֵינוּ עַל־זֹאת וַיֵּעָתֵר לָנוּ:

24 Then I selected twelve of the chiefs of the *Kohanim*, namely Sherebiah and Hashabiah with ten of their brothers,

כד וָאַבְדִּילָה מִשָּׂרֵי הַכֹּהֲנִים שְׁנֵים עָשָׂר לְשֵׁרֵבְיָה חֲשַׁבְיָה וְעִמָּהֶם מֵאֲחֵיהֶם עֲשָׂרָה:

25 and I weighed out to them the silver, the gold, and the vessels, the contribution to the House of our God which the king, his counselors and officers, and all *Yisrael* who were present had made.

כה וָאֶשְׁקוֹלָה [וָאֶשְׁקֲלָה] לָהֶם אֶת־הַכֶּסֶף וְאֶת־הַזָּהָב וְאֶת־הַכֵּלִים תְּרוּמַת בֵּית־אֱלֹהֵינוּ הַהֵרִימוּ הַמֶּלֶךְ וְיֹעֲצָיו וְשָׂרָיו וְכָל־יִשְׂרָאֵל הַנִּמְצָאִים:

26 I entrusted to their safekeeping the weight of six hundred and fifty talents of silver, one hundred silver vessels of one talent each, one hundred talents of gold;

כו וָאֶשְׁקֲלָה עַל־יָדָם כֶּסֶף כִּכָּרִים שֵׁשׁ־מֵאוֹת וַחֲמִשִּׁים וּכְלֵי־כֶסֶף מֵאָה לְכִכָּרִים זָהָב מֵאָה כִכָּר:

27 also, twenty gold bowls worth one thousand darics and two vessels of good, shining bronze, as precious as gold.

כז וּכְפֹרֵי זָהָב עֶשְׂרִים לַאֲדַרְכֹנִים אָלֶף וּכְלֵי נְחֹשֶׁת מֻצְהָב טוֹבָה שְׁנַיִם חֲמוּדֹת כַּזָּהָב:

28 I said to them, "You are consecrated to *Hashem*, and the vessels are consecrated, and the silver and gold are a freewill offering to God of your fathers.

כח וָאֹמְרָה אֲלֵהֶם אַתֶּם קֹדֶשׁ לַיהוָה וְהַכֵּלִים קֹדֶשׁ וְהַכֶּסֶף וְהַזָּהָב נְדָבָה לַיהוָה אֱלֹהֵי אֲבֹתֵיכֶם:

29 Guard them diligently until such time as you weigh them out in the presence of the officers of the *Kohanim* and the *Leviim* and the officers of the clans of *Yisrael* in *Yerushalayim* in the chambers of the House of *Hashem*."

כט שִׁקְדוּ וְשִׁמְרוּ עַד־תִּשְׁקְלוּ לִפְנֵי שָׂרֵי הַכֹּהֲנִים וְהַלְוִיִּם וְשָׂרֵי הָאָבוֹת לְיִשְׂרָאֵל בִּירוּשָׁלִָם הַלְּשָׁכוֹת בֵּית יְהוָה:

³⁰ So the *Kohanim* and the *Leviim* received the cargo of silver and gold and vessels by weight, to bring them to *Yerushalayim* to the House of our God.

ל וְקִבְּלוּ הַכֹּהֲנִים וְהַלְוִיִּם מִשְׁקַל הַכֶּסֶף וְהַזָּהָב וְהַכֵּלִים לְהָבִיא לִירוּשָׁלַ͏ִם לְבֵית אֱלֹהֵֽינוּ׃

³¹ We set out for *Yerushalayim* from the Ahava River on the twelfth of the first month. We enjoyed the care of our God, who saved us from enemy ambush on the journey.

לא וַנִּסְעָה מִנְּהַר אַֽהֲוָא בִּשְׁנֵים עָשָׂר לַחֹדֶשׁ הָרִאשׁוֹן לָלֶכֶת יְרוּשָׁלָ͏ִם וְיַד־אֱלֹהֵינוּ הָיְתָה עָלֵינוּ וַיַּצִּילֵנוּ מִכַּף אוֹיֵב וְאוֹרֵב עַל־הַדָּֽרֶךְ׃

> *va-nis-AH mi-n'-HAR a-ha-VA bish-NAYM a-SAR la-KHO-desh
> ha-ri-SHON la-LE-khet y'-ru-sha-LA-im v'-YAD e-lo-HAY-nu ha-y'-TAH
> a-LAY-nu va-ya-tzee-LAY-nu mi-KAF o-YAYV v'-o-RAYV al ha-DA-rekh*

³² We arrived in *Yerushalayim* and stayed there three days.

לב וַנָּבוֹא יְרוּשָׁלָ͏ִם וַנֵּשֶׁב שָׁם יָמִים שְׁלֹשָֽׁה׃

³³ On the fourth day the silver, gold, and vessels were weighed out in the House of our God into the keeping of Meremoth son of *Uriya* the *Kohen*, with whom was *Elazar* son of *Pinchas*. Yozavad son of *Yeshua*, and Noadiah son of Binnui, the *Leviim*, were with them.

לג וּבַיּוֹם הָרְבִיעִי נִשְׁקַל הַכֶּסֶף וְהַזָּהָב וְהַכֵּלִים בְּבֵית אֱלֹהֵינוּ עַל יַד־מְרֵמוֹת בֶּן־אוּרִיָּה הַכֹּהֵן וְעִמּוֹ אֶלְעָזָר בֶּן־פִּֽינְחָס וְעִמָּהֶם יוֹזָבָד בֶּן־יֵשׁוּעַ וְנוֹעַדְיָה בֶן־בִּנּוּי הַלְוִיִּֽם׃

³⁴ Everything accorded as to number and weight, the entire cargo being recorded at that time.

לד בְּמִסְפָּר בְּמִשְׁקָל לַכֹּל וַיִּכָּתֵב כָּל־הַמִּשְׁקָל בָּעֵת הַהִֽיא׃

³⁵ The returning exiles who arrived from captivity made burnt offerings to the God of *Yisrael*: twelve bulls for all *Yisrael*, ninety-six rams, seventy-seven lambs and twelve he-goats as a purification offering, all this a burnt offering to *Hashem*.

לה הַבָּאִים מֵֽהַשְּׁבִי בְנֵֽי־הַגּוֹלָה הִקְרִיבוּ עֹלוֹת לֵאלֹהֵי יִשְׂרָאֵל פָּרִים שְׁנֵים־עָשָׂר עַל־כָּל־יִשְׂרָאֵל אֵילִים תִּשְׁעִים וְשִׁשָּׁה כְּבָשִׂים שִׁבְעִים וְשִׁבְעָה צְפִירֵי חַטָּאת שְׁנֵים עָשָׂר הַכֹּל עוֹלָה לַיהוָֽה׃

³⁶ They handed the royal orders to the king's satraps and the governors of the province of Beyond the River who gave support to the people and the House of *Hashem*.

לו וַֽיִּתְּנוּ אֶת־דָּתֵי הַמֶּלֶךְ לַאֲחַשְׁדַּרְפְּנֵי הַמֶּלֶךְ וּפַחֲווֹת עֵבֶר הַנָּהָר וְנִשְּׂאוּ אֶת־הָעָם וְאֶת־בֵּית־הָאֱלֹהִֽים׃

9 ¹ When this was over, the officers approached me, saying, "The people of *Yisrael* and the *Kohanim* and *Leviim* have not separated themselves from the peoples of the land whose abhorrent practices are like those of the Canaanites, the Hittites, the Perizzites, the Jebusites, the Ammonites, the Moabites, the Egyptians, and the Amorites.

ט א וּכְכַלּוֹת אֵלֶּה נִגְּשׁוּ אֵלַי הַשָּׂרִים לֵאמֹר לֹא־נִבְדְּלוּ הָעָם יִשְׂרָאֵל וְהַכֹּהֲנִים וְהַלְוִיִּם מֵעַמֵּי הָאֲרָצוֹת כְּתוֹעֲבֹֽתֵיהֶם לַכְּנַעֲנִי הַחִתִּי הַפְּרִזִּי הַיְבוּסִי הָֽעַמֹּנִי הַמֹּֽאָבִי הַמִּצְרִי וְהָאֱמֹרִֽי׃

Ezra/Nehemiah

8:31 We set out for *Yerushalayim* For the People of Israel, the past and present fuse together to create the most extraordinary future. Through *Ezra's* actions, it is clear that a carefully choreographed event was planned and designed to reflect the earlier exodus from Egypt. Just as the Jews left Egypt in the first month, the Hebrew month of *Nisan*, and crossed the Sea of Reeds, *Ezra's* exodus departed from a river in the first month. Certainly, the symbolism of recreating such a formative occurrence wasn't lost on the members of the entourage, giving them great courage and hope. In modern times, almost the entire Iraqi-Babylonian Jewish community immigrated to Israel in the early 1950s, essentially ending a continual presence there which had lasted for over 2800. This modern-day miracle was aptly named 'Operation Ezra and Nechemya.'

Iraqi immigrants arriving in Israel, 1950

2 They have taken their daughters as wives for themselves and for their sons, so that the holy seed has become intermingled with the peoples of the land; and it is the officers and prefects who have taken the lead in this trespass."

ב כִּי־נָשְׂאוּ מִבְּנֹתֵיהֶם לָהֶם וְלִבְנֵיהֶם וְהִתְעָרְבוּ זֶרַע הַקֹּדֶשׁ בְּעַמֵּי הָאֲרָצוֹת וְיַד הַשָּׂרִים וְהַסְּגָנִים הָיְתָה בַּמַּעַל הַזֶּה רִאשׁוֹנָה:

3 When I heard this, I rent my garment and robe, I tore hair out of my head and beard, and I sat desolate.

ג וּכְשָׁמְעִי אֶת־הַדָּבָר הַזֶּה קָרַעְתִּי אֶת־בִּגְדִי וּמְעִילִי וָאֶמְרְטָה מִשְּׂעַר רֹאשִׁי וּזְקָנִי וָאֵשְׁבָה מְשׁוֹמֵם:

4 Around me gathered all who were concerned over the words of the God of *Yisrael* because of the returning exiles' trespass, while I sat desolate until the evening offering.

ד וְאֵלַי יֵאָסְפוּ כֹּל חָרֵד בְּדִבְרֵי אֱלֹהֵי־יִשְׂרָאֵל עַל מַעַל הַגּוֹלָה וַאֲנִי יֹשֵׁב מְשׁוֹמֵם עַד לְמִנְחַת הָעָרֶב:

5 At the time of the evening offering I ended my self-affliction; still in my torn garment and robe, I got down on my knees and spread out my hands to *Hashem* my God,

ה וּבְמִנְחַת הָעֶרֶב קַמְתִּי מִתַּעֲנִיתִי וּבְקָרְעִי בִגְדִי וּמְעִילִי וָאֶכְרְעָה עַל־בִּרְכַּי וָאֶפְרְשָׂה כַפַּי אֶל־יְהוָה אֱלֹהָי:

6 and said, "O my God, I am too ashamed and mortified to lift my face to You, O my God, for our iniquities are overwhelming and our guilt has grown high as heaven.

ו וָאֹמְרָה אֱלֹהַי בֹּשְׁתִּי וְנִכְלַמְתִּי לְהָרִים אֱלֹהַי פָּנַי אֵלֶיךָ כִּי עֲוֹנֹתֵינוּ רָבוּ לְמַעְלָה רֹּאשׁ וְאַשְׁמָתֵנוּ גָדְלָה עַד לַשָּׁמָיִם:

7 From the time of our fathers to this very day we have been deep in guilt. Because of our iniquities, we, our kings, and our *Kohanim* have been handed over to foreign kings, to the sword, to captivity, to pillage, and to humiliation, as is now the case.

ז מִימֵי אֲבֹתֵינוּ אֲנַחְנוּ בְּאַשְׁמָה גְדֹלָה עַד הַיּוֹם הַזֶּה וּבַעֲוֹנֹתֵינוּ נִתַּנּוּ אֲנַחְנוּ מְלָכֵינוּ כֹהֲנֵינוּ בְּיַד מַלְכֵי הָאֲרָצוֹת בַּחֶרֶב בַּשְּׁבִי וּבַבִּזָּה וּבְבֹשֶׁת פָּנִים כְּהַיּוֹם הַזֶּה:

8 "But now, for a short while, there has been a reprieve from *Hashem* our God, who has granted us a surviving remnant and given us a stake in His holy place; our God has restored the luster to our eyes and furnished us with a little sustenance in our bondage.

ח וְעַתָּה כִּמְעַט־רֶגַע הָיְתָה תְחִנָּה מֵאֵת יְהוָה אֱלֹהֵינוּ לְהַשְׁאִיר לָנוּ פְּלֵיטָה וְלָתֶת־לָנוּ יָתֵד בִּמְקוֹם קָדְשׁוֹ לְהָאִיר עֵינֵינוּ אֱלֹהֵינוּ וּלְתִתֵּנוּ מִחְיָה מְעַט בְּעַבְדֻתֵנוּ:

v'-a-TAH kim-at RE-ga ha-y'-TAH t'-khi-NAH may-AYT a-do-NAI e-lo-HAY-nu l'-hash-EER LA-nu p'-lay-TAH v'-la-tet LA-nu ya-TAYD bim-KOM kod-SHO l'-ha-EER ay-NAY-nu e-lo-HAY-nu ul-ti-TAY-nu mikh-YAH m'-AT b'-av-du-TAY-nu

North American immigrants arrive in Israel

9:8 A Surviving Remnant In his admonition of the people who have returned to the Land of Israel only to abandon *Hashem* and intermarry with local women, *Ezra* praises God for providing them a reprieve from the years of exile and persecution. He thanks *Hashem* for causing the king of Persia to look favorably upon His people, and for the remnant of the nation that survived. However, even though Cyrus had granted permission to those who survived the destruc- tion and exile, the "surviving remnant," to return home and reconstruct the *Beit Hamikdash*, a mere 42,360 people heeded the initial call to return and rebuild (Ezra 2:64). In just a short time, the Jews had become accustomed to living in exile, and had embraced its lifestyle. As

9 For bondsmen we are, though even in our bondage *Hashem* has not forsaken us, but has disposed the king of Persia favorably toward us, to furnish us with sustenance and to raise again the House of our God, repairing its ruins and giving us a hold in *Yehuda* and *Yerushalayim*.

ט כִּי־עֲבָדִים אֲנַחְנוּ וּבְעַבְדֻתֵנוּ לֹא עֲזָבָנוּ אֱלֹהֵינוּ וַיַּט־עָלֵינוּ חֶסֶד לִפְנֵי מַלְכֵי פָרַס לָתֶת־לָנוּ מִחְיָה לְרוֹמֵם אֶת־בֵּית אֱלֹהֵינוּ וּלְהַעֲמִיד אֶת־חָרְבֹתָיו וְלָתֶת־לָנוּ גָדֵר בִּיהוּדָה וּבִירוּשָׁלָ͏ִם׃

10 "Now, what can we say in the face of this, O our God, for we have forsaken Your commandments,

י וְעַתָּה מַה־נֹּאמַר אֱלֹהֵינוּ אַחֲרֵי־זֹאת כִּי עָזַבְנוּ מִצְוֺתֶיךָ׃

11 which You gave us through Your servants the *Neviim* when You said, 'The land that you are about to possess is a land unclean through the uncleanness of the peoples of the land, through their abhorrent practices with which they, in their impurity, have filled it from one end to the other.

יא אֲשֶׁר צִוִּיתָ בְּיַד עֲבָדֶיךָ הַנְּבִיאִים לֵאמֹר הָאָרֶץ אֲשֶׁר אַתֶּם בָּאִים לְרִשְׁתָּהּ אֶרֶץ נִדָּה הִיא בְּנִדַּת עַמֵּי הָאֲרָצוֹת בְּתוֹעֲבֹתֵיהֶם אֲשֶׁר מִלְאוּהָ מִפֶּה אֶל־פֶּה בְּטֻמְאָתָם׃

12 Now then, do not give your daughters in marriage to their sons or let their daughters marry your sons; do nothing for their well-being or advantage, then you will be strong and enjoy the bounty of the land and bequeath it to your children forever.'

יב וְעַתָּה בְּנוֹתֵיכֶם אַל־תִּתְּנוּ לִבְנֵיהֶם וּבְנֹתֵיהֶם אַל־תִּשְׂאוּ לִבְנֵיכֶם וְלֹא־תִדְרְשׁוּ שְׁלֹמָם וְטוֹבָתָם עַד־עוֹלָם לְמַעַן תֶּחֶזְקוּ וַאֲכַלְתֶּם אֶת־טוּב הָאָרֶץ וְהוֹרַשְׁתֶּם לִבְנֵיכֶם עַד־עוֹלָם׃

13 After all that has happened to us because of our evil deeds and our deep guilt – though You, our God, have been forbearing, [punishing us] less than our iniquity [deserves] in that You have granted us such a remnant as this –

יג וְאַחֲרֵי כָּל־הַבָּא עָלֵינוּ בְּמַעֲשֵׂינוּ הָרָעִים וּבְאַשְׁמָתֵנוּ הַגְּדֹלָה כִּי אַתָּה אֱלֹהֵינוּ חָשַׂכְתָּ לְמַטָּה מֵעֲוֺנֵנוּ וְנָתַתָּה לָנוּ פְּלֵיטָה כָּזֹאת׃

14 shall we once again violate Your commandments by intermarrying with these peoples who follow such abhorrent practices? Will You not rage against us till we are destroyed without remnant or survivor?

יד הֲנָשׁוּב לְהָפֵר מִצְוֺתֶיךָ וּלְהִתְחַתֵּן בְּעַמֵּי הַתֹּעֵבוֹת הָאֵלֶּה הֲלוֹא תֶאֱנַף־בָּנוּ עַד־כַּלֵּה לְאֵין שְׁאֵרִית וּפְלֵיטָה׃

15 *Hashem*, God of *Yisrael*, You are benevolent, for we have survived as a remnant, as is now the case. We stand before You in all our guilt, for we cannot face You on this account."

טו יְהֹוָה אֱלֹהֵי יִשְׂרָאֵל צַדִּיק אַתָּה כִּי־נִשְׁאַרְנוּ פְלֵיטָה כְּהַיּוֹם הַזֶּה הִנְנוּ לְפָנֶיךָ בְּאַשְׁמָתֵינוּ כִּי אֵין לַעֲמוֹד לְפָנֶיךָ עַל־זֹאת׃

10 1 While *Ezra* was praying and making confession, weeping and prostrating himself before the House of *Hashem*, a very great crowd of Israelites gathered about him, men, women, and children; the people were weeping bitterly.

י א וּכְהִתְפַּלֵּל עֶזְרָא וּכְהִתְוַדֹּתוֹ בֹּכֶה וּמִתְנַפֵּל לִפְנֵי בֵּית הָאֱלֹהִים נִקְבְּצוּ אֵלָיו מִיִּשְׂרָאֵל קָהָל רַב־מְאֹד אֲנָשִׁים וְנָשִׁים וִילָדִים כִּי־בָכוּ הָעָם הַרְבֵּה־בֶכֶה׃

Rabbi Yehuda Halevi writes in his work *The Kuzari*: "In reality, however, only a small portion returned. The majority remained in *Bavel*, willfully accepting the exile, as they did not wish to leave their homes and businesses…" This is no less true in our own day and age. Jews have become very comfortable living in the Diaspora, yet they must take heed of *Ezra's* stirring words to recognize the kindness *Hashem* has done for His people and return with their families to *Eretz Yisrael*.

2 Then *Shechanya* son of *Yechiel* of the family of Elam spoke up and said to *Ezra*, "We have trespassed against our God by bringing into our homes foreign women from the peoples of the land; but there is still hope for *Yisrael* despite this.

ב וַיַּעַן שְׁכַנְיָה בֶן־יְחִיאֵל מִבְּנֵי עולם [עֵילָם] וַיֹּאמֶר לְעֶזְרָא אֲנַחְנוּ מָעַלְנוּ בֵאלֹהֵינוּ וַנֹּשֶׁב נָשִׁים נָכְרִיּוֹת מֵעַמֵּי הָאָרֶץ וְעַתָּה יֵשׁ־מִקְוֶה לְיִשְׂרָאֵל עַל־זֹאת:

3 Now then, let us make a covenant with our God to expel all these women and those who have been born to them, in accordance with the bidding of *Hashem* and of all who are concerned over the commandment of our God, and let the Teaching be obeyed.

ג וְעַתָּה נִכְרָת־בְּרִית לֵאלֹהֵינוּ לְהוֹצִיא כָל־נָשִׁים וְהַנּוֹלָד מֵהֶם בַּעֲצַת אֲדֹנָי וְהַחֲרֵדִים בְּמִצְוַת אֱלֹהֵינוּ וְכַתּוֹרָה יֵעָשֶׂה:

4 Take action, for the responsibility is yours and we are with you. Act with resolve!"

ד קוּם כִּי־עָלֶיךָ הַדָּבָר וַאֲנַחְנוּ עִמָּךְ חֲזַק וַעֲשֵׂה:

5 So *Ezra* at once put the officers of the *Kohanim* and the *Leviim* and all *Yisrael* under oath to act accordingly, and they took the oath.

ה וַיָּקָם עֶזְרָא וַיַּשְׁבַּע אֶת־שָׂרֵי הַכֹּהֲנִים הַלְוִיִּם וְכָל־יִשְׂרָאֵל לַעֲשׂוֹת כַּדָּבָר הַזֶּה וַיִּשָּׁבֵעוּ:

6 Then *Ezra* rose from his place in front of the House of *Hashem* and went into the Hamber of *Yehochanan* son of *Elyashiv*; there, he ate no bread and drank no water, for he was in mourning over the trespass of those who had returned from exile.

ו וַיָּקָם עֶזְרָא מִלִּפְנֵי בֵּית הָאֱלֹהִים וַיֵּלֶךְ אֶל־לִשְׁכַּת יְהוֹחָנָן בֶּן־אֶלְיָשִׁיב וַיֵּלֶךְ שָׁם לֶחֶם לֹא־אָכַל וּמַיִם לֹא־שָׁתָה כִּי מִתְאַבֵּל עַל־מַעַל הַגּוֹלָה:

7 Then a proclamation was issued in *Yehuda* and *Yerushalayim* that all who had returned from the exile should assemble in *Yerushalayim*,

ז וַיַּעֲבִירוּ קוֹל בִּיהוּדָה וִירוּשָׁלַ͏ִם לְכֹל בְּנֵי הַגּוֹלָה לְהִקָּבֵץ יְרוּשָׁלָ͏ִם:

8 and that anyone who did not come in three days would, by decision of the officers and elders, have his property confiscated and himself excluded from the congregation of the returning exiles.

ח וְכֹל אֲשֶׁר לֹא־יָבוֹא לִשְׁלֹשֶׁת הַיָּמִים כַּעֲצַת הַשָּׂרִים וְהַזְּקֵנִים יָחֳרַם כָּל־רְכוּשׁוֹ וְהוּא יִבָּדֵל מִקְּהַל הַגּוֹלָה:

9 All the men of *Yehuda* and *Binyamin* assembled in *Yerushalayim* in three days; it was the ninth month, the twentieth of the month. All the people sat in the square of the House of *Hashem*, trembling on account of the event and because of the rains.

ט וַיִּקָּבְצוּ כָל־אַנְשֵׁי־יְהוּדָה וּבִנְיָמִן יְרוּשָׁלַ͏ִם לִשְׁלֹשֶׁת הַיָּמִים הוּא חֹדֶשׁ הַתְּשִׁיעִי בְּעֶשְׂרִים בַּחֹדֶשׁ וַיֵּשְׁבוּ כָל־הָעָם בִּרְחוֹב בֵּית הָאֱלֹהִים מַרְעִידִים עַל־הַדָּבָר וּמֵהַגְּשָׁמִים:

va-yi-ka-v'-TZU khol an-SHAY y'-hu-DAH u-vin-ya-MIN y'-ru-sha-LA-im
lish-LO-shet ha-ya-MEEM HU KHO-desh ha-t'-shee-EE b'-es-REEM
ba-KHO-desh va-yay-sh'-VU khol ha-AM bir-KHOV BAYT ha-e-lo-HEEM
mar-ee-DEEM al ha-da-VAR u-may-ha-g'-sha-MEEM

10:9 All the men of *Yehuda* and *Binyamin* assembled in *Yerushalayim* This verse only mentions the tribes of *Yehuda* and *Binyamin*, the two tribes that made up the ancient kingdom of *Yehuda* that had been exiled to Babylon. The other ten tribes who had formed the kingdom of *Yisrael* had been exiled earlier by the Assyrians, forced to assimilate and became lost to the Nation of Israel. Although today, almost all Jews are descendants of the ancient tribe of *Yehuda*, the modern Jewish state was called "Israel" and not "Judah." The supra-

10 Then *Ezra* the *Kohen* got up and said to them, "You have trespassed by bringing home foreign women, thus aggravating the guilt of *Yisrael*.

11 So now, make confession to *Hashem*, God of your fathers, and do His will, and separate yourselves from the peoples of the land and from the foreign women."

12 The entire congregation responded in a loud voice, "We must surely do just as you say.

13 However, many people are involved, and it is the rainy season; it is not possible to remain out in the open, nor is this the work of a day or two, because we have transgressed extensively in this matter.

14 Let our officers remain on behalf of the entire congregation, and all our townspeople who have brought home foreign women shall appear before them at scheduled times, together with the elders and judges of each town, in order to avert the burning anger of our God from us on this account."

15 Only *Yonatan* son of *Asael* and Jahzeiah son of Tikvah remained for this purpose, assisted by Meshullam and Shabbethai, the *Leviim*.

16 The returning exiles did so. *Ezra* the *Kohen* and the men who were the chiefs of the ancestral clans – all listed by name – sequestered themselves on the first day of the tenth month to study the matter.

17 By the first day of the first month they were done with all the men who had brought home foreign women.

18 Among the priestly families who were found to have brought foreign women were *Yeshua* son of *Yotzadak* and his brothers Maaseiah, *Eliezer*, Jarib, and *Gedalia*.

י וַיָּקָם עֶזְרָא הַכֹּהֵן וַיֹּאמֶר אֲלֵהֶם אַתֶּם מְעַלְתֶּם וַתֹּשִׁיבוּ נָשִׁים נָכְרִיּוֹת לְהוֹסִיף עַל־אַשְׁמַת יִשְׂרָאֵל:

יא וְעַתָּה תְּנוּ תוֹדָה לַיהוָה אֱלֹהֵי־אֲבֹתֵיכֶם וַעֲשׂוּ רְצוֹנוֹ וְהִבָּדְלוּ מֵעַמֵּי הָאָרֶץ וּמִן־הַנָּשִׁים הַנָּכְרִיּוֹת:

יב וַיַּעֲנוּ כָל־הַקָּהָל וַיֹּאמְרוּ קוֹל גָּדוֹל כֵּן כדבריך [כִּדְבָרְךָ] עָלֵינוּ לַעֲשׂוֹת:

יג אֲבָל הָעָם רָב וְהָעֵת גְּשָׁמִים וְאֵין כֹּחַ לַעֲמוֹד בַּחוּץ וְהַמְּלָאכָה לֹא־לְיוֹם אֶחָד וְלֹא לִשְׁנַיִם כִּי־הִרְבִּינוּ לִפְשֹׁעַ בַּדָּבָר הַזֶּה:

יד יַעֲמְדוּ־נָא שָׂרֵינוּ לְכָל־הַקָּהָל וְכֹל אֲשֶׁר בֶּעָרֵינוּ הַהֹשִׁיב נָשִׁים נָכְרִיּוֹת יָבֹא לְעִתִּים מְזֻמָּנִים וְעִמָּהֶם זִקְנֵי־עִיר וָעִיר וְשֹׁפְטֶיהָ עַד לְהָשִׁיב חֲרוֹן אַף־אֱלֹהֵינוּ מִמֶּנּוּ עַד לַדָּבָר הַזֶּה:

טו אַךְ יוֹנָתָן בֶּן־עֲשָׂהאֵל וְיַחְזְיָה בֶן־תִּקְוָה עָמְדוּ עַל־זֹאת וּמְשֻׁלָּם וְשַׁבְּתַי הַלֵּוִי עֲזָרֻם:

טז וַיַּעֲשׂוּ־כֵן בְּנֵי הַגּוֹלָה וַיִּבָּדְלוּ עֶזְרָא הַכֹּהֵן אֲנָשִׁים רָאשֵׁי הָאָבוֹת לְבֵית אֲבֹתָם וְכֻלָּם בְּשֵׁמוֹת וַיֵּשְׁבוּ בְּיוֹם אֶחָד לַחֹדֶשׁ הָעֲשִׂירִי לְדַרְיוֹשׁ הַדָּבָר:

יז וַיְכַלּוּ בַכֹּל אֲנָשִׁים הַהֹשִׁיבוּ נָשִׁים נָכְרִיּוֹת עַד יוֹם אֶחָד לַחֹדֶשׁ הָרִאשׁוֹן:

יח וַיִּמָּצֵא מִבְּנֵי הַכֹּהֲנִים אֲשֶׁר הֹשִׁיבוּ נָשִׁים נָכְרִיּוֹת מִבְּנֵי יֵשׁוּעַ בֶּן־יוֹצָדָק וְאֶחָיו מַעֲשֵׂיָה וֶאֱלִיעֶזֶר וְיָרִיב וּגְדַלְיָה:

tribal name "Israel" provides the most comprehensive framework for the realization of *Yechezkel's* vision: "Thus said *Hashem*: I am going to take the stick of *Yosef* – which is in the hand of *Efraim* and of the tribes of *Yisrael* associated with him – and I will place the stick of *Yehudah* upon it and make them into one stick; they shall be joined in My hand.... I will make them a single nation in the land, on the hills of *Yisrael*, and one king shall be king of them all. Never again shall they be two nations, and never again shall they be divided into two kingdoms" (Ezekiel 37:19, 22). The State's founders wished to be as inclusive as possible, allowing room for the vast cultural and ethnic diversity of the incoming exiles and thus fulfilling a role in the prophetic return of the lost ten tribes, along with the tribes of *Yehuda* and *Binyamin*, to the Land of Israel.

Members of the lost tribe of Menashe upon arrival at Ben Gurion airport

19 They gave their word to expel their wives and, acknowledging their guilt, offered a ram from the flock to expiate it.

יט וַיִּתְּנוּ יָדָם לְהוֹצִיא נְשֵׁיהֶם וַאֲשֵׁמִים אֵיל־צֹאן עַל־אַשְׁמָתָם:

20 Of the sons of Immer: *Chanani* and Zebadiah;

כ וּמִבְּנֵי אִמֵּר חֲנָנִי וּזְבַדְיָה:

21 of the sons of Harim: Maaseiah, *Eliyahu, Shemaya, Yechiel*, and *Uzziyahu*;

כא וּמִבְּנֵי חָרִם מַעֲשֵׂיָה וְאֵלִיָּה וּשְׁמַעְיָה וִיחִיאֵל וְעֻזִּיָּה:

22 of the sons of Pashhur: Elioenai, Maaseiah, Ishmael, Nethanel, *Yozavad*, and Elasah;

כב וּמִבְּנֵי פַשְׁחוּר אֶלְיוֹעֵינַי מַעֲשֵׂיָה יִשְׁמָעֵאל נְתַנְאֵל יוֹזָבָד וְאֶלְעָשָׂה:

23 of the *Leviim*: *Yozavad, Shim'i*, Kelaiah who is Kelita, Pethahiah, *Yehuda*, and *Eliezer*.

כג וּמִן־הַלְוִיִּם יוֹזָבָד וְשִׁמְעִי וְקֵלָיָה הוּא קְלִיטָא פְּתַחְיָה יְהוּדָה וֶאֱלִיעֶזֶר:

24 Of the singers: *Elyashiv*. Of the gatekeepers: *Shalum*, Telem, and *Uri*.

כד וּמִן־הַמְשֹׁרְרִים אֶלְיָשִׁיב וּמִן־הַשֹּׁעֲרִים שַׁלֻּם וָטֶלֶם וְאוּרִי:

25 Of the Israelites: of the sons of Parosh: Ramiah, Izziah, Malchijah, Mijamin, *Elazar*, Malchijah, and Benaiah;

כה וּמִיִּשְׂרָאֵל מִבְּנֵי פַרְעֹשׁ רַמְיָה וְיִזִּיָּה וּמַלְכִּיָּה וּמִיָּמִן וְאֶלְעָזָר וּמַלְכִּיָּה וּבְנָיָה:

26 of the sons of Elam: Mattaniah, *Zecharya, Yechiel*, Abdi, Jeremoth, and *Eliyahu*;

כו וּמִבְּנֵי עֵילָם מַתַּנְיָה זְכַרְיָה וִיחִיאֵל וְעַבְדִּי וִירֵמוֹת וְאֵלִיָּה:

27 of the sons of Zattu: Elioenai, *Elyashiv*, Mattaniah, Jeremoth, Zabad, and Aziza;

כז וּמִבְּנֵי זַתּוּא אֶלְיוֹעֵנַי אֶלְיָשִׁיב מַתַּנְיָה וִירֵמוֹת וְזָבָד וַעֲזִיזָא:

28 of the sons of Bebai: *Yehochanan, Chananya*, Zabbai, and Athlai;

כח וּמִבְּנֵי בֵּבָי יְהוֹחָנָן חֲנַנְיָה זַבַּי עַתְלָי:

29 of the sons of Bani: Meshullam, Malluch, Adaiah, Yashuv, Sheal, and Ramoth;

כט וּמִבְּנֵי בָנִי מְשֻׁלָּם מַלּוּךְ וַעֲדָיָה יָשׁוּב וּשְׁאָל ירמות [וְרָמוֹת:]

30 of the sons of Pahathmoab: Adna, Chelal, Benaiah, Maaseiah, Mattaniah, *Betzalel*, Binnui, and *Menashe*;

ל וּמִבְּנֵי פַּחַת מוֹאָב עַדְנָא וּכְלָל בְּנָיָה מַעֲשֵׂיָה מַתַּנְיָה בְצַלְאֵל וּבִנּוּי וּמְנַשֶּׁה:

31 of the sons of Harim: *Eliezer*, Isshijah, Malchijah, Shemaya, and Shimeon;

לא וּבְנֵי חָרִם אֱלִיעֶזֶר יִשִּׁיָּה מַלְכִּיָּה שְׁמַעְיָה שִׁמְעוֹן:

32 also *Binyamin*, Malluch, and Shemariah;

לב בְּנְיָמִן מַלּוּךְ שְׁמַרְיָה:

33 of the sons of Hashum: Mattenai, Mattattah, Zabad, Eliphelet, Jeremai, *Menashe*, and *Shim'i*;

לג מִבְּנֵי חָשֻׁם מַתְּנַי מַתַּתָּה זָבָד אֱלִיפֶלֶט יְרֵמַי מְנַשֶּׁה שִׁמְעִי:

34 of the sons of Bani: Maadai, *Amram*, and Uel;

לד מִבְּנֵי בָנִי מַעֲדַי עַמְרָם וְאוּאֵל:

35 also Benaiah, Bedeiah, Cheluhu,

לה בְּנָיָה בֵדְיָה כלהי [כְּלוּהוּ:]

36 Vaniah, Meremoth, *Elyashiv*

לו וַנְיָה מְרֵמוֹת אֶלְיָשִׁיב:

37 Mattaniah, Mattenai, Jaasai,

לז מַתַּנְיָה מַתְּנַי ויעשו [וְיַעֲשָׂי:]

38 Bani, Binnui, *Shim'i*,

לח וּבָנִי וּבִנּוּי שִׁמְעִי:

39 Shelemiah, *Natan*, Adaiah,

לט וְשֶׁלֶמְיָה וְנָתָן וַעֲדָיָה:

40 Machnadebai, Shashai, Sharai,

מ מַכְנַדְבַי שָׁשַׁי שָׁרָי:

41 Azarel, Shelemiah, Shemariah,

מא עֲזַרְאֵל וְשֶׁלֶמְיָהוּ שְׁמַרְיָה:

42 *Shalum*, Amariah, and *Yosef*;

מב שַׁלּוּם אֲמַרְיָה יוֹסֵף:

43 of the sons of Nebo: Jeiel, Mattithiah, Zabad, Zebina, Jaddai, *Yoel*, and Benaiah.

מג מִבְּנֵי נְבוֹ יְעִיאֵל מַתִּתְיָה זָבָד זְבִינָא ידו [יַדַּי] וְיוֹאֵל בְּנָיָה:

44 All these had married foreign women, among whom were some women who had borne children.

מד כָּל־אֵלֶּה נשאי [נָשְׂאוּ] נָשִׁים נָכְרִיּוֹת וְיֵשׁ מֵהֶם נָשִׁים וַיָּשִׂימוּ בָּנִים:

1 ¹ The narrative of *Nechemya* son of *Chachalya*: In the month of *Kislev* of the twentieth year, when I was in the fortress of Shushan,

א דִּבְרֵי נְחֶמְיָה בֶּן־חֲכַלְיָה וַיְהִי בְחֹדֶשׁ־ כִּסְלֵו [כַּסְלֵיו] שְׁנַת עֶשְׂרִים וַאֲנִי הָיִיתִי בְּשׁוּשַׁן הַבִּירָה:

² *Chanani*, one of my brothers, together with some men of *Yehuda*, arrived, and I asked them about the *Yehudim*, the remnant who had survived the captivity, and about *Yerushalayim*.

ב וַיָּבֹא חֲנָנִי אֶחָד מֵאַחַי הוּא וַאֲנָשִׁים מִיהוּדָה וָאֶשְׁאָלֵם עַל־הַיְּהוּדִים הַפְּלֵיטָה אֲשֶׁר־נִשְׁאֲרוּ מִן־הַשֶּׁבִי וְעַל־ יְרוּשָׁלָ‍ִם:

³ They replied, "The survivors who have survived the captivity there in the province are in dire trouble and disgrace; *Yerushalayim*'s wall is full of breaches, and its gates have been destroyed by fire."

ג וַיֹּאמְרוּ לִי הַנִּשְׁאָרִים אֲשֶׁר־נִשְׁאֲרוּ מִן־הַשֶּׁבִי שָׁם בַּמְּדִינָה בְּרָעָה גְדֹלָה וּבְחֶרְפָּה וְחוֹמַת יְרוּשָׁלַ‍ִם מְפֹרָצֶת וּשְׁעָרֶיהָ נִצְּתוּ בָאֵשׁ:

⁴ When I heard that, I sat and wept, and was in mourning for days, fasting and praying to the God of Heaven.

ד וַיְהִי כְּשָׁמְעִי אֶת־הַדְּבָרִים הָאֵלֶּה יָשַׁבְתִּי וָאֶבְכֶּה וָאֶתְאַבְּלָה יָמִים וָאֱהִי צָם וּמִתְפַּלֵּל לִפְנֵי אֱלֹהֵי הַשָּׁמָיִם:

⁵ I said, "*Hashem*, God of Heaven, great and awesome *Hashem*, who stays faithful to His covenant with those who love Him and keep His commandments!

ה וָאֹמַר אָנָּא יְהֹוָה אֱלֹהֵי הַשָּׁמַיִם הָאֵל הַגָּדוֹל וְהַנּוֹרָא שֹׁמֵר הַבְּרִית וָחֶסֶד לְאֹהֲבָיו וּלְשֹׁמְרֵי מִצְוֹתָיו:

⁶ Let Your ear be attentive and Your eyes open to receive the prayer of Your servant that I am praying to You now, day and night, on behalf of the Israelites, Your servants, confessing the sins that we Israelites have committed against You, sins that I and my father's house have committed.

ו תְּהִי נָא אָזְנְךָ־קַשֶּׁבֶת וְעֵינֶיךָ פְתֻחוֹת לִשְׁמֹעַ אֶל־תְּפִלַּת עַבְדְּךָ אֲשֶׁר אָנֹכִי מִתְפַּלֵּל לְפָנֶיךָ הַיּוֹם יוֹמָם וָלַיְלָה עַל־ בְּנֵי יִשְׂרָאֵל עֲבָדֶיךָ וּמִתְוַדֶּה עַל־חַטֹּאות בְּנֵי־יִשְׂרָאֵל אֲשֶׁר חָטָאנוּ לָךְ וַאֲנִי וּבֵית־ אָבִי חָטָאנוּ:

⁷ We have offended You by not keeping the commandments, the laws, and the rules that You gave to Your servant *Moshe*.

ז חֲבֹל חָבַלְנוּ לָךְ וְלֹא־שָׁמַרְנוּ אֶת־הַמִּצְוֹת וְאֶת־הַחֻקִּים וְאֶת־הַמִּשְׁפָּטִים אֲשֶׁר צִוִּיתָ אֶת־מֹשֶׁה עַבְדֶּךָ:

⁸ Be mindful of the promise You gave to Your servant *Moshe*: 'If you are unfaithful, I will scatter you among the peoples;

ח זְכָר־נָא אֶת־הַדָּבָר אֲשֶׁר צִוִּיתָ אֶת־ מֹשֶׁה עַבְדְּךָ לֵאמֹר אַתֶּם תִּמְעָלוּ אֲנִי אָפִיץ אֶתְכֶם בָּעַמִּים:

⁹ but if you turn back to Me, faithfully keep My commandments, even if your dispersed are at the ends of the earth, I will gather them from there and bring them to the place where I have chosen to establish My name.'

ט וְשַׁבְתֶּם אֵלַי וּשְׁמַרְתֶּם מִצְוֹתַי וַעֲשִׂיתֶם אֹתָם אִם־יִהְיֶה נִדַּחֲכֶם בִּקְצֵה הַשָּׁמַיִם מִשָּׁם אֲקַבְּצֵם והבואתים [וַהֲבִיאוֹתִים] אֶל־הַמָּקוֹם אֲשֶׁר בָּחַרְתִּי לְשַׁכֵּן אֶת־שְׁמִי שָׁם:

v'-shav-TEM ay-LAI ush-mar-TEM mitz-vo-TAI va-a-see-TEM o-TAM im yih-YEH ni-da-kha-KHEM bik-TZAY ha-sha-MA-yim mi-SHAM a-ka-b'-TZAYM va-ha-vee-o-TEEM el ha-ma-KOM a-SHER ba-KHAR-tee l'-sha-KAYN et sh'-MEE SHAM

המקום

1:9 And bring them to the place where I have chosen to establish My name One thing that sets Judaism apart from other religions is the concept of a "chosen place." Many biblical commandments are relevant only in the Holy Land, and according to some Jewish philosophers, even other biblical laws have a qualitative superiority when performed in the land. Additionally, as seen in this verse, *Eretz*

The Temple Mount, site of the *Beit Hamikdash*

27

10 For they are Your servants and Your people whom You redeemed by Your great power and Your mighty hand.

י וְהֵם עֲבָדֶיךָ וְעַמֶּךָ אֲשֶׁר פָּדִיתָ בְּכֹחֲךָ הַגָּדוֹל וּבְיָדְךָ הַחֲזָקָה:

11 O *Hashem*! Let Your ear be attentive to the prayer of Your servant, and to the prayer of Your servants who desire to hold Your name in awe. Grant Your servant success today, and dispose that man to be compassionate toward him!" I was the king's cupbearer at the time.

יא אָנָּא אֲדֹנָי תְּהִי נָא אָזְנְךָ־קַשֶּׁבֶת אֶל־תְּפִלַּת עַבְדְּךָ וְאֶל־תְּפִלַּת עֲבָדֶיךָ הַחֲפֵצִים לְיִרְאָה אֶת־שְׁמֶךָ וְהַצְלִיחָה־נָּא לְעַבְדְּךָ הַיּוֹם וּתְנֵהוּ לְרַחֲמִים לִפְנֵי הָאִישׁ הַזֶּה וַאֲנִי הָיִיתִי מַשְׁקֶה לַמֶּלֶךְ:

2 1 In the month of *Nisan*, in the twentieth year of King Artaxerxes, wine was set before him; I took the wine and gave it to the king – I had never been out of sorts in his presence.

ב א וַיְהִי בְּחֹדֶשׁ נִיסָן שְׁנַת עֶשְׂרִים לְאַרְתַּחְשַׁסְתְּא הַמֶּלֶךְ יַיִן לְפָנָיו וָאֶשָּׂא אֶת־הַיַּיִן וָאֶתְּנָה לַמֶּלֶךְ וְלֹא־הָיִיתִי רַע לְפָנָיו:

2 The king said to me, "How is it that you look bad, though you are not ill? It must be bad thoughts." I was very frightened,

ב וַיֹּאמֶר לִי הַמֶּלֶךְ מַדּוּעַ פָּנֶיךָ רָעִים וְאַתָּה אֵינְךָ חוֹלֶה אֵין זֶה כִּי־אִם רֹעַ לֵב וָאִירָא הַרְבֵּה מְאֹד:

3 but I answered the king, "May the king live forever! How should I not look bad when the city of the graveyard of my ancestors lies in ruins, and its gates have been consumed by fire?"

ג וָאֹמַר לַמֶּלֶךְ הַמֶּלֶךְ לְעוֹלָם יִחְיֶה מַדּוּעַ לֹא־יֵרְעוּ פָנַי אֲשֶׁר הָעִיר בֵּית־קִבְרוֹת אֲבֹתַי חֲרֵבָה וּשְׁעָרֶיהָ אֻכְּלוּ בָאֵשׁ:

4 The king said to me, "What is your request?" With a prayer to the God of Heaven,

ד וַיֹּאמֶר לִי הַמֶּלֶךְ עַל־מַה־זֶּה אַתָּה מְבַקֵּשׁ וָאֶתְפַּלֵּל אֶל־אֱלֹהֵי הַשָּׁמָיִם:

5 I answered the king, "If it please the king, and if your servant has found favor with you, send me to *Yehuda*, to the city of my ancestors' graves, to rebuild it."

ה וָאֹמַר לַמֶּלֶךְ אִם־עַל־הַמֶּלֶךְ טוֹב וְאִם־יִיטַב עַבְדְּךָ לְפָנֶיךָ אֲשֶׁר תִּשְׁלָחֵנִי אֶל־יְהוּדָה אֶל־עִיר קִבְרוֹת אֲבֹתַי וְאֶבְנֶנָּה:

6 With the consort seated at his side, the king said to me, "How long will you be gone and when will you return?" So it was agreeable to the king to send me, and I gave him a date.

ו וַיֹּאמֶר לִי הַמֶּלֶךְ וְהַשֵּׁגַל יוֹשֶׁבֶת אֶצְלוֹ עַד־מָתַי יִהְיֶה מַהֲלָכְךָ וּמָתַי תָּשׁוּב וַיִּיטַב לִפְנֵי־הַמֶּלֶךְ וַיִּשְׁלָחֵנִי וָאֶתְּנָה לוֹ זְמָן:

7 Then I said to the king, "If it please the king, let me have letters to the governors of the province of Beyond the River, directing them to grant me passage until I reach *Yehuda*;

ז וָאוֹמַר לַמֶּלֶךְ אִם־עַל־הַמֶּלֶךְ טוֹב אִגְּרוֹת יִתְּנוּ־לִי עַל־פַּחֲווֹת עֵבֶר הַנָּהָר אֲשֶׁר יַעֲבִירוּנִי עַד אֲשֶׁר־אָבוֹא אֶל־יְהוּדָה:

8 likewise, a letter to *Asaf*, the keeper of the King's Park, directing him to give me timber for roofing the gatehouses of the temple fortress and the city walls and for the house I shall occupy." The king gave me these, thanks to my God's benevolent care for me.

ח וְאִגֶּרֶת אֶל־אָסָף שֹׁמֵר הַפַּרְדֵּס אֲשֶׁר לַמֶּלֶךְ אֲשֶׁר יִתֶּן־לִי עֵצִים לְקָרוֹת אֶת־שַׁעֲרֵי הַבִּירָה אֲשֶׁר־לַבַּיִת וּלְחוֹמַת הָעִיר וְלַבַּיִת אֲשֶׁר־אָבוֹא אֵלָיו וַיִּתֶּן־לִי הַמֶּלֶךְ כְּיַד־אֱלֹהַי הַטּוֹבָה עָלָי:

Yisrael is meant to play a central role in the national redemption process, as it is the destination for the ingathering of the exiles. In the *Tanakh*, "the place," or *hamakom* (המקום) in Hebrew, refers both to the Land of Israel and the site of the *Beit Hamikdash*. Perhaps unsurprisingly, the Sages teach that this word is also one of God's seventy names.

9 When I came to the governors of the province of Beyond the River I gave them the king's letters. The king also sent army officers and cavalry with me.

ט וָאָבוֹא אֶל־פַּחֲווֹת עֵבֶר הַנָּהָר וָאֶתְּנָה לָהֶם אֵת אִגְּרוֹת הַמֶּלֶךְ וַיִּשְׁלַח עִמִּי הַמֶּלֶךְ שָׂרֵי חַיִל וּפָרָשִׁים:

10 When Sanballat the Horonite and Tobiah the Ammonite servant heard, it displeased them greatly that someone had come, intent on improving the condition of the Israelites.

י וַיִּשְׁמַע סַנְבַלַּט הַחֹרֹנִי וְטוֹבִיָּה הָעֶבֶד הָעַמֹּנִי וַיֵּרַע לָהֶם רָעָה גְדֹלָה אֲשֶׁר־בָּא אָדָם לְבַקֵּשׁ טוֹבָה לִבְנֵי יִשְׂרָאֵל:

11 I arrived in *Yerushalayim*. After I was there three days

יא וָאָבוֹא אֶל־יְרוּשָׁלָ͏ִם וָאֱהִי־שָׁם יָמִים שְׁלֹשָׁה:

12 I got up at night, I and a few men with me, and telling no one what my God had put into my mind to do for *Yerushalayim*, and taking no other beast than the one on which I was riding,

יב וָאָקוּם לַיְלָה אֲנִי וַאֲנָשִׁים מְעַט עִמִּי וְלֹא־הִגַּדְתִּי לְאָדָם מָה אֱלֹהַי נֹתֵן אֶל־לִבִּי לַעֲשׂוֹת לִירוּשָׁלָ͏ִם וּבְהֵמָה אֵין עִמִּי כִּי אִם־הַבְּהֵמָה אֲשֶׁר אֲנִי רֹכֵב בָּהּ:

13 I went out by the Valley Gate, at night, toward the Jackals' Spring and the Dung Gate; and I surveyed the walls of *Yerushalayim* that were breached, and its gates, consumed by fire.

יג וָאֵצְאָה בְשַׁעַר־הַגַּיְא לַיְלָה וְאֶל־פְּנֵי עֵין הַתַּנִּין וְאֶל־שַׁעַר הָאַשְׁפֹּת וָאֱהִי שֹׂבֵר בְּחוֹמֹת יְרוּשָׁלַ͏ִם אֲשֶׁר־הַמְפֹרוּצִים [הֵם פְּרוּצִים] וּשְׁעָרֶיהָ אֻכְּלוּ בָאֵשׁ:

14 I proceeded to the Fountain Gate and to the King's Pool, where there was no room for the beast under me to continue.

יד וָאֶעֱבֹר אֶל־שַׁעַר הָעַיִן וְאֶל־בְּרֵכַת הַמֶּלֶךְ וְאֵין־מָקוֹם לַבְּהֵמָה לַעֲבֹר תַּחְתָּי:

15 So I went up the wadi by night, surveying the wall, and, entering again by the Valley Gate, I returned.

טו וָאֱהִי עֹלֶה בַנַּחַל לַיְלָה וָאֱהִי שֹׂבֵר בַּחוֹמָה וָאָשׁוּב וָאָבוֹא בְּשַׁעַר הַגַּיְא וָאָשׁוּב:

16 The prefects knew nothing of where I had gone or what I had done, since I had not yet divulged it to the *Yehudim* – the *Kohanim*, the nobles, the prefects, or the rest of the officials.

טז וְהַסְּגָנִים לֹא יָדְעוּ אָנָה הָלַכְתִּי וּמֶה אֲנִי עֹשֶׂה וְלַיְּהוּדִים וְלַכֹּהֲנִים וְלַחֹרִים וְלַסְּגָנִים וּלְיֶתֶר עֹשֵׂה הַמְּלָאכָה עַד־כֵּן לֹא הִגַּדְתִּי:

17 Then I said to them, "You see the bad state we are in – *Yerushalayim* lying in ruins and its gates destroyed by fire. Come, let us rebuild the wall of *Yerushalayim* and suffer no more disgrace."

יז וָאוֹמַר אֲלֵהֶם אַתֶּם רֹאִים הָרָעָה אֲשֶׁר אֲנַחְנוּ בָהּ אֲשֶׁר יְרוּשָׁלַ͏ִם חֲרֵבָה וּשְׁעָרֶיהָ נִצְּתוּ בָאֵשׁ לְכוּ וְנִבְנֶה אֶת־חוֹמַת יְרוּשָׁלַ͏ִם וְלֹא־נִהְיֶה עוֹד חֶרְפָּה:

va-o-MAR a-lay-HEM a-TEM ro-EEM ha-ra-AH a-SHER a-NAKH-nu VAH
a-SHER y'-ru-sha-LA-im kha-ray-VAH ush-a-RE-ha ni-tz'-TU va-AYSH l'-KHU
v'-niv-NEH et KHO-mat y'-ru-sha-LA-im v'-lo nih-YEH OD kher-PAH

2:17 Come, let us rebuild the wall of *Yerushalayim* One of the Jewish prayers recited on the ninth day of the Hebrew month of *Av*, the day of the destruction of the *Beit Hamikdash*, states: "You destroyed Jerusalem by fire, so too will You rebuild it with fire." Near the Western Wall, archeologists uncovered a complex destroyed in the Roman fires of 70 CE, and spear-pierced skeletal remains found there gave silent testimony to the tragedy. Destruction by fire is comprehensible, but the idea of construction by fire is more difficult to understand.

Perhaps it indicates the degree of passion necessary to engage in such a task. If this is the case, indeed we have merited living in a time where the latter fire is burning brighter, and many are answering *Nechemya*'s call: "Come, let us rebuild!"

Walls of the Old City of *Yerushalayim*

18 I told them of my God's benevolent care for me, also of the things that the king had said to me, and they said, "Let us start building!" They were encouraged by [His] benevolence.

יח וָאַגִּיד לָהֶם אֶת־יַד אֱלֹהַי אֲשֶׁר־הִיא טוֹבָה עָלַי וְאַף־דִּבְרֵי הַמֶּלֶךְ אֲשֶׁר אָמַר־לִי וַיֹּאמְרוּ נָקוּם וּבָנִינוּ וַיְחַזְּקוּ יְדֵיהֶם לַטּוֹבָה:

19 When Sanballat the Horonite and Tobiah the Ammonite servant and *Geshem* the Arab heard, they mocked us and held us in contempt and said, "What is this that you are doing? Are you rebelling against the king?"

יט וַיִּשְׁמַע סַנְבַלַּט הַחֹרֹנִי וְטֹבִיָּה הָעֶבֶד הָעַמּוֹנִי וְגֶשֶׁם הָעַרְבִי וַיַּלְעִגוּ לָנוּ וַיִּבְזוּ עָלֵינוּ וַיֹּאמְרוּ מָה־הַדָּבָר הַזֶּה אֲשֶׁר אַתֶּם עֹשִׂים הַעַל הַמֶּלֶךְ אַתֶּם מֹרְדִים:

20 I said to them in reply, "The God of Heaven will grant us success, and we, His servants, will start building. But you have no share or claim or stake in *Yerushalayim*!"

כ וָאָשִׁיב אוֹתָם דָּבָר וָאוֹמַר לָהֶם אֱלֹהֵי הַשָּׁמַיִם הוּא יַצְלִיחַ לָנוּ וַאֲנַחְנוּ עֲבָדָיו נָקוּם וּבָנִינוּ וְלָכֶם אֵין־חֵלֶק וּצְדָקָה וְזִכָּרוֹן בִּירוּשָׁלָ͏ִם:

3 ¹ Then *Elyashiv* the *Kohen Gadol* and his fellow *Kohanim* set to and rebuilt the Sheep Gate; they consecrated it and set up its doors, consecrating it as far as the Hundred's Tower, as far as the Tower of Hananel.

ג א וַיָּקָם אֶלְיָשִׁיב הַכֹּהֵן הַגָּדוֹל וְאֶחָיו הַכֹּהֲנִים וַיִּבְנוּ אֶת־שַׁעַר הַצֹּאן הֵמָּה קִדְּשׁוּהוּ וַיַּעֲמִידוּ דַּלְתֹתָיו וְעַד־מִגְדַּל הַמֵּאָה קִדְּשׁוּהוּ עַד מִגְדַּל חֲנַנְאֵל:

² Next to him, the men of *Yericho* built. Next to them, Zaccur son of Imri.

ב וְעַל־יָדוֹ בָנוּ אַנְשֵׁי יְרֵחוֹ וְעַל־יָדוֹ בָנָה זַכּוּר בֶּן־אִמְרִי:

³ The sons of Hassenaah rebuilt the Fish Gate; they roofed it and set up its doors, locks, and bars.

ג וְאֵת שַׁעַר הַדָּגִים בָּנוּ בְּנֵי הַסְּנָאָה הֵמָּה קֵרוּהוּ וַיַּעֲמִידוּ דַּלְתֹתָיו מַנְעוּלָיו וּבְרִיחָיו:

⁴ Next to them, Meremoth son of *Uriya* son of Hakkoz repaired; and next to him, Meshullam son of *Berechya* son of Meshezabel. Next to him, *Tzadok* son of Baana repaired.

ד וְעַל־יָדָם הֶחֱזִיק מְרֵמוֹת בֶּן־אוּרִיָּה בֶּן־הַקּוֹץ וְעַל־יָדָם הֶחֱזִיק מְשֻׁלָּם בֶּן־בֶּרֶכְיָה בֶּן־מְשֵׁיזַבְאֵל וְעַל־יָדָם הֶחֱזִיק צָדוֹק בֶּן־בַּעֲנָא:

⁵ Next to him, the Tekoites repaired, though their nobles would not take upon their shoulders the work of their lord.

ה וְעַל־יָדָם הֶחֱזִיקוּ הַתְּקוֹעִים וְאַדִּירֵיהֶם לֹא־הֵבִיאוּ צַוָּרָם בַּעֲבֹדַת אֲדֹנֵיהֶם:

⁶ Joiada son of Paseah and Meshullam son of Besodeiah repaired the Jeshanah Gate; they roofed it and set up its doors, locks, and bars.

ו וְאֵת שַׁעַר הַיְשָׁנָה הֶחֱזִיקוּ יוֹיָדָע בֶּן־פָּסֵחַ וּמְשֻׁלָּם בֶּן־בְּסוֹדְיָה הֵמָּה קֵרוּהוּ וַיַּעֲמִידוּ דַּלְתֹתָיו וּמַנְעֻלָיו וּבְרִיחָיו:

⁷ Next to them, Melatiah the Givonite and Jadon the Meronothite repaired, [with] the men of *Givon* and *Mitzpa*, under the jurisdiction of the governor of the province of Beyond the River.

ז וְעַל־יָדָם הֶחֱזִיק מְלַטְיָה הַגִּבְעֹנִי וְיָדוֹן הַמֵּרֹנֹתִי אַנְשֵׁי גִבְעוֹן וְהַמִּצְפָּה לְכִסֵּא פַּחַת עֵבֶר הַנָּהָר:

⁸ Next to them, Uzziel son of Harhaiah, [of the] smiths, repaired. Next to him, *Chananya*, of the perfumers. They restored *Yerushalayim* as far as the Broad Wall.

ח עַל־יָדוֹ הֶחֱזִיק עֻזִּיאֵל בֶּן־חַרְהֲיָה צוֹרְפִים וְעַל־יָדוֹ הֶחֱזִיק חֲנַנְיָה בֶּן־הָרַקָּחִים וַיַּעַזְבוּ יְרוּשָׁלַ͏ִם עַד הַחוֹמָה הָרְחָבָה:

⁹ Next to them, Rephaiah son of *Chur*, chief of half the district of *Yerushalayim*, repaired.

ט וְעַל־יָדָם הֶחֱזִיק רְפָיָה בֶן־חוּר שַׂר חֲצִי פֶּלֶךְ יְרוּשָׁלָ͏ִם:

10 Next to him, Jedaiah son of Harumaph repaired in front of his house. Next to him, Hattush son of Hashabneiah repaired.

י וְעַל־יָדָם הֶחֱזִיק יְדָיָה בֶן־חֲרוּמַף וְנֶגֶד בֵּיתוֹ וְעַל־יָדוֹ הֶחֱזִיק חַטּוּשׁ בֶּן־חֲשַׁבְנְיָה:

11 Malchijah son of Harim and Hasshub son of Pahath-moab repaired a second stretch, including the Tower of Ovens.

יא מִדָּה שֵׁנִית הֶחֱזִיק מַלְכִּיָּה בֶן־חָרִם וְחַשּׁוּב בֶּן־פַּחַת מוֹאָב וְאֵת מִגְדַּל הַתַּנּוּרִים:

12 Next to them, *Shalum* son of Hallohesh, chief of half the district of *Yerushalayim*, repaired – he and his daughters.

יב וְעַל־יָדוֹ הֶחֱזִיק שַׁלּוּם בֶּן־הַלּוֹחֵשׁ שַׂר חֲצִי פֶּלֶךְ יְרוּשָׁלָ͏ִם הוּא וּבְנוֹתָיו:

13 Hanun and the inhabitants of *Zanoach* repaired the Valley Gate; they rebuilt it and set up its doors, locks, and bars. And [they also repaired] a thousand *amot* of wall to the Dung Gate.

יג אֵת שַׁעַר הַגַּיְא הֶחֱזִיק חָנוּן וְיֹשְׁבֵי זָנוֹחַ הֵמָּה בָנוּהוּ וַיַּעֲמִידוּ דַּלְתֹתָיו מַנְעֻלָיו וּבְרִיחָיו וְאֶלֶף אַמָּה בַּחוֹמָה עַד שַׁעַר הָשְׁפוֹת:

14 Malchijah son of Rechab, chief of the district of Beth-haccerem, repaired the Dung Gate; he rebuilt it and set up its doors, locks, and bars.

יד וְאֵת שַׁעַר הָאַשְׁפּוֹת הֶחֱזִיק מַלְכִּיָּה בֶן־רֵכָב שַׂר פֶּלֶךְ בֵּית־הַכָּרֶם הוּא יִבְנֶנּוּ וְיַעֲמִיד דַּלְתֹתָיו מַנְעֻלָיו וּבְרִיחָיו:

15 Shallun son of Col-hozeh, chief of the district of *Mitzpa*, repaired the Fountain Gate; he rebuilt it and covered it, and set up its doors, locks, and bars, as well as the wall of the irrigation pool of the King's Garden as far as the steps going down from the City of *David*.

טו וְאֵת שַׁעַר הָעַיִן הֶחֱזִיק שַׁלּוּן בֶּן־כָּל־חֹזֶה שַׂר פֶּלֶךְ הַמִּצְפָּה הוּא יִבְנֶנּוּ וִיטַלְלֶנּוּ וְיַעֲמִידוּ [וְיַעֲמִיד] דַּלְתֹתָיו מַנְעֻלָיו וּבְרִיחָיו וְאֵת חוֹמַת בְּרֵכַת הַשֶּׁלַח לְגַן־הַמֶּלֶךְ וְעַד־הַמַּעֲלוֹת הַיּוֹרְדוֹת מֵעִיר דָּוִיד:

v'-AYT SHA-ar ha-A-yin he-khe-ZEEK sha-LUN ben kol kho-ZEH SAR PE-lekh ha-mitz-PAH HU yiv-NE-nu vee-ta-l'-LE-nu v'-ya-a-MEED dal-to-TAV man-u-LAV uv-ree-KHAV v'-AYT kho-MAT b'-ray-KHAT ha-SHE-lakh l'-gan ha-ME-lekh v'-ad ha-ma-a-LOT ha-yo-r'-DOT may-EER da-VEED

16 After him, *Nechemya* son of Azbuk, chief of half the district of Beth-zur, repaired, from in front of the graves of *David* as far as the artificial pool, and as far as the House of the Warriors.

טז אַחֲרָיו הֶחֱזִיק נְחֶמְיָה בֶן־עַזְבּוּק שַׂר חֲצִי פֶּלֶךְ בֵּית־צוּר עַד־נֶגֶד קִבְרֵי דָוִיד וְעַד־הַבְּרֵכָה הָעֲשׂוּיָה וְעַד בֵּית הַגִּבֹּרִים:

17 After him, the *Leviim* repaired: Rehum son of Bani. Next to him, Hashabiah, chief of half the district of Keilah, repaired for his district.

יז אַחֲרָיו הֶחֱזִיקוּ הַלְוִיִּם רְחוּם בֶּן־בָּנִי עַל־יָדוֹ הֶחֱזִיק חֲשַׁבְיָה שַׂר־חֲצִי־פֶלֶךְ קְעִילָה לְפִלְכּוֹ:

3:15 As far as the steps going down from the City of *David* The most extraordinary site where one can see the merging of biblical text with archeology is Jerusalem's City of David National Park. Although identified in the mid-nineteenth century, many answers to biblical riddles still lay locked beneath its soil. In 2005, Israeli archeologist Eilat Mazar discover a large stone structure that she believes to be the foundations of King David's palace, illuminating the verse "*David* captured the str onghold of *Tzion*; it is now the City of *David*"

(II Samuel 5:7). As one stands in this spot and gazes at the mountains in all directions, King David's words come to life: "*Yerushalayim*, hills enfold it, and *Hashem* enfolds His people now and forever" (Psalms 125:2).

Excavations at City of David National Park in *Yerushalayim*

¹⁸ After him, their brothers repaired: Bavvai son of Henadad, chief of half the district of Keilah.

יח אַחֲרָיו הֶחֱזִיקוּ אֲחֵיהֶם בַּוַּי בֶּן־חֵנָדָד שַׂר חֲצִי פֶּלֶךְ קְעִילָה:

¹⁹ Next to him, Ezer son of *Yeshua*, the chief of *Mitzpa*, repaired a second stretch, from in front of the ascent to the armory [at] the angle [of the wall].

יט וַיְחַזֵּק עַל־יָדוֹ עֵזֶר בֶּן־יֵשׁוּעַ שַׂר הַמִּצְפָּה מִדָּה שֵׁנִית מִנֶּגֶד עֲלֹת הַנֶּשֶׁק הַמִּקְצֹעַ:

²⁰ After him, *Baruch* son of Zaccai zealously repaired a second stretch, from the angle to the entrance to the house of *Elyashiv*, the *Kohen Gadol*.

כ אַחֲרָיו הֶחֱרָה הֶחֱזִיק בָּרוּךְ בֶּן־זַבַּי [זַכַּי] מִדָּה שֵׁנִית מִן־הַמִּקְצוֹעַ עַד־פֶּתַח בֵּית אֶלְיָשִׁיב הַכֹּהֵן הַגָּדוֹל:

²¹ After him, Meremoth son of *Uriya* son of Hakkoz repaired a second stretch, from the entrance to *Elyashiv*'s house to the end of *Elyashiv*'s house.

כא אַחֲרָיו הֶחֱזִיק מְרֵמוֹת בֶּן־אוּרִיָּה בֶּן־הַקּוֹץ מִדָּה שֵׁנִית מִפֶּתַח בֵּית אֶלְיָשִׁיב וְעַד־תַּכְלִית בֵּית אֶלְיָשִׁיב:

²² After him, the *Kohanim*, inhabitants of the plain, repaired.

כב וְאַחֲרָיו הֶחֱזִיקוּ הַכֹּהֲנִים אַנְשֵׁי הַכִּכָּר:

²³ After them, *Binyamin* and Hasshub repaired in front of their houses. After them, *Azarya* son of Maaseiah son of Ananiah repaired beside his house.

כג אַחֲרָיו הֶחֱזִיק בִּנְיָמִן וְחַשּׁוּב נֶגֶד בֵּיתָם אַחֲרָיו הֶחֱזִיק עֲזַרְיָה בֶן־מַעֲשֵׂיָה בֶּן־עֲנָנְיָה אֵצֶל בֵּיתוֹ:

²⁴ After him, Binnui son of Henadad repaired a second stretch, from the house of *Azarya* to the angle, to the corner.

כד אַחֲרָיו הֶחֱזִיק בִּנּוּי בֶּן־חֵנָדָד מִדָּה שֵׁנִית מִבֵּית עֲזַרְיָה עַד־הַמִּקְצוֹעַ וְעַד־הַפִּנָּה:

²⁵ Palal son of Uzai – from in front of the angle and the tower that juts out of the house of the king, the upper [tower] of the prison compound. After him, Pedaiah son of Parosh.

כה פָּלָל בֶּן־אוּזַי מִנֶּגֶד הַמִּקְצוֹעַ וְהַמִּגְדָּל הַיּוֹצֵא מִבֵּית הַמֶּלֶךְ הָעֶלְיוֹן אֲשֶׁר לַחֲצַר הַמַּטָּרָה אַחֲרָיו פְּדָיָה בֶן־פַּרְעֹשׁ:

²⁶ The temple servants were living on the Ophel, as far as a point in front of the Water Gate in the east, and the jutting tower.)

כו וְהַנְּתִינִים הָיוּ יֹשְׁבִים בָּעֹפֶל עַד נֶגֶד שַׁעַר הַמַּיִם לַמִּזְרָח וְהַמִּגְדָּל הַיּוֹצֵא:

²⁷ After him, the Tekoites repaired a second stretch, from in front of the great jutting tower to the wall of the Ophel.

כז אַחֲרָיו הֶחֱזִיקוּ הַתְּקֹעִים מִדָּה שֵׁנִית מִנֶּגֶד הַמִּגְדָּל הַגָּדוֹל הַיּוֹצֵא וְעַד חוֹמַת הָעֹפֶל:

²⁸ Above the Horse Gate, the *Kohanim* repaired, each in front of his house.

כח מֵעַל שַׁעַר הַסּוּסִים הֶחֱזִיקוּ הַכֹּהֲנִים אִישׁ לְנֶגֶד בֵּיתוֹ:

²⁹ After them, *Tzadok* son of Immer repaired in front of his house. After him, *Shemaya* son of Shechaniah, keeper of the East Gate, repaired.

כט אַחֲרָיו הֶחֱזִיק צָדוֹק בֶּן־אִמֵּר נֶגֶד בֵּיתוֹ וְאַחֲרָיו הֶחֱזִיק שְׁמַעְיָה בֶן־שְׁכַנְיָה שֹׁמֵר שַׁעַר הַמִּזְרָח:

³⁰ After him, *Chananya* son of Shelemiah and Hanun, the sixth son of Zalaph, repaired a second stretch. After them, Meshullam son of *Berechya* repaired in front of his chamber.

ל אַחֲרֵי [אַחֲרָיו] הֶחֱזִיק חֲנַנְיָה בֶן־שֶׁלֶמְיָה וְחָנוּן בֶּן־צָלָף הַשִּׁשִּׁי מִדָּה שֵׁנִי אַחֲרָיו הֶחֱזִיק מְשֻׁלָּם בֶּן־בֶּרֶכְיָה נֶגֶד נִשְׁכָּתוֹ:

³¹ After him, Malchijah of the smiths repaired as far as the house of the temple servants and the merchants, [from] in front of the Muster Gate to the corner loft.

לא אַחֲרֵי [אַחֲרָיו] הֶחֱזִיק מַלְכִּיָּה בֶּן־הַצֹּרְפִי עַד־בֵּית הַנְּתִינִים וְהָרֹכְלִים נֶגֶד שַׁעַר הַמִּפְקָד וְעַד עֲלִיַּת הַפִּנָּה:

32 And between the corner loft to the Sheep Gate the smiths and the merchants repaired.

לב וּבֵין עֲלִיַּת הַפִּנָּה לְשַׁעַר הַצֹּאן הֶחֱזִיקוּ הַצֹּרְפִים וְהָרֹכְלִים:

33 When Sanballat heard that we were rebuilding the wall, it angered him, and he was extremely vexed. He mocked the *Yehudim*,

לג וַיְהִי כַּאֲשֶׁר שָׁמַע סַנְבַלַּט כִּי־אֲנַחְנוּ בוֹנִים אֶת־הַחוֹמָה וַיִּחַר לוֹ וַיִּכְעַס הַרְבֵּה וַיַּלְעֵג עַל־הַיְּהוּדִים:

34 saying in the presence of his brothers and the Shomron force, "What are the miserable *Yehudim* doing? Will they restore, offer sacrifice, and finish one day? Can they revive those stones out of the dust heaps, burned as they are?"

לד וַיֹּאמֶר לִפְנֵי אֶחָיו וְחֵיל שֹׁמְרוֹן וַיֹּאמֶר מָה הַיְּהוּדִים הָאֲמֵלָלִים עֹשִׂים הֲיַעַזְבוּ לָהֶם הֲיִזְבָּחוּ הַיְכַלּוּ בַיּוֹם הַיְחַיּוּ אֶת־הָאֲבָנִים מֵעֲרֵמוֹת הֶעָפָר וְהֵמָּה שְׂרוּפוֹת:

35 Tobiah the Ammonite, alongside him, said, "That stone wall they are building – if a fox climbed it he would breach it!"

לה וְטוֹבִיָּה הָעַמֹּנִי אֶצְלוֹ וַיֹּאמֶר גַּם אֲשֶׁר־הֵם בּוֹנִים אִם־יַעֲלֶה שׁוּעָל וּפָרַץ חוֹמַת אַבְנֵיהֶם:

36 Hear, our God, how we have become a mockery, and return their taunts upon their heads! Let them be taken as spoil to a land of captivity!

לו שְׁמַע אֱלֹהֵינוּ כִּי־הָיִינוּ בוּזָה וְהָשֵׁב חֶרְפָּתָם אֶל־רֹאשָׁם וּתְנֵם לְבִזָּה בְּאֶרֶץ שִׁבְיָה:

37 Do not cover up their iniquity or let their sin be blotted out before You, for they hurled provocations at the builders.

לז וְאַל־תְּכַס עַל־עֲוֹנָם וְחַטָּאתָם מִלְּפָנֶיךָ אַל־תִּמָּחֶה כִּי הִכְעִיסוּ לְנֶגֶד הַבּוֹנִים:

38 We rebuilt the wall till it was continuous all around to half its height; for the people's heart was in the work.

לח וַנִּבְנֶה אֶת־הַחוֹמָה וַתִּקָּשֵׁר כָּל־הַחוֹמָה עַד־חֶצְיָהּ וַיְהִי לֵב לָעָם לַעֲשׂוֹת:

ד

4 1 When Sanballat and Tobiah, and the Arabs, the Ammonites, and the Ashdodites heard that healing had come to the walls of *Yerushalayim*, that the breached parts had begun to be filled, it angered them very much,

א וַיְהִי כַאֲשֶׁר שָׁמַע סַנְבַלַּט וְטוֹבִיָּה וְהָעַרְבִים וְהָעַמֹּנִים וְהָאַשְׁדּוֹדִים כִּי־עָלְתָה אֲרוּכָה לְחֹמוֹת יְרוּשָׁלַםִ כִּי־הֵחֵלּוּ הַפְּרֻצִים לְהִסָּתֵם וַיִּחַר לָהֶם מְאֹד:

2 and they all conspired together to come and fight against *Yerushalayim* and to throw it into confusion.

ב וַיִּקְשְׁרוּ כֻלָּם יַחְדָּו לָבוֹא לְהִלָּחֵם בִּירוּשָׁלָםִ וְלַעֲשׂוֹת לוֹ תּוֹעָה:

3 Because of them we prayed to our God, and set up a watch over them day and night.

ג וַנִּתְפַּלֵּל אֶל־אֱלֹהֵינוּ וַנַּעֲמִיד מִשְׁמָר עֲלֵיהֶם יוֹמָם וָלַיְלָה מִפְּנֵיהֶם:

4 *Yehuda* was saying, "The strength of the basket-carrier has failed, And there is so much rubble; We are not able ourselves To rebuild the wall."

ד וַיֹּאמֶר יְהוּדָה כָּשַׁל כֹּחַ הַסַּבָּל וְהֶעָפָר הַרְבֵּה וַאֲנַחְנוּ לֹא נוּכַל לִבְנוֹת בַּחוֹמָה:

5 And our foes were saying, "Before they know or see it, we shall be in among them and kill them, and put a stop to the work."

ה וַיֹּאמְרוּ צָרֵינוּ לֹא יֵדְעוּ וְלֹא יִרְאוּ עַד אֲשֶׁר־נָבוֹא אֶל־תּוֹכָם וַהֲרַגְנוּם וְהִשְׁבַּתְנוּ אֶת־הַמְּלָאכָה:

6 When the *Yehudim* living near them would arrive, they would tell us time and again "...from all the places where...you shall come back to us..."

ו וַיְהִי כַּאֲשֶׁר־בָּאוּ הַיְּהוּדִים הַיֹּשְׁבִים אֶצְלָם וַיֹּאמְרוּ לָנוּ עֶשֶׂר פְּעָמִים מִכָּל־הַמְּקֹמוֹת אֲשֶׁר־תָּשׁוּבוּ עָלֵינוּ:

7 I stationed, on the lower levels of the place, behind the walls, on the bare rock – I stationed the people by families with their swords, their lances, and their bows.

ז וָאַעֲמִיד מִתַּחְתִּיּוֹת לַמָּקוֹם מֵאַחֲרֵי לַחוֹמָה בצחחיים [בַּצְּחִיחִים] וָאַעֲמִיד אֶת־הָעָם לְמִשְׁפָּחוֹת עִם־חַרְבֹתֵיהֶם רָמְחֵיהֶם וְקַשְּׁתֹתֵיהֶם:

8 Then I decided to exhort the nobles, the prefects, and the rest of the people, "Do not be afraid of them! Think of the great and awesome *Hashem*, and fight for your brothers, your sons and daughters, your wives and homes!"

ח וָאֵרֶא וָאָקוּם וָאֹמַר אֶל־הַחֹרִים וְאֶל־הַסְּגָנִים וְאֶל־יֶתֶר הָעָם אַל־תִּירְאוּ מִפְּנֵיהֶם אֶת־אֲדֹנָי הַגָּדוֹל וְהַנּוֹרָא זְכֹרוּ וְהִלָּחֲמוּ עַל־אֲחֵיכֶם בְּנֵיכֶם וּבְנֹתֵיכֶם נְשֵׁיכֶם וּבָתֵּיכֶם:

9 When our enemies learned that it had become known to us, since *Hashem* had thus frustrated their plan, we could all return to the wall, each to his work.

ט וַיְהִי כַּאֲשֶׁר־שָׁמְעוּ אוֹיְבֵינוּ כִּי־נוֹדַע לָנוּ וַיָּפֶר הָאֱלֹהִים אֶת־עֲצָתָם ונשוב [וַנָּשָׁב] כֻּלָּנוּ אֶל־הַחוֹמָה אִישׁ אֶל־מְלַאכְתּוֹ:

10 From that day on, half my servants did work and half held lances and shields, bows and armor. And the officers stood behind the whole house of *Yehuda*

י וַיְהִי מִן־הַיּוֹם הַהוּא חֲצִי נְעָרַי עֹשִׂים בַּמְּלָאכָה וְחֶצְיָם מַחֲזִיקִים וְהָרְמָחִים הַמָּגִנִּים וְהַקְּשָׁתוֹת וְהַשִּׁרְיֹנִים וְהַשָּׂרִים אַחֲרֵי כָּל־בֵּית יְהוּדָה:

11 who were rebuilding the wall. The basket-carriers were burdened, doing work with one hand while the other held a weapon.

יא הַבּוֹנִים בַּחוֹמָה וְהַנֹּשְׂאִים בַּסֶּבֶל עֹמְשִׂים בְּאַחַת יָדוֹ עֹשֶׂה בַמְּלָאכָה וְאַחַת מַחֲזֶקֶת הַשָּׁלַח:

ha-bo-NEEM ba-kho-MAH v'-ha-no-s'-EEM ba-SE-vel o-m'-SEEM b'-a-KHAT
ya-DO o-SEH va-m'-la-KHAH v'-a-KHAT ma-kha-ZE-ket ha-SHA-lakh

12 As for the builders, each had his sword girded at his side as he was building. The trumpeter stood beside me.

יב וְהַבּוֹנִים אִישׁ חַרְבּוֹ אֲסוּרִים עַל־מָתְנָיו וּבוֹנִים וְהַתּוֹקֵעַ בַּשּׁוֹפָר אֶצְלִי:

13 I said to the nobles, the prefects, and the rest of the people, "There is much work and it is spread out; we are scattered over the wall, far from one another.

יג וָאֹמַר אֶל־הַחֹרִים וְאֶל־הַסְּגָנִים וְאֶל־יֶתֶר הָעָם הַמְּלָאכָה הַרְבֵּה וּרְחָבָה וַאֲנַחְנוּ נִפְרָדִים עַל־הַחוֹמָה רְחוֹקִים אִישׁ מֵאָחִיו:

A new IDF recruit holding a *Tanakh* and a gun

4:11 Doing work with one hand while the other held a weapon Throughout the *Tanakh*, God does wonders and miracles to save the Jewish people. Although perhaps one would think that a nation under *Hashem's* direct protection should not need arms to defend itself, it is His will that people conduct themselves in a natural manner. Only when necessary will *Hashem* intervene with open miracles. This verse describes how in *Nechemya's* time, those rebuilding the walls of *Yerushalayim* would work with one hand while holding weapons of self-defense in the other. Though they rely on their own strength for protection, they remember that the Lord is the source of their might and their success. As described earlier in verse 3, first they "prayed to our God," and then they "set up a watch" against their enemies. Today, the soldiers of the Israel Defense Forces are the ones protecting the Nation of Israel. At IDF swearing-in ceremonies, each soldier is given a *Tanakh* to hold in one hand, and a gun in the other. In this way, Israeli soldiers are the spiritual descendants of *Nechemya's* work force who are reminded that it is not their strength alone that protects the nation, but *Hashem* above.

14 When you hear a trumpet call, gather yourselves to me at that place; our God will fight for us!"

בִּמְקוֹם אֲשֶׁר תִּשְׁמְעוּ אֶת־קוֹל הַשּׁוֹפָר שָׁמָּה תִּקָּבְצוּ אֵלֵינוּ אֱלֹהֵינוּ יִלָּחֶם לָנוּ: יד

15 And so we worked on, while half were holding lances, from the break of day until the stars appeared.

וַאֲנַחְנוּ עֹשִׂים בַּמְּלָאכָה וְחֶצְיָם מַחֲזִיקִים בָּרְמָחִים מֵעֲלוֹת הַשַּׁחַר עַד צֵאת הַכּוֹכָבִים: טו

16 I further said to the people at that time, "Let every man with his servant lodge in *Yerushalayim*, that we may use the night to stand guard and the day to work."

גַּם בָּעֵת הַהִיא אָמַרְתִּי לָעָם אִישׁ וְנַעֲרוֹ יָלִינוּ בְּתוֹךְ יְרוּשָׁלִָם וְהָיוּ־לָנוּ הַלַּיְלָה מִשְׁמָר וְהַיּוֹם מְלָאכָה: טז

17 Nor did I, my brothers, my servants, or the guards following me ever take off our clothes, [or] each his weapon, even at the water.

וְאֵין אֲנִי וְאַחַי וּנְעָרַי וְאַנְשֵׁי הַמִּשְׁמָר אֲשֶׁר אַחֲרָי אֵין־אֲנַחְנוּ פֹשְׁטִים בְּגָדֵינוּ אִישׁ שִׁלְחוֹ הַמָּיִם: יז

5 1 There was a great outcry by the common folk and their wives against their brother *Yehudim*.

וַתְּהִי צַעֲקַת הָעָם וּנְשֵׁיהֶם גְּדוֹלָה אֶל־ אֲחֵיהֶם הַיְּהוּדִים: א **ה**

2 Some said, "Our sons and daughters are numerous; we must get grain to eat in order that we may live!"

וְיֵשׁ אֲשֶׁר אֹמְרִים בָּנֵינוּ וּבְנֹתֵינוּ אֲנַחְנוּ רַבִּים וְנִקְחָה דָגָן וְנֹאכְלָה וְנִחְיֶה: ב

3 Others said, "We must pawn our fields, our vineyards, and our homes to get grain to stave off hunger."

וְיֵשׁ אֲשֶׁר אֹמְרִים שְׂדֹתֵינוּ וּכְרָמֵינוּ וּבָתֵּינוּ אֲנַחְנוּ עֹרְבִים וְנִקְחָה דָגָן בָּרָעָב: ג

4 Yet others said, "We have borrowed money against our fields and vineyards to pay the king's tax.

וְיֵשׁ אֲשֶׁר אֹמְרִים לָוִינוּ כֶסֶף לְמִדַּת הַמֶּלֶךְ שְׂדֹתֵינוּ וּכְרָמֵינוּ: ד

5 Now we are as good as our brothers, and our children as good as theirs; yet here we are subjecting our sons and daughters to slavery – some of our daughters are already subjected – and we are powerless, while our fields and vineyards belong to others."

וְעַתָּה כִּבְשַׂר אַחֵינוּ בְּשָׂרֵנוּ כִּבְנֵיהֶם בָּנֵינוּ וְהִנֵּה אֲנַחְנוּ כֹבְשִׁים אֶת־בָּנֵינוּ וְאֶת־בְּנֹתֵינוּ לַעֲבָדִים וְיֵשׁ מִבְּנֹתֵינוּ נִכְבָּשׁוֹת וְאֵין לְאֵל יָדֵנוּ וּשְׂדֹתֵינוּ וּכְרָמֵינוּ לַאֲחֵרִים: ה

6 It angered me very much to hear their outcry and these complaints.

וַיִּחַר לִי מְאֹד כַּאֲשֶׁר שָׁמַעְתִּי אֶת־ זַעֲקָתָם וְאֵת הַדְּבָרִים הָאֵלֶּה: ו

7 After pondering the matter carefully, I censured the nobles and the prefects, saying, "Are you pressing claims on loans made to your brothers?" Then I raised a large crowd against them

וַיִּמָּלֵךְ לִבִּי עָלַי וָאָרִיבָה אֶת־הַחֹרִים וְאֶת־הַסְּגָנִים וָאֹמְרָה לָהֶם מַשָּׁא אִישׁ־ בְּאָחִיו אַתֶּם נֹשִׁאים [נֹשִׁים] וָאֶתֵּן עֲלֵיהֶם קְהִלָּה גְדוֹלָה: ז

8 and said to them, "We have done our best to buy back our Yehudiish brothers who were sold to the nations; will you now sell your brothers so that they must be sold [back] to us?" They kept silent, for they found nothing to answer.

וָאֹמְרָה לָהֶם אֲנַחְנוּ קָנִינוּ אֶת־אַחֵינוּ הַיְּהוּדִים הַנִּמְכָּרִים לַגּוֹיִם כְּדֵי בָנוּ וְגַם־ אַתֶּם תִּמְכְּרוּ אֶת־אֲחֵיכֶם וְנִמְכְּרוּ־לָנוּ וַיַּחֲרִישׁוּ וְלֹא מָצְאוּ דָּבָר: ח

9 So I continued, "What you are doing is not right. You ought to act in a *Hashem*-fearing way so as not to give our enemies, the nations, room to reproach us.

וַיֹּאמֶר [וָאוֹמַר] לֹא־טוֹב הַדָּבָר אֲשֶׁר־ אַתֶּם עֹשִׂים הֲלוֹא בְּיִרְאַת אֱלֹהֵינוּ תֵּלֵכוּ מֵחֶרְפַּת הַגּוֹיִם אוֹיְבֵינוּ: ט

10 I, my brothers, and my servants also have claims of money and grain against them; let us now abandon those claims!

י וְגַם־אֲנִי אַחַי וּנְעָרַי נֹשִׁים בָּהֶם כֶּסֶף וְדָגָן נַעַזְבָה־נָּא אֶת־הַמַּשָּׁא הַזֶּה:

11 Give back at once their fields, their vineyards, their olive trees, and their homes, and [abandon] the claims for the hundred pieces of silver, the grain, the wine, and the oil that you have been pressing against them!"

יא הָשִׁיבוּ נָא לָהֶם כְּהַיּוֹם שְׂדֹתֵיהֶם כַּרְמֵיהֶם זֵיתֵיהֶם וּבָתֵּיהֶם וּמְאַת הַכֶּסֶף וְהַדָּגָן הַתִּירוֹשׁ וְהַיִּצְהָר אֲשֶׁר אַתֶּם נֹשִׁים בָּהֶם:

12 They replied, "We shall give them back, and not demand anything of them; we shall do just as you say." Summoning the *Kohanim*, I put them under oath to keep this promise.

יב וַיֹּאמְרוּ נָשִׁיב וּמֵהֶם לֹא נְבַקֵּשׁ כֵּן נַעֲשֶׂה כַּאֲשֶׁר אַתָּה אוֹמֵר וָאֶקְרָא אֶת־הַכֹּהֲנִים וָאַשְׁבִּיעֵם לַעֲשׂוֹת כַּדָּבָר הַזֶּה:

13 I also shook out the bosom of my garment and said, "So may *Hashem* shake free of his household and property any man who fails to keep this promise; may he be thus shaken out and stripped." All the assembled answered, "*Amen*," and praised *Hashem*. The people kept this promise.

יג גַּם־חָצְנִי נָעַרְתִּי וָאֹמְרָה כָּכָה יְנַעֵר הָאֱלֹהִים אֶת־כָּל־הָאִישׁ אֲשֶׁר לֹא־יָקִים אֶת־הַדָּבָר הַזֶּה מִבֵּיתוֹ וּמִיגִיעוֹ וְכָכָה יִהְיֶה נָעוּר וָרֵק וַיֹּאמְרוּ כָל־הַקָּהָל אָמֵן וַיְהַלְלוּ אֶת־יְהוָה וַיַּעַשׂ הָעָם כַּדָּבָר הַזֶּה:

14 Furthermore, from the day I was commissioned to be governor in the land of *Yehuda* – from the twentieth year of King Artaxerxes until his thirty-second year, twelve years in all – neither I nor my brothers ever ate of the governor's food allowance.

יד גַּם מִיּוֹם אֲשֶׁר־צִוָּה אֹתִי לִהְיוֹת פֶּחָם בְּאֶרֶץ יְהוּדָה מִשְּׁנַת עֶשְׂרִים וְעַד שְׁנַת שְׁלֹשִׁים וּשְׁתַּיִם לְאַרְתַּחְשַׁסְתְּא הַמֶּלֶךְ שָׁנִים שְׁתֵּים עֶשְׂרֵה אֲנִי וְאַחַי לֶחֶם הַפֶּחָה לֹא אָכַלְתִּי:

15 The former governors who preceded me laid heavy burdens on the people, and took from them for bread and wine more than forty *shekalim* of silver. Their servants also tyrannized over the people. But I, out of the fear of *Hashem*, did not do so.

טו וְהַפַּחוֹת הָרִאשֹׁנִים אֲשֶׁר־לְפָנַי הִכְבִּידוּ עַל־הָעָם וַיִּקְחוּ מֵהֶם בְּלֶחֶם וָיַיִן אַחַר כֶּסֶף־שְׁקָלִים אַרְבָּעִים גַּם נַעֲרֵיהֶם שָׁלְטוּ עַל־הָעָם וַאֲנִי לֹא־עָשִׂיתִי כֵן מִפְּנֵי יִרְאַת אֱלֹהִים:

*v'-ha-pa-KHOT ha-ri-sho-NEEM a-sher l'-fa-NAI hikh-BEE-du al
ha-AM va-yik-KHU may-HEM b'-LE-khem va-YA-yin a-KHAR KE-sef
sh'-ka-LEEM ar-ba-EEM GAM na-a-ray-HEM sha-l'-TU al ha-AM
va-a-NEE lo a-SEE-tee KHAYN mi-p'-NAY yir-AT e-lo-HEEM*

Ezra/Nehemiah

5:15 And took from them for bread and wine
More than any other food, bread and wine were the staples of ancient society. Bread provides basic nourishment, and wine, while in our lives considered a luxury, was an important source of calories, sugar and iron. Jews recite special benedictions over both bread and wine, and they are both utilized in spiritual rituals: Grains and wine were offered as Temple sacrifices, and today they are both used to mark the sanctity of the Shabbat and Jewish festivals, thus strengthening the connection between physical and spiritual sustenance. In addition, wheat and grapes are two of the seven special agricultural products associated with the Land of Israel (Deuteronomy 8:8). Today, after two thousand years of desolation, Israel boasts a booming agricultural industry and over 200 wineries that produce award-winning kosher wines.

Golan Heights Winery in Katzrin

16 I also supported the work on this wall; we did not buy any land, and all my servants were gathered there at the work.

טז וְגַם בִּמְלֶאכֶת הַחוֹמָה הַזֹּאת הֶחֱזַקְתִּי וְשָׂדֶה לֹא קָנִינוּ וְכָל־נְעָרַי קְבוּצִים שָׁם עַל־הַמְּלָאכָה:

17 Although there were at my table, between *Yehudim* and prefects, one hundred and fifty men in all, beside those who came to us from surrounding nations;

יז וְהַיְּהוּדִים וְהַסְּגָנִים מֵאָה וַחֲמִשִּׁים אִישׁ וְהַבָּאִים אֵלֵינוּ מִן־הַגּוֹיִם אֲשֶׁר־סְבִיבֹתֵינוּ עַל־שֻׁלְחָנִי:

18 and although what was prepared for each day came to one ox, six select sheep, and fowl, all prepared for me, and at ten-day intervals all sorts of wine in abundance – yet I did not resort to the governor's food allowance, for the [king's] service lay heavily on the people.

יח וַאֲשֶׁר הָיָה נַעֲשֶׂה לְיוֹם אֶחָד שׁוֹר אֶחָד צֹאן שֵׁשׁ־בְּרֻרוֹת וְצִפֳּרִים נַעֲשׂוּ־לִי וּבֵין עֲשֶׂרֶת יָמִים בְּכָל־יַיִן לְהַרְבֵּה וְעִם־זֶה לֶחֶם הַפֶּחָה לֹא בִקַּשְׁתִּי כִּי־כָבְדָה הָעֲבֹדָה עַל־הָעָם הַזֶּה:

19 O my God, remember to my credit all that I have done for this people!

יט זָכְרָה־לִּי אֱלֹהַי לְטוֹבָה כֹּל אֲשֶׁר־עָשִׂיתִי עַל־הָעָם הַזֶּה:

6 1 When word reached Sanballat, Tobiah, *Geshem* the Arab, and the rest of our enemies that I had rebuilt the wall and not a breach remained in it – though at that time I had not yet set up doors in the gateways –

ו א וַיְהִי כַאֲשֶׁר נִשְׁמַע לְסַנְבַלַּט וְטוֹבִיָּה וּלְגֶשֶׁם הָעַרְבִי וּלְיֶתֶר אֹיְבֵינוּ כִּי בָנִיתִי אֶת־הַחוֹמָה וְלֹא־נוֹתַר בָּהּ פָּרֶץ גַּם עַד־הָעֵת הַהִיא דְּלָתוֹת לֹא־הֶעֱמַדְתִּי בַשְּׁעָרִים:

vai-HEE kha-a-SHER nish-MA l'-san-va-LAT v'-to-vi-YAH ul-GE-shem ha-ar-VEE ul-YE-ter o-y'-VAY-nu KEE va-NEE-tee et ha-kho-MAH v'-lo NO-tar BAH PA-retz GAM ad ha-AYT ha-HEE d'-la-TOT lo he-e-MAD-tee va-sh'-a-REEM

2 Sanballat and *Geshem* sent a message to me, saying, "Come, let us get together in Kephirim in the Ono valley"; they planned to do me harm.

ב וַיִּשְׁלַח סַנְבַלַּט וְגֶשֶׁם אֵלַי לֵאמֹר לְכָה וְנִוָּעֲדָה יַחְדָּו בַּכְּפִירִים בְּבִקְעַת אוֹנוֹ וְהֵמָּה חֹשְׁבִים לַעֲשׂוֹת לִי רָעָה:

3 I sent them messengers, saying, "I am engaged in a great work and cannot come down, for the work will stop if I leave it in order to come down to you."

ג וָאֶשְׁלְחָה עֲלֵיהֶם מַלְאָכִים לֵאמֹר מְלָאכָה גְדוֹלָה אֲנִי עֹשֶׂה וְלֹא אוּכַל לָרֶדֶת לָמָּה תִשְׁבַּת הַמְּלָאכָה כַּאֲשֶׁר אַרְפֶּהָ וְיָרַדְתִּי אֲלֵיכֶם:

4 They sent me the same message four times, and I gave them the same answer.

ד וַיִּשְׁלְחוּ אֵלַי כַּדָּבָר הַזֶּה אַרְבַּע פְּעָמִים וָאָשִׁיב אוֹתָם כַּדָּבָר הַזֶּה:

Jerusalem's Old City walls

6:1 I had rebuilt the wall and not a breach remained in it Built, destroyed and rebuilt – this has repeatedly been the fate of *Yerushalayim's* walls. Today's iconic Old City walls were renovated in 1538–42 by the Ottoman sultan Suleiman the Magnificent, whose dedicatory inscription adorns the Jaffa Gate. A more modest Hebrew inscription indicates another repair in 1970, quoting *Nechemya*, "Healing had come to the walls of *Yerushalayim*" (Nehemiah 4:1). Jerusalem's walls are significant in ways beyond what meets the eye; on a simple level, of course, they provide protection for the city. But on a more mystical plane, these walls provide a separation between what is inside and that which is outside. Though *Yerushalayim* and its inhabitants are supposed to influence the rest of the world with holiness and spirituality, the walls remind us that it is also important to separate and focus inward. Everyone has an obligation to make an impact and a contribution to the rest of the world, but one must remember not to neglect themselves and their own needs in the process.

5 Sanballat sent me the same message a fifth time by his servant, who had an open letter with him.

ה וַיִּשְׁלַח אֵלַי סַנְבַלַּט כַּדָּבָר הַזֶּה פַּעַם חֲמִישִׁית אֶת־נַעֲרוֹ וְאִגֶּרֶת פְּתוּחָה בְּיָדוֹ:

6 Its text was: "Word has reached the nations, and *Geshem* too says that you and the *Yehudim* are planning to rebel – for which reason you are building the wall – and that you are to be their king. Such is the word.

ו כָּתוּב בָּהּ בַּגּוֹיִם נִשְׁמָע וְגַשְׁמוּ אֹמֵר אַתָּה וְהַיְּהוּדִים חֹשְׁבִים לִמְרוֹד עַל־כֵּן אַתָּה בוֹנֶה הַחוֹמָה וְאַתָּה הֹוֶה לָהֶם לְמֶלֶךְ כַּדְּבָרִים הָאֵלֶּה:

7 You have also set up *Neviim* in *Yerushalayim* to proclaim about you, 'There is a king in *Yehuda*!' Word of these things will surely reach the king; so come, let us confer together."

ז וְגַם־נְבִיאִים הֶעֱמַדְתָּ לִקְרֹא עָלֶיךָ בִירוּשָׁלַ͏ִם לֵאמֹר מֶלֶךְ בִּיהוּדָה וְעַתָּה יִשָּׁמַע לַמֶּלֶךְ כַּדְּבָרִים הָאֵלֶּה וְעַתָּה לְכָה וְנִוָּעֲצָה יַחְדָּו:

8 I sent back a message to him, saying, "None of these things you mention has occurred; they are figments of your imagination" –

ח וָאֶשְׁלְחָה אֵלָיו לֵאמֹר לֹא נִהְיָה כַּדְּבָרִים הָאֵלֶּה אֲשֶׁר אַתָּה אוֹמֵר כִּי מִלִּבְּךָ אַתָּה בוֹדָאם:

9 for they all wished to intimidate us, thinking, "They will desist from the work, and it will not get done." Now strengthen my hands!

ט כִּי כֻלָּם מְיָרְאִים אוֹתָנוּ לֵאמֹר יִרְפּוּ יְדֵיהֶם מִן־הַמְּלָאכָה וְלֹא תֵעָשֶׂה וְעַתָּה חַזֵּק אֶת־יָדָי:

10 Then I visited *Shemaya* son of Delaiah son of Mehetabel when he was housebound, and he said, "Let us meet in the House of *Hashem*, inside the sanctuary, And let us shut the doors of the sanctuary, for they are coming to kill you, By night they are coming to kill you."

י וַאֲנִי־בָאתִי בֵּית שְׁמַעְיָה בֶן־דְּלָיָה בֶּן־מְהֵיטַבְאֵל וְהוּא עָצוּר וַיֹּאמֶר נִוָּעֵד אֶל־בֵּית הָאֱלֹהִים אֶל־תּוֹךְ הַהֵיכָל וְנִסְגְּרָה דַּלְתוֹת הַהֵיכָל כִּי בָּאִים לְהָרְגֶךָ וְלַיְלָה בָּאִים לְהָרְגֶךָ:

11 I replied, "Will a man like me take flight? Besides, who such as I can go into the sanctuary and live? I will not go in."

יא וָאֹמְרָה הַאִישׁ כָּמוֹנִי יִבְרָח וּמִי כָמוֹנִי אֲשֶׁר־יָבוֹא אֶל־הַהֵיכָל וָחָי לֹא אָבוֹא:

12 Then I realized that it was not *Hashem* who sent him, but that he uttered that prophecy about me – Tobiah and Sanballat having hired him –

יב וָאַכִּירָה וְהִנֵּה לֹא־אֱלֹהִים שְׁלָחוֹ כִּי הַנְּבוּאָה דִּבֶּר עָלַי וְטוֹבִיָּה וְסַנְבַלַּט שְׂכָרוֹ:

13 because he was a hireling, that I might be intimidated and act thus and commit a sin, and so provide them a scandal with which to reproach me.

יג לְמַעַן שָׂכוּר הוּא לְמַעַן־אִירָא וְאֶעֱשֶׂה־כֵּן וְחָטָאתִי וְהָיָה לָהֶם לְשֵׁם רָע לְמַעַן יְחָרְפוּנִי:

14 "O my God, remember against Tobiah and Sanballat these deeds of theirs, and against Noadiah the prophetess, and against the other prophets that they wished to intimidate me!"

יד זָכְרָה אֱלֹהַי לְטוֹבִיָּה וּלְסַנְבַלַּט כְּמַעֲשָׂיו אֵלֶּה וְגַם לְנוֹעַדְיָה הַנְּבִיאָה וּלְיֶתֶר הַנְּבִיאִים אֲשֶׁר הָיוּ מְיָרְאִים אוֹתִי:

15 The wall was finished on the twenty-fifth of Elul, after fifty-two days.

טו וַתִּשְׁלַם הַחוֹמָה בְּעֶשְׂרִים וַחֲמִשָּׁה לֶאֱלוּל לַחֲמִשִּׁים וּשְׁנַיִם יוֹם:

16 When all our enemies heard it, and all the nations round about us were intimidated, and fell very low in their own estimation; they realized that this work had been accomplished by the help of our God.

טז וַיְהִי כַּאֲשֶׁר שָׁמְעוּ כָּל־אוֹיְבֵינוּ וַיִּרְאוּ כָּל־הַגּוֹיִם אֲשֶׁר סְבִיבֹתֵינוּ וַיִּפְּלוּ מְאֹד בְּעֵינֵיהֶם וַיֵּדְעוּ כִּי מֵאֵת אֱלֹהֵינוּ נֶעֶשְׂתָה הַמְּלָאכָה הַזֹּאת:

17 Also in those days, the nobles of *Yehuda* kept up a brisk correspondence with Tobiah, and Tobiah with them.

יז גַּם בַּיָּמִים הָהֵם מַרְבִּים חֹרֵי יְהוּדָה אִגְּרֹתֵיהֶם הוֹלְכוֹת עַל־טוֹבִיָּה וַאֲשֶׁר לְטוֹבִיָּה בָּאוֹת אֲלֵיהֶם:

18 Many in *Yehuda* were his confederates, for he was a son-in-law of *Shechanya* son of Arah, and his son *Yehochanan* had married the daughter of Meshullam son of *Berechya*.

יח כִּי־רַבִּים בִּיהוּדָה בַּעֲלֵי שְׁבוּעָה לוֹ כִּי־חָתָן הוּא לִשְׁכַנְיָה בֶן־אָרַח וִיהוֹחָנָן בְּנוֹ לָקַח אֶת־בַּת־מְשֻׁלָּם בֶּן בֶּרֶכְיָה:

19 They would also speak well of him to me, and would divulge my affairs to him. Tobiah sent letters to intimidate me.

יט גַּם טוֹבֹתָיו הָיוּ אֹמְרִים לְפָנַי וּדְבָרַי הָיוּ מוֹצִיאִים לוֹ אִגְּרוֹת שָׁלַח טוֹבִיָּה לְיָרְאֵנִי:

7 1 When the wall was rebuilt and I had set up the doors, tasks were assigned to the gatekeepers, the singers, and the *Leviim*.

ז א וַיְהִי כַּאֲשֶׁר נִבְנְתָה הַחוֹמָה וָאַעֲמִיד הַדְּלָתוֹת וַיִּפָּקְדוּ הַשּׁוֹעֲרִים וְהַמְשֹׁרְרִים וְהַלְוִיִּם:

2 I put *Chanani* my brother and *Chananya*, the captain of the fortress, in charge of *Yerushalayim*, for he was a more trustworthy and *Hashem*-fearing man than most.

ב וָאֲצַוֶּה אֶת־חֲנָנִי אָחִי וְאֶת־חֲנַנְיָה שַׂר הַבִּירָה עַל־יְרוּשָׁלָ͏ִם כִּי־הוּא כְּאִישׁ אֱמֶת וְיָרֵא אֶת־הָאֱלֹהִים מֵרַבִּים:

3 I said to them, "The gates of *Yerushalayim* are not to be opened until the heat of the day, and before you leave your posts let the doors be closed and barred. And assign the inhabitants of *Yerushalayim* to watches, each man to his watch, and each in front of his own house."

ג וַיֹּאמֶר [וָאֹמַר] לָהֶם לֹא יִפָּתְחוּ שַׁעֲרֵי יְרוּשָׁלַ͏ִם עַד־חֹם הַשֶּׁמֶשׁ וְעַד הֵם עֹמְדִים יָגִיפוּ הַדְּלָתוֹת וֶאֱחֹזוּ וְהַעֲמֵיד מִשְׁמְרוֹת יֹשְׁבֵי יְרוּשָׁלַ͏ִם אִישׁ בְּמִשְׁמָרוֹ וְאִישׁ נֶגֶד בֵּיתוֹ:

4 The city was broad and large, the people in it were few, and houses were not yet built.

ד וְהָעִיר רַחֲבַת יָדַיִם וּגְדוֹלָה וְהָעָם מְעַט בְּתוֹכָהּ וְאֵין בָּתִּים בְּנוּיִם:

*v'-ha-EER ra-kha-VAT ya-DA-yim ug-do-LAH v'-ha-AM
m'-AT b'-to-KHAH v'-AYN ba-TEEM b'-nu-YIM*

5 My *Hashem* put it into my mind to assemble the nobles, the prefects, and the people, in order to register them by families. I found the genealogical register of those who were the first to come up, and there I found written:

ה וַיִּתֵּן אֱלֹהַי אֶל־לִבִּי וָאֶקְבְּצָה אֶת־הַחֹרִים וְאֶת־הַסְּגָנִים וְאֶת־הָעָם לְהִתְיַחֵשׂ וָאֶמְצָא סֵפֶר הַיַּחַשׂ הָעוֹלִים בָּרִאשׁוֹנָה וָאֶמְצָא כָּתוּב בּוֹ:

7:4 The city was broad and large, the people in it were few There must be a proper proportion between a city's size and its population. *Nechemya* is concerned that since too few people were living in *Yerushalayim*, it would be difficult to defend, even though it was surrounded by a wall. He therefore looks for more people to inhabit the city. Conversely, if the borders of a city encompass too small an area, it will become overcrowded. This was the case in the 1850s when, in a miraculous reversal of *Nechemya's* time, *Yerusha-* layim became so full of inhabitants that it was necessary to expand and build new neighborhoods outside the Old City walls, beginning with the neighborhood of *Mishkenot Sha'ananim* in 1860. As a land, however, the Land of Israel will always have room to contain her children. Also named *Eretz Hatzvi*, 'The Land of the Gazelle,' the Talmud (*Ketubot* 112a) states that just as a gazelle's hide stretches according to need, so too the Land of Israel will stretch to sustain any number of its people. Furthermore, King Solomon writes "my beloved is like a gazelle" (Song of Songs 2:9), inferring that just as a gazelle finds its way home from the ends of the world, so too will the dispersed Jews return. And when they do, *Eretz Yisrael* will contain them all.

A street in the *Mishkenot Sha'ananim* neighborhood of *Yerushalayim*

6 These are the people of the province who came up from among the captive exiles that Nebuchadnezzar, king of Babylon, had deported, and who returned to *Yerushalayim* and to *Yehuda*, each to his own city,

א אֵלֶּה ׀ בְּנֵי הַמְּדִינָה הָעֹלִים מִשְּׁבִי הַגּוֹלָה אֲשֶׁר הֶגְלָה נְבוּכַדְנֶצַּר מֶלֶךְ בָּבֶל וַיָּשׁוּבוּ לִירוּשָׁלַ͏ִם וְלִיהוּדָה אִישׁ לְעִירוֹ:

7 who came with *Zerubavel*, *Yeshua*, *Nechemya*, *Azarya*, Raamiah, Nahamani, *Mordechai*, Bilshan, Mispereth, Bigvai, Nehum, Baanah. The number of the men of the people of *Yisrael*:

ז הַבָּאִים עִם־זְרֻבָּבֶל יֵשׁוּעַ נְחֶמְיָה עֲזַרְיָה רַעַמְיָה נַחֲמָנִי מׇרְדֳּכַי בִּלְשָׁן מִסְפֶּרֶת בִּגְוַי נְחוּם בַּעֲנָה מִסְפַּר אַנְשֵׁי עַם יִשְׂרָאֵל:

8 the sons of Parosh – 2,172;

ח בְּנֵי פַרְעֹשׁ אַלְפַּיִם מֵאָה וְשִׁבְעִים וּשְׁנָיִם:

9 the sons of Shephatiah – 372;

ט בְּנֵי שְׁפַטְיָה שְׁלֹשׁ מֵאוֹת שִׁבְעִים וּשְׁנָיִם:

10 the sons of Arah – 652;

י בְּנֵי אָרַח שֵׁשׁ מֵאוֹת חֲמִשִּׁים וּשְׁנָיִם:

11 the sons of Pahath-moab: the sons of *Yeshua* and Yoav – 2,818;

יא בְּנֵי־פַחַת מוֹאָב לִבְנֵי יֵשׁוּעַ וְיוֹאָב אַלְפַּיִם וּשְׁמֹנֶה מֵאוֹת שְׁמֹנָה עָשָׂר:

12 the sons of Elam – 1,254;

יב בְּנֵי עֵילָם אֶלֶף מָאתַיִם חֲמִשִּׁים וְאַרְבָּעָה:

13 the sons of Zattu – 845;

יג בְּנֵי זַתּוּא שְׁמֹנֶה מֵאוֹת אַרְבָּעִים וַחֲמִשָּׁה:

14 the sons of Zaccai – 760;

יד בְּנֵי זַכָּי שְׁבַע מֵאוֹת וְשִׁשִּׁים:

15 the sons of Binnui – 648;

טו בְּנֵי בִנּוּי שֵׁשׁ מֵאוֹת אַרְבָּעִים וּשְׁמֹנָה:

16 the sons of Bebai – 628;

טז בְּנֵי בֵבָי שֵׁשׁ מֵאוֹת עֶשְׂרִים וּשְׁמֹנָה:

17 the sons of Azgad – 2,322;

יז בְּנֵי עַזְגָּד אַלְפַּיִם שְׁלֹשׁ מֵאוֹת עֶשְׂרִים וּשְׁנָיִם:

18 the sons of Adonikam – 667;

יח בְּנֵי אֲדֹנִיקָם שֵׁשׁ מֵאוֹת שִׁשִּׁים וְשִׁבְעָה:

19 the sons of Bigvai – 2,067;

יט בְּנֵי בִגְוָי אַלְפַּיִם שִׁשִּׁים וְשִׁבְעָה:

20 the sons of Adin – 655;

כ בְּנֵי עָדִין שֵׁשׁ מֵאוֹת חֲמִשִּׁים וַחֲמִשָּׁה:

21 the sons of Ater: *Chizkiyahu* – 98;

כא בְּנֵי־אָטֵר לְחִזְקִיָּה תִּשְׁעִים וּשְׁמֹנָה:

22 the sons of Hashum – 328;

כב בְּנֵי חָשֻׁם שְׁלֹשׁ מֵאוֹת עֶשְׂרִים וּשְׁמֹנָה:

23 the sons of Bezai – 324;

כג בְּנֵי בֵצָי שְׁלֹשׁ מֵאוֹת עֶשְׂרִים וְאַרְבָּעָה:

24 the sons of Hariph – 112;

כד בְּנֵי חָרִיף מֵאָה שְׁנֵים עָשָׂר:

25 the sons of *Givon* – 95;

כה בְּנֵי גִבְעוֹן תִּשְׁעִים וַחֲמִשָּׁה:

26 the men of *Beit Lechem* and Netophah – 188;

כו אַנְשֵׁי בֵית־לֶחֶם וּנְטֹפָה מֵאָה שְׁמֹנִים וּשְׁמֹנָה:

27 the men of *Anatot* – 128;

כז אַנְשֵׁי עֲנָתוֹת מֵאָה עֶשְׂרִים וּשְׁמֹנָה:

28 the men of Beth-azmaveth – 42;

כח אַנְשֵׁי בֵית־עַזְמָוֶת אַרְבָּעִים וּשְׁנָיִם:

29 the men of *Kiryat Ye'arim*, Chephirah, and Beeroth – 743;

כט אַנְשֵׁי קִרְיַת יְעָרִים כְּפִירָה וּבְאֵרוֹת שְׁבַע מֵאוֹת אַרְבָּעִים וּשְׁלֹשָׁה:

30 the men of *Rama* and Geba – 621;

ל אַנְשֵׁי הָרָמָה וָגֶבַע שֵׁשׁ מֵאוֹת עֶשְׂרִים וְאֶחָד:

31 the men of Michmas – 122;

לא אַנְשֵׁי מִכְמָס מֵאָה וְעֶשְׂרִים וּשְׁנָיִם:

32 the men of *Beit El* and Ai – 123;

לב אַנְשֵׁי בֵית־אֵל וְהָעָי מֵאָה עֶשְׂרִים וּשְׁלֹשָׁה:

33 the men of the other Nebo – 52;

לג אַנְשֵׁי נְבוֹ אַחֵר חֲמִשִּׁים וּשְׁנָיִם:

34 the sons of the other Elam – 1,254;

לד בְּנֵי עֵילָם אַחֵר אֶלֶף מָאתַיִם חֲמִשִּׁים וְאַרְבָּעָה:

35 the sons of Harim – 320;

לה בְּנֵי חָרִם שְׁלֹשׁ מֵאוֹת וְעֶשְׂרִים:

36 the sons of *Yericho* – 345;

לו בְּנֵי יְרֵחוֹ שְׁלֹשׁ מֵאוֹת אַרְבָּעִים וַחֲמִשָּׁה:

37 the sons of Lod, Hadid, and Ono – 721;

לז בְּנֵי־לֹד חָדִיד וְאוֹנוֹ שְׁבַע מֵאוֹת וְעֶשְׂרִים וְאֶחָד:

38 the sons of Senaah – 3,930.

לח בְּנֵי סְנָאָה שְׁלֹשֶׁת אֲלָפִים תְּשַׁע מֵאוֹת וּשְׁלֹשִׁים:

39 The *Kohanim*: the sons of Jedaiah: the house of *Yeshua* – 973;

לט הַכֹּהֲנִים בְּנֵי יְדַעְיָה לְבֵית יֵשׁוּעַ תְּשַׁע מֵאוֹת שִׁבְעִים וּשְׁלֹשָׁה:

40 the sons of Immer – 1,052;

מ בְּנֵי אִמֵּר אֶלֶף חֲמִשִּׁים וּשְׁנָיִם:

41 the sons of Pashhur – 1,247;

מא בְּנֵי פַשְׁחוּר אֶלֶף מָאתַיִם אַרְבָּעִים וְשִׁבְעָה:

42 the sons of Harim – 1,017.

מב בְּנֵי חָרִם אֶלֶף שִׁבְעָה עָשָׂר:

43 The *Leviim*: the sons of *Yeshua*: *Kadmiel*, the sons of Hodeiah – 74.

מג הַלְוִיִּם בְּנֵי־יֵשׁוּעַ לְקַדְמִיאֵל לִבְנֵי לְהוֹדְוָה שִׁבְעִים וְאַרְבָּעָה:

44 The singers: the sons of *Asaf* – 148.

מד הַמְשֹׁרְרִים בְּנֵי אָסָף מֵאָה אַרְבָּעִים וּשְׁמֹנָה:

45 The gatekeepers: the sons of *Shalum*, the sons of Ater, the sons of Talmon, the sons of Akkub, the sons of Hatita, the sons of Shobai – 138.

מה הַשֹּׁעֲרִים בְּנֵי־שַׁלּוּם בְּנֵי־אָטֵר בְּנֵי־טַלְמֹן בְּנֵי־עַקּוּב בְּנֵי חֲטִיטָא בְּנֵי שֹׁבָי מֵאָה שְׁלֹשִׁים וּשְׁמֹנָה:

46 The temple servants: the sons of Ziha, the sons of Hasupha, the sons of Tabbaoth,

מו הַנְּתִינִים בְּנֵי־צִחָא בְנֵי־חֲשֻׂפָא בְּנֵי טַבָּעוֹת:

47 the sons of Keros, the sons of Siah, the sons of Padon,

מז בְּנֵי־קֵירֹס בְּנֵי־סִיעָא בְּנֵי פָדוֹן:

48 the sons of Lebanah, the sons of Hagabah, the sons of Shalmai,

מח בְּנֵי־לְבָנָה בְנֵי־חֲגָבָה בְּנֵי שַׁלְמָי:

49 the sons of Hanan, the sons of Giddel, the sons of Gahar,

מט בְּנֵי־חָנָן בְּנֵי־גִדֵּל בְּנֵי־גָחַר׃

50 the sons of Reaiah, the sons of Rezin, the sons of Nekoda,

נ בְּנֵי־רְאָיָה בְנֵי־רְצִין בְּנֵי נְקוֹדָא׃

51 the sons of Gazzam, the sons of Uzza, the sons of Paseah,

נא בְּנֵי־גַזָּם בְּנֵי־עֻזָּא בְּנֵי פָסֵחַ׃

52 the sons of Besai, the sons of Meunim, the sons of Nephishesim,

נב בְּנֵי־בֵסַי בְּנֵי־מְעוּנִים בְּנֵי נְפוּשְׁסִים
[נְפִישְׁסִים]׃

53 the sons of Bakbuk, the sons of Hakupha, the sons of Harhur,

נג בְּנֵי־בַקְבּוּק בְּנֵי־חֲקוּפָא בְּנֵי חַרְחוּר׃

54 the sons of Bazlith, the sons of Mehida, the sons of Harsha,

נד בְּנֵי־בַצְלִית בְּנֵי־מְחִידָא בְּנֵי חַרְשָׁא׃

55 the sons of Barkos, the sons of Sisera, the sons of Temah,

נה בְּנֵי־בַרְקוֹס בְּנֵי־סִיסְרָא בְּנֵי־תָמַח׃

56 the sons of Neziah, the sons of Hatipha.

נו בְּנֵי נְצִיחַ בְּנֵי חֲטִיפָא׃

57 The sons of *Shlomo*'s servants: the sons of Sotai, the sons of Sophereth, the sons of Perida,

נז בְּנֵי עַבְדֵי שְׁלֹמֹה בְּנֵי־סוֹטַי בְּנֵי־סוֹפֶרֶת
בְּנֵי פְרִידָא׃

58 the sons of Jala, the sons of Darkon, the sons of Giddel,

נח בְּנֵי־יַעְלָא בְנֵי־דַרְקוֹן בְּנֵי גִדֵּל׃

59 the sons of Shephatiah, the sons of Hattil, the sons of Pochereth-hazzebaim, the sons of Ammon.

נט בְּנֵי שְׁפַטְיָה בְנֵי־חַטִּיל בְּנֵי פֹּכֶרֶת
הַצְּבָיִים בְּנֵי אָמוֹן׃

60 The total of temple servants and the sons of *Shlomo*'s servants – 392.

ס כָּל־הַנְּתִינִים וּבְנֵי עַבְדֵי שְׁלֹמֹה שְׁלֹשׁ
מֵאוֹת תִּשְׁעִים וּשְׁנָיִם׃

61 The following were those who came up from Tel-melah, Tel-harsha, Cherub, Addon, and Immer – they were unable to tell whether their father's house and descent were Israelite:

סא וְאֵלֶּה הָעוֹלִים מִתֵּל מֶלַח תֵּל חַרְשָׁא
כְּרוּב אַדּוֹן וְאִמֵּר וְלֹא יָכְלוּ לְהַגִּיד בֵּית־
אֲבוֹתָם וְזַרְעָם אִם מִיִּשְׂרָאֵל הֵם׃

62 the sons of Delaiah, the sons of Tobiah, the sons of Nekoda – 642.

סב בְּנֵי־דְלָיָה בְנֵי־טוֹבִיָּה בְּנֵי נְקוֹדָא שֵׁשׁ
מֵאוֹת וְאַרְבָּעִים וּשְׁנָיִם׃

63 Of the *Kohanim*: the sons of Habaiah, the sons of Hakkoz, the sons of *Barzilai* who had married a daughter of *Barzilai* the Giladite and had taken his name –

סג וּמִן־הַכֹּהֲנִים בְּנֵי חֲבַיָּה בְּנֵי הַקּוֹץ בְּנֵי
בַרְזִלַּי אֲשֶׁר לָקַח מִבְּנוֹת בַּרְזִלַּי הַגִּלְעָדִי
אִשָּׁה וַיִּקָּרֵא עַל־שְׁמָם׃

64 these searched for their genealogical records, but they could not be found, so they were disqualified for the priesthood.

סד אֵלֶּה בִּקְשׁוּ כְתָבָם הַמִּתְיַחְשִׂים וְלֹא
נִמְצָא וַיְגֹאֲלוּ מִן־הַכְּהֻנָּה׃

65 The Tirshatha ordered them not to eat of the most holy things until a *Kohen* with Urim and Thummim should appear.

סה וַיֹּאמֶר הַתִּרְשָׁתָא לָהֶם אֲשֶׁר לֹא־
יֹאכְלוּ מִקֹּדֶשׁ הַקֳּדָשִׁים עַד עֲמֹד הַכֹּהֵן
לְאוּרִים וְתֻמִּים׃

66 The sum of the entire community was 42,360,

סו כָּל־הַקָּהָל כְּאֶחָד אַרְבַּע רִבּוֹא אַלְפַּיִם
שְׁלֹשׁ־מֵאוֹת וְשִׁשִּׁים׃

67 not counting their male and female servants, these being 7,337; they also had 245 male and female singers.

סז מִלְּבַד עַבְדֵיהֶם וְאַמְהֹתֵיהֶם אֵלֶּה שִׁבְעַת אֲלָפִים שְׁלֹשׁ מֵאוֹת שְׁלֹשִׁים וְשִׁבְעָה וְלָהֶם מְשֹׁרְרִים וּמְשֹׁרֲרוֹת מָאתַיִם וְאַרְבָּעִים וַחֲמִשָּׁה:

68 [Their horses – 736, their mules – 245,] camels – 435, asses – 6,720.

סח גְּמַלִּים אַרְבַּע מֵאוֹת שְׁלֹשִׁים וַחֲמִשָּׁה חֲמֹרִים שֵׁשֶׁת אֲלָפִים שְׁבַע מֵאוֹת וְעֶשְׂרִים:

69 Some of the heads of the clans made donations for the work. The Tirshatha donated to the treasury: gold – 1,000 drachmas, basins – 50, priestly robes – 530.

סט וּמִקְצָת רָאשֵׁי הָאָבוֹת נָתְנוּ לַמְּלָאכָה הַתִּרְשָׁתָא נָתַן לָאוֹצָר זָהָב דַּרְכְּמֹנִים אֶלֶף מִזְרָקוֹת חֲמִשִּׁים כָּתְנוֹת כֹּהֲנִים שְׁלֹשִׁים וַחֲמֵשׁ מֵאוֹת:

70 Some of the heads of the clans donated to the work treasury: gold – 20,000 drachmas, and silver – 2,200 *manim*.

ע וּמֵרָאשֵׁי הָאָבוֹת נָתְנוּ לְאוֹצַר הַמְּלָאכָה זָהָב דַּרְכְּמוֹנִים שְׁתֵּי רִבּוֹת וְכֶסֶף מָנִים אַלְפַּיִם וּמָאתָיִם:

71 The rest of the people donated: gold – 20,000 drachmas, silver – 2,000, and priestly robes – 67.

עא וַאֲשֶׁר נָתְנוּ שְׁאֵרִית הָעָם זָהָב דַּרְכְּמוֹנִים שְׁתֵּי רִבּוֹא וְכֶסֶף מָנִים אַלְפָּיִם וְכָתְנֹת כֹּהֲנִים שִׁשִּׁים וְשִׁבְעָה:

72 The *Kohanim*, the *Leviim*, the gatekeepers, the singers, some of the people, the temple servants, and all *Yisrael* took up residence in their towns. When the seventh month arrived – the Israelites being [settled] in their towns –

עב וַיֵּשְׁבוּ הַכֹּהֲנִים וְהַלְוִיִּם וְהַשּׁוֹעֲרִים וְהַמְשֹׁרְרִים וּמִן הָעָם וְהַנְּתִינִים וְכָל יִשְׂרָאֵל בְּעָרֵיהֶם וַיִּגַּע הַחֹדֶשׁ הַשְּׁבִיעִי וּבְנֵי יִשְׂרָאֵל בְּעָרֵיהֶם:

8 1 the entire people assembled as one man in the square before the Water Gate, and they asked *Ezra* the scribe to bring the scroll of the Teaching of *Moshe* with which *Hashem* had charged *Yisrael*.

ח א וַיֵּאָסְפוּ כָל הָעָם כְּאִישׁ אֶחָד אֶל הָרְחוֹב אֲשֶׁר לִפְנֵי שַׁעַר הַמָּיִם וַיֹּאמְרוּ לְעֶזְרָא הַסֹּפֵר לְהָבִיא אֶת סֵפֶר תּוֹרַת מֹשֶׁה אֲשֶׁר צִוָּה יְהוָה אֶת יִשְׂרָאֵל:

2 On the first day of the seventh month, *Ezra* the *Kohen* brought the Teaching before the congregation, men and women and all who could listen with understanding.

ב וַיָּבִיא עֶזְרָא הַכֹּהֵן אֶת הַתּוֹרָה לִפְנֵי הַקָּהָל מֵאִישׁ וְעַד אִשָּׁה וְכֹל מֵבִין לִשְׁמֹעַ בְּיוֹם אֶחָד לַחֹדֶשׁ הַשְּׁבִיעִי:

3 He read from it, facing the square before the Water Gate, from the first light until midday, to the men and the women and those who could understand; the ears of all the people were given to the scroll of the Teaching.

ג וַיִּקְרָא בוֹ לִפְנֵי הָרְחוֹב אֲשֶׁר לִפְנֵי שַׁעַר הַמַּיִם מִן הָאוֹר עַד מַחֲצִית הַיּוֹם נֶגֶד הָאֲנָשִׁים וְהַנָּשִׁים וְהַמְּבִינִים וְאָזְנֵי כָל הָעָם אֶל סֵפֶר הַתּוֹרָה:

4 *Ezra* the scribe stood upon a wooden tower made for the purpose, and beside him stood Mattithiah, Shema, Anaiah, *Uriya*, *Chilkiyahu*, and Maaseiah at his right, and at his left Pedaiah, *Mishael*, Malchijah, Hashum, Hashbaddanah, *Zecharya*, Meshullam.

ד וַיַּעֲמֹד עֶזְרָא הַסֹּפֵר עַל מִגְדַּל עֵץ אֲשֶׁר עָשׂוּ לַדָּבָר וַיַּעֲמֹד אֶצְלוֹ מַתִּתְיָה וְשֶׁמַע וַעֲנָיָה וְאוּרִיָּה וְחִלְקִיָּה וּמַעֲשֵׂיָה עַל יְמִינוֹ וּמִשְּׂמֹאלוֹ פְּדָיָה וּמִישָׁאֵל וּמַלְכִּיָּה וְחָשֻׁם וְחַשְׁבַּדָּנָה זְכַרְיָה מְשֻׁלָּם:

5 *Ezra* opened the scroll in the sight of all the people, for he was above all the people; as he opened it, all the people stood up.

ה וַיִּפְתַּח עֶזְרָא הַסֵּפֶר לְעֵינֵי כָל־הָעָם כִּי־מֵעַל כָּל־הָעָם הָיָה וּכְפִתְחוֹ עָמְדוּ כָל־הָעָם:

6 *Ezra* blessed *Hashem*, the great *Hashem*, and all the people answered, "*Amen, Amen*," with hands upraised. Then they bowed their heads and prostrated themselves before *Hashem* with their faces to the ground.

ו וַיְבָרֶךְ עֶזְרָא אֶת־יְהֹוָה הָאֱלֹהִים הַגָּדוֹל וַיַּעֲנוּ כָל־הָעָם אָמֵן אָמֵן בְּמֹעַל יְדֵיהֶם וַיִּקְּדוּ וַיִּשְׁתַּחֲוֻ לַיהֹוָה אַפַּיִם אָרְצָה:

7 *Yeshua*, Bani, Sherebiah, Jamin, Akkub, Shabbethai, Hodiah, Maaseiah, Kelita, *Azarya*, *Yozavad*, Hanan, Pelaiah, and the *Leviim* explained the Teaching to the people, while the people stood in their places.

ז וְיֵשׁוּעַ וּבָנִי וְשֵׁרֵבְיָה יָמִין עַקּוּב שַׁבְּתַי הוֹדִיָּה מַעֲשֵׂיָה קְלִיטָא עֲזַרְיָה יוֹזָבָד חָנָן פְּלָאיָה וְהַלְוִיִּם מְבִינִים אֶת־הָעָם לַתּוֹרָה וְהָעָם עַל־עָמְדָם:

8 They read from the scroll of the Teaching of *Hashem*, translating it and giving the sense; so they understood the reading.

ח וַיִּקְרְאוּ בַסֵּפֶר בְּתוֹרַת הָאֱלֹהִים מְפֹרָשׁ וְשׂוֹם שֶׂכֶל וַיָּבִינוּ בַּמִּקְרָא:

9 *Nechemya* the Tirshatha, *Ezra* the *Kohen* and scribe, and the *Leviim* who were explaining to the people said to all the people, "This day is holy to *Hashem* your God: you must not mourn or weep," for all the people were weeping as they listened to the words of the Teaching.

ט וַיֹּאמֶר נְחֶמְיָה הוּא הַתִּרְשָׁתָא וְעֶזְרָא הַכֹּהֵן הַסֹּפֵר וְהַלְוִיִּם הַמְּבִינִים אֶת־הָעָם לְכָל־הָעָם הַיּוֹם קָדֹשׁ־הוּא לַיהֹוָה אֱלֹהֵיכֶם אַל־תִּתְאַבְּלוּ וְאַל־תִּבְכּוּ כִּי בוֹכִים כָּל־הָעָם כְּשָׁמְעָם אֶת־דִּבְרֵי הַתּוֹרָה:

10 He further said to them, "Go, eat choice foods and drink sweet drinks and send portions to whoever has nothing prepared, for the day is holy to our Lord. Do not be sad, for your rejoicing in *Hashem* is the source of your strength."

י וַיֹּאמֶר לָהֶם לְכוּ אִכְלוּ מַשְׁמַנִּים וּשְׁתוּ מַמְתַּקִּים וְשִׁלְחוּ מָנוֹת לְאֵין נָכוֹן לוֹ כִּי־קָדוֹשׁ הַיּוֹם לַאֲדֹנֵינוּ וְאַל־תֵּעָצֵבוּ כִּי־חֶדְוַת יְהֹוָה הִיא מָעֻזְּכֶם:

11 The *Leviim* were quieting the people, saying, "Hush, for the day is holy; do not be sad."

יא וְהַלְוִיִּם מַחְשִׁים לְכָל־הָעָם לֵאמֹר הַסּוּ כִּי הַיּוֹם קָדֹשׁ וְאַל־תֵּעָצֵבוּ:

12 Then all the people went to eat and drink and send portions and make great merriment, for they understood the things they were told.

יב וַיֵּלְכוּ כָל־הָעָם לֶאֱכֹל וְלִשְׁתּוֹת וּלְשַׁלַּח מָנוֹת וְלַעֲשׂוֹת שִׂמְחָה גְדוֹלָה כִּי הֵבִינוּ בַּדְּבָרִים אֲשֶׁר הוֹדִיעוּ לָהֶם:

13 On the second day, the heads of the clans of all the people and the *Kohanim* and *Leviim* gathered to *Ezra* the scribe to study the words of the Teaching.

יג וּבַיּוֹם הַשֵּׁנִי נֶאֶסְפוּ רָאשֵׁי הָאָבוֹת לְכָל־הָעָם הַכֹּהֲנִים וְהַלְוִיִּם אֶל־עֶזְרָא הַסֹּפֵר וּלְהַשְׂכִּיל אֶל־דִּבְרֵי הַתּוֹרָה:

14 They found written in the Teaching that *Hashem* had commanded *Moshe* that the Israelites must dwell in booths during the festival of the seventh month,

יד וַיִּמְצְאוּ כָּתוּב בַּתּוֹרָה אֲשֶׁר צִוָּה יְהֹוָה בְּיַד־מֹשֶׁה אֲשֶׁר יֵשְׁבוּ בְנֵי־יִשְׂרָאֵל בַּסֻּכּוֹת בֶּחָג בַּחֹדֶשׁ הַשְּׁבִיעִי:

15 and that they must announce and proclaim throughout all their towns and *Yerushalayim* as follows, "Go out to the mountains and bring leafy branches of olive trees, pine trees, myrtles, palms and [other] leafy trees to make booths, as it is written."

טו וַאֲשֶׁר יַשְׁמִיעוּ וְיַעֲבִירוּ קוֹל בְּכָל־עָרֵיהֶם וּבִירוּשָׁלַ͏ִם לֵאמֹר צְאוּ הָהָר וְהָבִיאוּ עֲלֵי־זַיִת וַעֲלֵי־עֵץ שֶׁמֶן וַעֲלֵי הֲדַס וַעֲלֵי תְמָרִים וַעֲלֵי עֵץ עָבֹת לַעֲשֹׂת סֻכֹּת כַּכָּתוּב:

va-a-SHER yash-MEE-u v'-ya-a-VEE-ru KOL b'-khol a-ray-HEM u-vee-ru-sha-LA-im lay-MOR tz'-U ha-HAR v'-ha-VEE-u a-lay ZA-yit va-a-lay AYTZ SHE-men va-a-LAY ha-DAS va-a-LAY t'-ma-REEM va-a-LAY AYTZ a-VOT la-a-SOT su-KOT ka-ka-TUV

16 So the people went out and brought them, and made themselves booths on their roofs, in their courtyards, in the courtyards of the House of *Hashem*, in the square of the Water Gate and in the square of the *Efraim* Gate.

טז וַיֵּצְאוּ הָעָם וַיָּבִיאוּ וַיַּעֲשׂוּ לָהֶם סֻכּוֹת אִישׁ עַל־גַּגּוֹ וּבְחַצְרֹתֵיהֶם וּבְחַצְרוֹת בֵּית הָאֱלֹהִים וּבִרְחוֹב שַׁעַר הַמָּיִם וּבִרְחוֹב שַׁעַר אֶפְרָיִם:

17 The whole community that returned from the captivity made booths and dwelt in the booths – the Israelites had not done so from the days of *Yehoshua* son of *Nun* to that day – and there was very great rejoicing.

יז וַיַּעֲשׂוּ כָל־הַקָּהָל הַשָּׁבִים מִן־הַשְּׁבִי סֻכּוֹת וַיֵּשְׁבוּ בַסֻּכּוֹת כִּי לֹא־עָשׂוּ מִימֵי יֵשׁוּעַ בִּן־נוּן כֵּן בְּנֵי יִשְׂרָאֵל עַד הַיּוֹם הַהוּא וַתְּהִי שִׂמְחָה גְדוֹלָה מְאֹד:

18 He read from the scroll of the Teaching of *Hashem* each day, from the first to the last day. They celebrated the festival seven days, and there was a solemn gathering on the eighth, as prescribed.

יח וַיִּקְרָא בְּסֵפֶר תּוֹרַת הָאֱלֹהִים יוֹם בְּיוֹם מִן־הַיּוֹם הָרִאשׁוֹן עַד הַיּוֹם הָאַחֲרוֹן וַיַּעֲשׂוּ־חָג שִׁבְעַת יָמִים וּבַיּוֹם הַשְּׁמִינִי עֲצֶרֶת כַּמִּשְׁפָּט:

9 1 On the twenty-fourth day of this month, the Israelites assembled, fasting, in sackcloth, and with earth upon them.

ט א וּבְיוֹם עֶשְׂרִים וְאַרְבָּעָה לַחֹדֶשׁ הַזֶּה נֶאֶסְפוּ בְנֵי־יִשְׂרָאֵל בְּצוֹם וּבְשַׂקִּים וַאֲדָמָה עֲלֵיהֶם:

2 Those of the stock of *Yisrael* separated themselves from all foreigners, and stood and confessed their sins and the iniquities of their fathers.

ב וַיִּבָּדְלוּ זֶרַע יִשְׂרָאֵל מִכֹּל בְּנֵי נֵכָר וַיַּעַמְדוּ וַיִּתְוַדּוּ עַל־חַטֹּאתֵיהֶם וַעֲוֹנוֹת אֲבֹתֵיהֶם:

Olive branches in the Galilee

8:15 Go out to the mountains and bring leafy branches of olive trees Any species of tree may be used to construct the *sukkah*, the booth used to observe the holiday of *Sukkot*. For this particular *Sukkot*, though, the people specifically looked for olive branches. Besides being one of the seven special agricultural species of the Land of Israel (Deuteronomy 8:8), the olive also plays a significant role in the story of *Noach's* flood. After the rain stopped falling, *Noach* sent out a dove to see if the flood waters had receded. When the dove returned with a freshly plucked olive leaf, "*Noach* knew that the waters had decreased on the earth" (Genesis 8:11). Additionally, the *menorah* 'lamp' in the *Beit Hamikdash* is kindled daily exclusively with olive oil, and this oil is also used ceremoniously to anoint a new king. The common theme of these events is renewal. After the flood, the world was given a new start. Each time the *menorah* is lit, it is kindled anew, without any reliance on previous lightings, and the coronation of a new monarch also begins a new era for the kingdom. This symbolism was certainly not lost on the people in *Nechemya's* time, who were renewing their traditions in the God-given land of their forefathers.

3 Standing in their places, they read from the scroll of the Teaching of *Hashem* their God for one-fourth of the day, and for another fourth they confessed and prostrated themselves before *Hashem* their God.

ג וַיָּקוּמוּ עַל־עָמְדָם וַיִּקְרְאוּ בְּסֵפֶר תּוֹרַת יְהוָֹה אֱלֹהֵיהֶם רְבִעִית הַיּוֹם וּרְבִעִית מִתְוַדִּים וּמִשְׁתַּחֲוִים לַיהוָֹה אֱלֹהֵיהֶם:

4 On the raised platform of the *Leviim* stood *Yeshua* and Bani, *Kadmiel*, Shebaniah, Bunni, Sherebiah, Bani, and Chenani, and cried in a loud voice to *Hashem* their God.

ד וַיָּקָם עַל־מַעֲלֵה הַלְוִיִּם יֵשׁוּעַ וּבָנִי קַדְמִיאֵל שְׁבַנְיָה בֻּנִּי שֵׁרֵבְיָה בָּנִי כְנָנִי וַיִּזְעֲקוּ בְּקוֹל גָּדוֹל אֶל־יְהוָֹה אֱלֹהֵיהֶם:

5 The *Leviim Yeshua*, *Kadmiel*, Bani, Hashabniah, Sherebiah, Hodiah, and Pethahiah said, "Rise, bless *Hashem* your God who is from eternity to eternity: 'May Your glorious name be blessed, exalted though it is above every blessing and praise!'

ה וַיֹּאמְרוּ הַלְוִיִּם יֵשׁוּעַ וְקַדְמִיאֵל בָּנִי חֲשַׁבְנְיָה שֵׁרֵבְיָה הוֹדִיָּה שְׁבַנְיָה פְּתַחְיָה קוּמוּ בָּרְכוּ אֶת־יְהוָֹה אֱלֹהֵיכֶם מִן־ הָעוֹלָם עַד־הָעוֹלָם וִיבָרְכוּ שֵׁם כְּבוֹדֶךָ וּמְרוֹמַם עַל־כָּל־בְּרָכָה וּתְהִלָּה:

6 "You alone are *Hashem*. You made the heavens, the highest heavens, and all their host, the earth and everything upon it, the seas and everything in them. You keep them all alive, and the host of heaven prostrate themselves before You.

ו אַתָּה־הוּא יְהוָֹה לְבַדֶּךָ אֶת [אַתָּה] עָשִׂיתָ אֶת־הַשָּׁמַיִם שְׁמֵי הַשָּׁמַיִם וְכָל־ צְבָאָם הָאָרֶץ וְכָל־אֲשֶׁר עָלֶיהָ הַיַּמִּים וְכָל־אֲשֶׁר בָּהֶם וְאַתָּה מְחַיֶּה אֶת־כֻּלָּם וּצְבָא הַשָּׁמַיִם לְךָ מִשְׁתַּחֲוִים:

7 You are *Hashem*, who chose *Avram*, who brought him out of Ur of the Chaldeans and changed his name to *Avraham*.

ז אַתָּה־הוּא יְהוָֹה הָאֱלֹהִים אֲשֶׁר בָּחַרְתָּ בְּאַבְרָם וְהוֹצֵאתוֹ מֵאוּר כַּשְׂדִּים וְשַׂמְתָּ שְּׁמוֹ אַבְרָהָם:

8 Finding his heart true to You, You made a covenant with him to give the land of the Canaanite, the Hittite, the Amorite, the Perizzite, the Jebusite, and the Girgashite – to give it to his descendants. And You kept Your word, for You are righteous.

ח וּמָצָאתָ אֶת־לְבָבוֹ נֶאֱמָן לְפָנֶיךָ וְכָרוֹת עִמּוֹ הַבְּרִית לָתֵת אֶת־אֶרֶץ הַכְּנַעֲנִי הַחִתִּי הָאֱמֹרִי וְהַפְּרִזִּי וְהַיְבוּסִי וְהַגִּרְגָּשִׁי לָתֵת לְזַרְעוֹ וַתָּקֶם אֶת־דְּבָרֶיךָ כִּי צַדִּיק אָתָּה:

9 You took note of our fathers' affliction in Egypt, and heard their cry at the Sea of Reeds.

ט וַתֵּרֶא אֶת־עֳנִי אֲבֹתֵינוּ בְּמִצְרָיִם וְאֶת־ זַעֲקָתָם שָׁמַעְתָּ עַל־יַם־סוּף:

10 You performed signs and wonders against Pharaoh, all his servants, and all the people of his land, for You knew that they acted presumptuously toward them. You made a name for Yourself that endures to this day.

י וַתִּתֵּן אֹתֹת וּמֹפְתִים בְּפַרְעֹה וּבְכָל־ עֲבָדָיו וּבְכָל־עַם אַרְצוֹ כִּי יָדַעְתָּ כִּי הֵזִידוּ עֲלֵיהֶם וַתַּעַשׂ־לְךָ שֵׁם כְּהַיּוֹם הַזֶּה:

11 You split the sea before them; they passed through the sea on dry land, but You threw their pursuers into the depths, like a stone into the raging waters.

יא וְהַיָּם בָּקַעְתָּ לִפְנֵיהֶם וַיַּעַבְרוּ בְתוֹךְ־ הַיָּם בַּיַּבָּשָׁה וְאֶת־רֹדְפֵיהֶם הִשְׁלַכְתָּ בִמְצוֹלֹת כְּמוֹ־אֶבֶן בְּמַיִם עַזִּים:

12 "You led them by day with a pillar of cloud, and by night with a pillar of fire, to give them light in the way they were to go.

יב וּבְעַמּוּד עָנָן הִנְחִיתָם יוֹמָם וּבְעַמּוּד אֵשׁ לַיְלָה לְהָאִיר לָהֶם אֶת־הַדֶּרֶךְ אֲשֶׁר יֵלְכוּ־בָהּ:

13 You came down on *Har Sinai* and spoke to them from heaven; You gave them right rules and true teachings, good laws and commandments.

יג וְעַל הַר־סִינַי יָרַדְתָּ וְדַבֵּר עִמָּהֶם מִשָּׁמָיִם וַתִּתֵּן לָהֶם מִשְׁפָּטִים יְשָׁרִים וְתוֹרוֹת אֱמֶת חֻקִּים וּמִצְוֹת טוֹבִים:

14 You made known to them Your holy *Shabbat*, and You ordained for them laws, commandments and Teaching, through *Moshe* Your servant.

יד וְאֶת־שַׁבַּת קָדְשְׁךָ הוֹדַעְתָּ לָהֶם וּמִצְווֹת וְחֻקִּים וְתוֹרָה צִוִּיתָ לָהֶם בְּיַד מֹשֶׁה עַבְדֶּךָ:

15 You gave them bread from heaven when they were hungry, and produced water from a rock when they were thirsty. You told them to go and possess the land that You swore to give them.

טו וְלֶחֶם מִשָּׁמַיִם נָתַתָּה לָהֶם לִרְעָבָם וּמַיִם מִסֶּלַע הוֹצֵאתָ לָהֶם לִצְמָאָם וַתֹּאמֶר לָהֶם לָבוֹא לָרֶשֶׁת אֶת־הָאָרֶץ אֲשֶׁר־נָשָׂאתָ אֶת־יָדְךָ לָתֵת לָהֶם:

16 But they – our fathers – acted presumptuously; they stiffened their necks and did not obey Your commandments.

טז וְהֵם וַאֲבֹתֵינוּ הֵזִידוּ וַיַּקְשׁוּ אֶת־עָרְפָּם וְלֹא שָׁמְעוּ אֶל־מִצְוֺתֶיךָ:

17 Refusing to obey, unmindful of Your wonders that You did for them, they stiffened their necks, and in their defiance resolved to return to their slavery. But You, being a forgiving *Hashem*, gracious and compassionate, long-suffering and abounding in faithfulness, did not abandon them.

יז וַיְמָאֲנוּ לִשְׁמֹעַ וְלֹא־זָכְרוּ נִפְלְאֹתֶיךָ אֲשֶׁר עָשִׂיתָ עִמָּהֶם וַיַּקְשׁוּ אֶת־עָרְפָּם וַיִּתְּנוּ־רֹאשׁ לָשׁוּב לְעַבְדֻתָם בְּמִרְיָם וְאַתָּה אֱלוֹהַּ סְלִיחוֹת חַנּוּן וְרַחוּם אֶרֶךְ־אַפַּיִם וְרַב־וחֶסֶד [חֶסֶד] וְלֹא עֲזַבְתָּם:

18 Even though they made themselves a molten calf and said, 'This is your God who brought you out of Egypt,' thus committing great impieties,

יח אַף כִּי־עָשׂוּ לָהֶם עֵגֶל מַסֵּכָה וַיֹּאמְרוּ זֶה אֱלֹהֶיךָ אֲשֶׁר הֶעֶלְךָ מִמִּצְרָיִם וַיַּעֲשׂוּ נֶאָצוֹת גְּדֹלוֹת:

19 You, in Your abundant compassion, did not abandon them in the wilderness. The pillar of cloud did not depart from them to lead them on the way by day, nor the pillar of fire by night to give them light in the way they were to go.

יט וְאַתָּה בְּרַחֲמֶיךָ הָרַבִּים לֹא עֲזַבְתָּם בַּמִּדְבָּר אֶת־עַמּוּד הֶעָנָן לֹא־סָר מֵעֲלֵיהֶם בְּיוֹמָם לְהַנְחֹתָם בְּהַדֶּרֶךְ וְאֶת־עַמּוּד הָאֵשׁ בְּלַיְלָה לְהָאִיר לָהֶם וְאֶת־הַדֶּרֶךְ אֲשֶׁר יֵלְכוּ־בָהּ:

20 You endowed them with Your good spirit to instruct them. You did not withhold Your manna from their mouth; You gave them water when they were thirsty.

כ וְרוּחֲךָ הַטּוֹבָה נָתַתָּ לְהַשְׂכִּילָם וּמַנְךָ לֹא־מָנַעְתָּ מִפִּיהֶם וּמַיִם נָתַתָּה לָהֶם לִצְמָאָם:

21 Forty years You sustained them in the wilderness so that they lacked nothing; their clothes did not wear out, and their feet did not swell.

כא וְאַרְבָּעִים שָׁנָה כִּלְכַּלְתָּם בַּמִּדְבָּר לֹא חָסֵרוּ שַׂלְמֹתֵיהֶם לֹא בָלוּ וְרַגְלֵיהֶם לֹא בָצֵקוּ:

22 "You gave them kingdoms and peoples, and allotted them territory. They took possession of the land of Sihon, the land of the king of Heshbon, and the land of Og, king of Bashan.

כב וַתִּתֵּן לָהֶם מַמְלָכוֹת וַעֲמָמִים וַתַּחְלְקֵם לְפֵאָה וַיִּירְשׁוּ אֶת־אֶרֶץ סִיחוֹן וְאֶת־אֶרֶץ מֶלֶךְ חֶשְׁבּוֹן וְאֶת־אֶרֶץ עוֹג מֶלֶךְ־הַבָּשָׁן:

23 You made their children as numerous as the stars of heaven, and brought them to the land which You told their fathers to go and possess.

כג וּבְנֵיהֶם הִרְבִּיתָ כְּכֹכְבֵי הַשָּׁמָיִם וַתְּבִיאֵם אֶל־הָאָרֶץ אֲשֶׁר־אָמַרְתָּ לַאֲבֹתֵיהֶם לָבוֹא לָרֶשֶׁת:

24 The sons came and took possession of the land: You subdued the Canaanite inhabitants of the land before them; You delivered them into their power, both their kings and the peoples of the land, to do with them as they pleased.

כד וַיָּבֹאוּ הַבָּנִים וַיִּירְשׁוּ אֶת־הָאָרֶץ וַתַּכְנַע לִפְנֵיהֶם אֶת־יֹשְׁבֵי הָאָרֶץ הַכְּנַעֲנִים וַתִּתְּנֵם בְּיָדָם וְאֶת־מַלְכֵיהֶם וְאֶת־עַמְמֵי הָאָרֶץ לַעֲשׂוֹת בָּהֶם כִּרְצוֹנָם:

Ezra/Nehemiah

25 They captured fortified cities and rich lands; they took possession of houses filled with every good thing, of hewn cisterns, vineyards, olive trees, and fruit trees in abundance. They ate, they were filled, they grew fat; they luxuriated in Your great bounty.

כה וַיִּלְכְּדוּ עָרִים בְּצֻרוֹת וַאֲדָמָה שְׁמֵנָה וַיִּירְשׁוּ בָּתִּים מְלֵאִים־כָּל־טוּב בֹּרוֹת חֲצוּבִים כְּרָמִים וְזֵיתִים וְעֵץ מַאֲכָל לָרֹב וַיֹּאכְלוּ וַיִּשְׂבְּעוּ וַיַּשְׁמִינוּ וַיִּתְעַדְּנוּ בְּטוּבְךָ הַגָּדוֹל:

26 Then, defying You, they rebelled; they cast Your Teaching behind their back. They killed Your *Neviim* who admonished them to turn them back to You; they committed great impieties.

כו וַיַּמְרוּ וַיִּמְרְדוּ בָּךְ וַיַּשְׁלִכוּ אֶת־תּוֹרָתְךָ אַחֲרֵי גַוָּם וְאֶת־נְבִיאֶיךָ הָרָגוּ אֲשֶׁר־הֵעִידוּ בָם לַהֲשִׁיבָם אֵלֶיךָ וַיַּעֲשׂוּ נֶאָצוֹת גְּדֹלֹת:

27 "You delivered them into the power of their adversaries who oppressed them. In their time of trouble they cried to You; You in heaven heard them, and in Your abundant compassion gave them saviors who saved them from the power of their adversaries.

כז וַתִּתְּנֵם בְּיַד צָרֵיהֶם וַיָּצֵרוּ לָהֶם וּבְעֵת צָרָתָם יִצְעֲקוּ אֵלֶיךָ וְאַתָּה מִשָּׁמַיִם תִּשְׁמָע וּכְרַחֲמֶיךָ הָרַבִּים תִּתֵּן לָהֶם מוֹשִׁיעִים וְיוֹשִׁיעוּם מִיַּד צָרֵיהֶם:

28 But when they had relief, they again did what was evil in Your sight, so You abandoned them to the power of their enemies, who subjugated them. Again they cried to You, and You in heaven heard and rescued them in Your compassion, time after time.

כח וּכְנוֹחַ לָהֶם יָשׁוּבוּ לַעֲשׂוֹת רַע לְפָנֶיךָ וַתַּעַזְבֵם בְּיַד אֹיְבֵיהֶם וַיִּרְדּוּ בָהֶם וַיָּשׁוּבוּ וַיִּזְעָקוּךָ וְאַתָּה מִשָּׁמַיִם תִּשְׁמַע וְתַצִּילֵם כְּרַחֲמֶיךָ רַבּוֹת עִתִּים:

29 You admonished them in order to turn them back to Your Teaching, but they acted presumptuously and disobeyed Your commandments, and sinned against Your rules, by following which a man shall live. They turned a defiant shoulder, stiffened their neck, and would not obey.

כט וַתָּעַד בָּהֶם לַהֲשִׁיבָם אֶל־תּוֹרָתֶךָ וְהֵמָּה הֵזִידוּ וְלֹא־שָׁמְעוּ לְמִצְוֹתֶיךָ וּבְמִשְׁפָּטֶיךָ חָטְאוּ־בָם אֲשֶׁר־יַעֲשֶׂה אָדָם וְחָיָה בָהֶם וַיִּתְּנוּ כָתֵף סוֹרֶרֶת וְעָרְפָּם הִקְשׁוּ וְלֹא שָׁמֵעוּ:

30 You bore with them for many years, admonished them by Your spirit through Your *Neviim*, but they would not give ear, so You delivered them into the power of the peoples of the lands.

ל וַתִּמְשֹׁךְ עֲלֵיהֶם שָׁנִים רַבּוֹת וַתָּעַד בָּם בְּרוּחֲךָ בְּיַד־נְבִיאֶיךָ וְלֹא הֶאֱזִינוּ וַתִּתְּנֵם בְּיַד עַמֵּי הָאֲרָצֹת:

31 Still, in Your great compassion You did not make an end of them or abandon them, for You are a gracious and compassionate *Hashem*.

לא וּבְרַחֲמֶיךָ הָרַבִּים לֹא־עֲשִׂיתָם כָּלָה וְלֹא עֲזַבְתָּם כִּי אֵל־חַנּוּן וְרַחוּם אָתָּה:

32 "And now, our God, great, mighty, and awesome *Hashem*, who stays faithful to His covenant, do not treat lightly all the suffering that has overtaken us – our kings, our officers, our *Kohanim*, our *Neviim*, our fathers, and all Your people – from the time of the Assyrian kings to this day.

לב וְעַתָּה אֱלֹהֵינוּ הָאֵל הַגָּדוֹל הַגִּבּוֹר וְהַנּוֹרָא שׁוֹמֵר הַבְּרִית וְהַחֶסֶד אַל־יִמְעַט לְפָנֶיךָ אֵת כָּל־הַתְּלָאָה אֲשֶׁר־מְצָאַתְנוּ לִמְלָכֵינוּ לְשָׂרֵינוּ וּלְכֹהֲנֵינוּ וְלִנְבִיאֵנוּ וְלַאֲבֹתֵינוּ וּלְכָל־עַמֶּךָ מִימֵי מַלְכֵי אַשּׁוּר עַד הַיּוֹם הַזֶּה:

33 Surely You are in the right with respect to all that has come upon us, for You have acted faithfully, and we have been wicked.

לג וְאַתָּה צַדִּיק עַל כָּל־הַבָּא עָלֵינוּ כִּי־אֱמֶת עָשִׂיתָ וַאֲנַחְנוּ הִרְשָׁעְנוּ:

Ezra/Nehemiah

34 Our kings, officers, *Kohanim*, and fathers did not follow Your Teaching, and did not listen to Your commandments or to the warnings that You gave them.

לד וְאֶת־מְלָכֵינוּ שָׂרֵינוּ כֹּהֲנֵינוּ וַאֲבֹתֵינוּ לֹא עָשׂוּ תּוֹרָתֶךָ וְלֹא הִקְשִׁיבוּ אֶל־מִצְוֺתֶיךָ וּלְעֵדְוֺתֶיךָ אֲשֶׁר הַעִידֹתָ בָּהֶם׃

35 When they had their own kings and enjoyed the good that You lavished upon them, and the broad and rich land that You put at their disposal, they would not serve You, and did not turn from their wicked deeds.

לה וְהֵם בְּמַלְכוּתָם וּבְטוּבְךָ הָרָב אֲשֶׁר־נָתַתָּ לָהֶם וּבְאֶרֶץ הָרְחָבָה וְהַשְּׁמֵנָה אֲשֶׁר־ נָתַתָּ לִפְנֵיהֶם לֹא עֲבָדוּךָ וְלֹא־שָׁבוּ מִמַּעַלְלֵיהֶם הָרָעִים׃

36 Today we are slaves, and the land that You gave our fathers to enjoy its fruit and bounty – here we are slaves on it!

לו הִנֵּה אֲנַחְנוּ הַיּוֹם עֲבָדִים וְהָאָרֶץ אֲשֶׁר־ נָתַתָּה לַאֲבֹתֵינוּ לֶאֱכֹל אֶת־פִּרְיָהּ וְאֶת־ טוּבָהּ הִנֵּה אֲנַחְנוּ עֲבָדִים עָלֶיהָ׃

*hi-NAY a-NAKH-nu ha-YOM a-va-DEEM v'-ha-A-retz
a-sher na-TA-tah la-a-vo-TAY-nu le-e-KHOL et pir-YAH v'-et
tu-VAH hi-NAY a-NAKH-nu a-va-DEEM a-LE-ha*

37 On account of our sins it yields its abundant crops to kings whom You have set over us. They rule over our bodies and our beasts as they please, and we are in great distress.

לז וּתְבוּאָתָהּ מַרְבָּה לַמְּלָכִים אֲשֶׁר־נָתַתָּה עָלֵינוּ בְּחַטֹּאותֵינוּ וְעַל גְּוִיֹּתֵינוּ מֹשְׁלִים וּבִבְהֶמְתֵּנוּ כִּרְצוֹנָם וּבְצָרָה גְדוֹלָה אֲנָחְנוּ׃

10 1 "In view of all this, we make this pledge and put it in writing; and on the sealed copy [are subscribed] our officials, our *Leviim*, and our *Kohanim*.

י א וּבְכָל־זֹאת אֲנַחְנוּ כֹּרְתִים אֲמָנָה וְכֹתְבִים וְעַל הֶחָתוּם שָׂרֵינוּ לְוִיֵּנוּ כֹּהֲנֵינוּ׃

2 "On the sealed copy [are subscribed]: *Nechemya* the Tirshatha son of *Chachalya* and *Tzidkiyahu*,

ב וְעַל הַחֲתוּמִים נְחֶמְיָה הַתִּרְשָׁתָא בֶּן־ חֲכַלְיָה וְצִדְקִיָּה׃

3 *Seraya, Azarya, Yirmiyahu,*

ג שְׂרָיָה עֲזַרְיָה יִרְמְיָה׃

4 Pashhur, Amariah, Malchijah,

ד פַּשְׁחוּר אֲמַרְיָה מַלְכִּיָּה׃

5 Hattush, Shebaniah, Malluch,

ה חַטּוּשׁ שְׁבַנְיָה מַלּוּךְ׃

6 Harim, Meremoth, *Ovadya,*

ו חָרִם מְרֵמוֹת עֹבַדְיָה׃

7 *Daniel,* Ginnethon, *Baruch,*

ז דָּנִיֵּאל גִּנְּתוֹן בָּרוּךְ׃

8 Meshullam, *Aviya,* Mijamin,

ח מְשֻׁלָּם אֲבִיָּה מִיָּמִן׃

9 Maaziah, Bilgai, *Shemaya;* these are the *Kohanim.*

ט מַעַזְיָה בִלְגַּי שְׁמַעְיָה אֵלֶּה הַכֹּהֲנִים׃

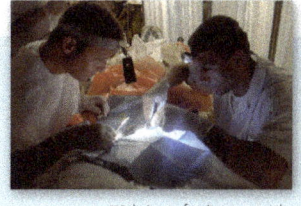
IDF doctors performing surgery at the IDF field hospital in Haiti, 2010

9:36 Here we are slaves on it This chapter speaks of *Hashem*'s original promise to *Avraham* to grant the Land of Israel to his descendants as an inheritance (verse 8). It then continues with an overview of history, including the exodus from Egypt, the years in the desert, the acquisition of *Eretz Yisrael* and the many trials and tribulations that were the plight of the Israelites for many centuries. One might assume that *Hashem* gave the land to the People of Israel so that they could rest in it at ease, and yet this verse states that in fact "we are slaves on it." The Land of Israel is not just a homeland or national territory. It is a tool, a vehicle through which the people can fulfill their ultimate purpose: To serve God and serve as a light unto the nations (Isaiah 42:6) – a mission requiring much hard work.

10 "And the *Leviim*: *Yeshua* son of Azaniah, Binnui of the sons of Henadad, and *Kadmiel*.

י וְהַלְוִיִּם וְיֵשׁוּעַ בֶּן־אֲזַנְיָה בִּנּוּי מִבְּנֵי חֵנָדָד קַדְמִיאֵל׃

11 And their brothers: Shebaniah, Hodiah, Kelita, Pelaiah, Hanan,

יא וַאֲחֵיהֶם שְׁבַנְיָה הוֹדִיָּה קְלִיטָא פְּלָאיָה חָנָן׃

12 Mica, Rehob, Hashabiah,

יב מִיכָא רְחוֹב חֲשַׁבְיָה׃

13 Zaccur, Sherebiah, Shebaniah,

יג זַכּוּר שֵׁרֵבְיָה שְׁבַנְיָה׃

14 Hodiah, Bani, and Beninu.

יד הוֹדִיָּה בָנִי בְּנִינוּ׃

15 "The heads of the people: Parosh, Pahath-moab, Elam, Zattu, Bani,

טו רָאשֵׁי הָעָם פַּרְעֹשׁ פַּחַת מוֹאָב עֵילָם זַתּוּא בָּנִי׃

16 Bunni, Azgad, Bebai,

טז בֻּנִּי עַזְגָּד בֵּבָי׃

17 *Adoniyahu*, Bigvai, Adin,

יז אֲדֹנִיָּה בִגְוַי עָדִין׃

18 Ater, *Chizkiyahu*, Azzur,

יח אָטֵר חִזְקִיָּה עַזּוּר׃

19 Hodiah, Hashum, Bezai,

יט הוֹדִיָּה חָשֻׁם בֵּצָי׃

20 Hariph, *Anatot*, Nebai,

כ חָרִיף עֲנָתוֹת נוֹבָי [נֵיבָי]׃

21 Magpiash, Meshullam, Hezir,

כא מַגְפִּיעָשׁ מְשֻׁלָּם חֵזִיר׃

22 Meshezabel, *Tzadok*, Jaddua,

כב מְשֵׁיזַבְאֵל צָדוֹק יַדּוּעַ׃

23 Pelatiah, Hanan, Anaiah,

כג פְּלַטְיָה חָנָן עֲנָיָה׃

24 *Hoshea, Chananya,* Hasshub,

כד הוֹשֵׁעַ חֲנַנְיָה חַשּׁוּב׃

25 Hallohesh, Pilha, Shobek,

כה הַלּוֹחֵשׁ פִּלְחָא שׁוֹבֵק׃

26 Rehum, Hashabnah, Maaseiah,

כו רְחוּם חֲשַׁבְנָה מַעֲשֵׂיָה׃

27 and Ahiah, Hanan, Anan,

כז וַאֲחִיָּה חָנָן עָנָן׃

28 Malluch, Harim, Baanah.

כח מַלּוּךְ חָרִם בַּעֲנָה׃

29 "And the rest of the people, the *Kohanim*, the *Leviim*, the gatekeepers, the singers, the temple servants, and all who separated themselves from the peoples of the lands to [follow] the Teaching of *Hashem*, their wives, sons and daughters, all who know enough to understand,

כט וּשְׁאָר הָעָם הַכֹּהֲנִים הַלְוִיִּם הַשּׁוֹעֲרִים הַמְשֹׁרְרִים הַנְּתִינִים וְכָל־הַנִּבְדָּל מֵעַמֵּי הָאֲרָצוֹת אֶל־תּוֹרַת הָאֱלֹהִים נְשֵׁיהֶם בְּנֵיהֶם וּבְנֹתֵיהֶם כֹּל יוֹדֵעַ מֵבִין׃

30 join with their noble brothers, and take an oath with sanctions to follow the Teaching of *Hashem*, given through *Moshe* the servant of *Hashem*, and to observe carefully all the commandments of *Hashem* our Lord, His rules and laws.

ל מַחֲזִיקִים עַל־אֲחֵיהֶם אַדִּירֵיהֶם וּבָאִים בְּאָלָה וּבִשְׁבוּעָה לָלֶכֶת בְּתוֹרַת הָאֱלֹהִים אֲשֶׁר נִתְּנָה בְּיַד מֹשֶׁה עֶבֶד־הָאֱלֹהִים וְלִשְׁמוֹר וְלַעֲשׂוֹת אֶת־כָּל־מִצְוֺת יְהוָה אֲדֹנֵינוּ וּמִשְׁפָּטָיו וְחֻקָּיו׃

31 "Namely: We will not give our daughters in marriage to the peoples of the land, or take their daughters for our sons.

לא וַאֲשֶׁר לֹא־נִתֵּן בְּנֹתֵינוּ לְעַמֵּי הָאָרֶץ וְאֶת־בְּנֹתֵיהֶם לֹא נִקַּח לְבָנֵינוּ׃

32 "The peoples of the land who bring their wares and all sorts of foodstuff for sale on the *Shabbat* day – we will not buy from them on the *Shabbat* or a holy day. "We will forgo [the produce of] the seventh year, and every outstanding debt.

לב וְעַמֵּי הָאָרֶץ הַמְבִיאִים אֶת־הַמַּקָּחוֹת וְכָל־שֶׁבֶר בְּיוֹם הַשַּׁבָּת לִמְכּוֹר לֹא־נִקַּח מֵהֶם בַּשַּׁבָּת וּבְיוֹם קֹדֶשׁ וְנִטֹּשׁ אֶת־ הַשָּׁנָה הַשְּׁבִיעִית וּמַשָּׁא כָל־יָד:

33 "We have laid upon ourselves obligations: To charge ourselves one-third of a *shekel* yearly for the service of the House of our God –

לג וְהֶעֱמַדְנוּ עָלֵינוּ מִצְוֹת לָתֵת עָלֵינוּ שְׁלִשִׁית הַשֶּׁקֶל בַּשָּׁנָה לַעֲבֹדַת בֵּית אֱלֹהֵינוּ:

34 for the rows of bread, for the regular meal offering and for the regular burnt offering, [for those of the] *Shabbatot*, new moons, festivals, for consecrations, for sin offerings to atone for *Yisrael*, and for all the work in the House of our God.

לד לְלֶחֶם הַמַּעֲרֶכֶת וּמִנְחַת הַתָּמִיד וּלְעוֹלַת הַתָּמִיד הַשַּׁבָּתוֹת הֶחֳדָשִׁים לַמּוֹעֲדִים וְלַקֳּדָשִׁים וְלַחַטָּאוֹת לְכַפֵּר עַל־יִשְׂרָאֵל וְכֹל מְלֶאכֶת בֵּית־אֱלֹהֵינוּ:

l'-LE-khem ha-ma-a-RE-khet u-min-KHAT ha-ta-MEED ul-o-LAT ha-ta-MEED ha-sha-ba-TOT he-kho-da-SHEEM la-mo-a-DEEM v'-la-ko-da-SHEEM v'-la-kha-TOT l'-kha-PAYR al yis-ra-AYL v'-KHOL m'-LE-khet bayt e-lo-HAY-nu

35 "We have cast lots [among] the *Kohanim*, the *Leviim*, and the people, to bring the wood offering to the House of our God by clans annually at set times in order to provide fuel for the *Mizbayach* of *Hashem* our God, as is written in the Teaching.

לה וְהַגּוֹרָלוֹת הִפַּלְנוּ עַל־קֻרְבַּן הָעֵצִים הַכֹּהֲנִים הַלְוִיִּם וְהָעָם לְהָבִיא לְבֵית אֱלֹהֵינוּ לְבֵית־אֲבֹתֵינוּ לְעִתִּים מְזֻמָּנִים שָׁנָה בְשָׁנָה לְבַעֵר עַל־מִזְבַּח יְהוָה אֱלֹהֵינוּ כַּכָּתוּב בַּתּוֹרָה:

36 "And [we undertake] to bring to the House of *Hashem* annually the first fruits of our soil, and of every fruit of every tree;

לו וּלְהָבִיא אֶת־בִּכּוּרֵי אַדְמָתֵנוּ וּבִכּוּרֵי כָל־ פְּרִי כָל־עֵץ שָׁנָה בְשָׁנָה לְבֵית יְהוָה:

37 also, the first-born of our sons and our beasts, as is written in the Teaching; and to bring the firstlings of our cattle and flocks to the House of our God for the *Kohanim* who minister in the House of our God.

לז וְאֶת־בְּכֹרוֹת בָּנֵינוּ וּבְהֶמְתֵּנוּ כַּכָּתוּב בַּתּוֹרָה וְאֶת־בְּכוֹרֵי בְקָרֵינוּ וְצֹאנֵינוּ לְהָבִיא לְבֵית אֱלֹהֵינוּ לַכֹּהֲנִים הַמְשָׁרְתִים בְּבֵית אֱלֹהֵינוּ:

38 "We will bring to the storerooms of the House of our God the first part of our dough, and our gifts [of grain], and of the fruit of every tree, wine and oil for the *Kohanim*, and the tithes of our land for the *Leviim* – the *Leviim* who collect the tithe in all our towns subject to royal service.

לח וְאֶת־רֵאשִׁית עֲרִיסֹתֵינוּ וּתְרוּמֹתֵינוּ וּפְרִי כָל־עֵץ תִּירוֹשׁ וְיִצְהָר נָבִיא לַכֹּהֲנִים אֶל־לִשְׁכוֹת בֵּית־אֱלֹהֵינוּ וּמַעְשַׂר אַדְמָתֵנוּ לַלְוִיִּם וְהֵם הַלְוִיִּם הַמְעַשְּׂרִים בְּכֹל עָרֵי עֲבֹדָתֵנוּ:

קרבן
קרוב

א **10:34 For the regular meal offering** The last ten verses of this chapter focus on the pledge to revive the many sacrificial obligations. The word for 'sacrifice' or 'offering', *korban* (קרבן), indicates its true purpose. *Korban* comes from the word *karov* (קרוב) which means 'close.' The *korban* facilitates a close relationship between man and God. Although the *korbanot* can only be brought in *Yerushalayim*, the core idea behind them is timeless and universal, intended for all humanity.

In the absence of the *Beit Hamikdash* and its sacrifices, we use prayer as a means of coming close to our Father in Heaven. As the verse is *Hoshea* says "Instead of bulls we will pay [the offering of] our lips" (Hosea 14:3).

Father and sons praying at the Western Wall

39 An Aaronite *Kohen* must be with the *Leviim* when they collect the tithe, and the *Leviim* must bring up a tithe of the tithe to the House of our God, to the storerooms of the treasury.

לט וְהָיָה הַכֹּהֵן בֶּן־אַהֲרֹן עִם־הַלְוִיִּם בַּעְשֵׂר הַלְוִיִּם וְהַלְוִיִּם יַעֲלוּ אֶת־מַעֲשַׂר הַמַּעֲשֵׂר לְבֵית אֱלֹהֵינוּ אֶל־הַלְּשָׁכוֹת לְבֵית הָאוֹצָר:

40 For it is to the storerooms that the Israelites and the *Leviim* must bring the gifts of grain, wine, and oil. The equipment of the sanctuary and of the ministering *Kohanim* and the gatekeepers and the singers is also there. "We will not neglect the House of our God."

מ כִּי אֶל־הַלְּשָׁכוֹת יָבִיאוּ בְנֵי־יִשְׂרָאֵל וּבְנֵי הַלֵּוִי אֶת־תְּרוּמַת הַדָּגָן הַתִּירוֹשׁ וְהַיִּצְהָר וְשָׁם כְּלֵי הַמִּקְדָּשׁ וְהַכֹּהֲנִים הַמְשָׁרְתִים וְהַשּׁוֹעֲרִים וְהַמְשֹׁרְרִים וְלֹא נַעֲזֹב אֶת־בֵּית אֱלֹהֵינוּ:

11 1 The officers of the people settled in *Yerushalayim*; the rest of the people cast lots for one out of ten to come and settle in the holy city of *Yerushalayim*, and the other nine-tenths to stay in the towns.

יא א וַיֵּשְׁבוּ שָׂרֵי־הָעָם בִּירוּשָׁלָםִ וּשְׁאָר הָעָם הִפִּילוּ גוֹרָלוֹת לְהָבִיא אֶחָד מִן־הָעֲשָׂרָה לָשֶׁבֶת בִּירוּשָׁלַםִ עִיר הַקֹּדֶשׁ וְתֵשַׁע הַיָּדוֹת בֶּעָרִים:

va-yay-sh'-VU sa-RAY ha-AM bee-ru-sha-LA-im ush-AR ha-AM
hi-PEE-lu go-ra-LOT l'-ha-VEE e-KHAD min ha-a-sa-RAH la-SHE-vet
bee-ru-sha-LA-im EER ha-KO-desh v'-TAY-sha ha-ya-DOT be-a-REEM

2 The people gave their blessing to all the men who willingly settled in *Yerushalayim*.

ב וַיְבָרְכוּ הָעָם לְכֹל הָאֲנָשִׁים הַמִּתְנַדְּבִים לָשֶׁבֶת בִּירוּשָׁלָםִ:

3 These are the heads of the province who lived in *Yerushalayim* – in the countryside of *Yehuda*, the people lived in their towns, each on his own property, Israelites, *Kohanim*, *Leviim*, temple servants, and the sons of *Shlomo*'s servants,

ג וְאֵלֶּה רָאשֵׁי הַמְּדִינָה אֲשֶׁר יָשְׁבוּ בִּירוּשָׁלָםִ וּבְעָרֵי יְהוּדָה יָשְׁבוּ אִישׁ בַּאֲחֻזָּתוֹ בְּעָרֵיהֶם יִשְׂרָאֵל הַכֹּהֲנִים וְהַלְוִיִּם וְהַנְּתִינִים וּבְנֵי עַבְדֵי שְׁלֹמֹה:

4 while in *Yerushalayim* some of the Judahites and some of the Benjaminites lived: Of the Judahites: Athaiah son of *Uzziyahu* son of *Zecharya* son of Amariah son of Shephatiah son of *Mehalalel*, of the clan of Periz,

ד וּבִירוּשָׁלַםִ יָשְׁבוּ מִבְּנֵי יְהוּדָה וּמִבְּנֵי בִנְיָמִן מִבְּנֵי יְהוּדָה עֲתָיָה בֶן־עֻזִּיָּה בֶּן־זְכַרְיָה בֶּן־אֲמַרְיָה בֶּן־שְׁפַטְיָה בֶּן־מַהֲלַלְאֵל מִבְּנֵי־פָרֶץ:

5 and Maaseiah son of *Baruch* son of Col-hozeh son of Hazaiah son of Adaiah son of Joiarib son of *Zecharya* son of the Shilohite.

ה וּמַעֲשֵׂיָה בֶן־בָּרוּךְ בֶּן־כָּל־חֹזֶה בֶּן־חֲזָיָה בֶן־עֲדָיָה בֶן־יוֹיָרִיב בֶּן־זְכַרְיָה בֶּן־הַשִּׁלֹנִי:

6 All the clan of Periz who were living in *Yerushalayim* – 468 valorous men.

ו כָּל־בְּנֵי־פֶרֶץ הַיֹּשְׁבִים בִּירוּשָׁלַםִ אַרְבַּע מֵאוֹת שִׁשִּׁים וּשְׁמֹנָה אַנְשֵׁי־חָיִל:

Ezra/Nehemiah

11:1 In the holy city of *Yerushalayim* In addition to *Yerushalayim*, Jews recognize three other holy cities, *Tzfat* (Safed), *Teveria* (Tiberias), and *Chevron* (Hebron). The idea of four holy cities originated after the Ottoman conquest of Israel, and corresponds to the four centers of Jewish life at the time. Each city is holy for a different reason, and each corresponds to one of the four elements from which the ancients believed the world was created. *Chevron* is the burial site of the Patriarchs and Matriarchs, symbolic of earth. *Teveria*, where the Jerusalem Talmud was compiled, resides by the shores of the *Kinneret* and corresponds to water. *Tzfat*, located high up on the mountains, is the renowned center of mystical Judaism, the *Kabbalah*, and is therefore associated with air. And *Yerushalayim*, the site of the Temples which contained the altars and the *menorah* lamp, is associated with fire. In this way, the four holy cities of Israel contain all the elements for everything in heaven and earth.

Aerial view of *Teveria* and the Sea of Galilee

7 These are the Binyaminites: Sallu son of Meshullam son of Joed son of Pedaiah son of Kolaiah son of Maaseiah son of *Itiel* son of Jesaiah.

וְאֵלֶּה בְּנֵי בִנְיָמִן סַלֻּא בֶּן־מְשֻׁלָּם בֶּן־
יוֹעֵד בֶּן־פְּדָיָה בֶּן־קוֹלָיָה בֶּן־מַעֲשֵׂיָה
בֶּן־אִיתִיאֵל בֶּן־יְשַׁעְיָה:

8 After him, Gabbai and Sallai – 928.

וְאַחֲרָיו גַּבַּי סַלָּי תְּשַׁע מֵאוֹת עֶשְׂרִים
וּשְׁמֹנָה:

9 *Yoel* son of Zichri was the official in charge of them, and *Yehuda* son of Hassenuah was the second-in-command of the city.

וְיוֹאֵל בֶּן־זִכְרִי פָּקִיד עֲלֵיהֶם וִיהוּדָה בֶּן־
הַסְּנוּאָה עַל־הָעִיר מִשְׁנֶה:

10 Of the *Kohanim*: Jedaiah son of Joiarib, Jachin,

מִן־הַכֹּהֲנִים יְדַעְיָה בֶן־יוֹיָרִיב יָכִין:

11 *Seraya* son of *Chilkiyahu* son of Meshullam son of *Tzadok* son of Meraioth son of *Achituv*, chief officer of the House of *Hashem*,

שְׂרָיָה בֶן־חִלְקִיָּה בֶּן־מְשֻׁלָּם בֶּן־
צָדוֹק בֶּן־מְרָיוֹת בֶּן־אֲחִיטוּב נְגִד בֵּית
הָאֱלֹהִים:

12 and their brothers, who did the work of the House – 822; and Adaiah son of Jeroham son of Pelaliah son of Amzi son of *Zecharya* son of Pashhur son of Malchijah,

וַאֲחֵיהֶם עֹשֵׂי הַמְּלָאכָה לַבַּיִת שְׁמֹנֶה
מֵאוֹת עֶשְׂרִים וּשְׁנָיִם וַעֲדָיָה בֶּן־יְרֹחָם
בֶּן־פְּלַלְיָה בֶּן־אַמְצִי בֶּן־זְכַרְיָה בֶּן־
פַּשְׁחוּר בֶּן־מַלְכִּיָּה:

13 and his brothers, heads of clans – 242; and Amashsai son of Azarel son of Ahzai son of Meshillemoth son of Immer,

וְאֶחָיו רָאשִׁים לְאָבוֹת מָאתַיִם אַרְבָּעִים
וּשְׁנָיִם וַעֲמַשְׁסַי בֶּן־עֲזַרְאֵל בֶּן־אַחְזַי בֶּן־
מְשִׁלֵּמוֹת בֶּן־אִמֵּר:

14 and their brothers, valorous warriors – 128. Zabdiel son of Haggedolim was the official in charge of them.

וַאֲחֵיהֶם גִּבּוֹרֵי חַיִל מֵאָה עֶשְׂרִים
וּשְׁמֹנָה וּפָקִיד עֲלֵיהֶם זַבְדִּיאֵל בֶּן־
הַגְּדוֹלִים:

15 Of the *Leviim*: Shemaya son of Hasshub son of Azrikam son of Hashabiah son of Bunni,

וּמִן־הַלְוִיִּם שְׁמַעְיָה בֶן־חַשּׁוּב בֶּן־
עַזְרִיקָם בֶּן־חֲשַׁבְיָה בֶּן־בּוּנִּי:

16 and Shabbethai and *Yozavad* of the heads of the *Leviim* were in charge of the external work of the House of *Hashem*.

וְשַׁבְּתַי וְיוֹזָבָד עַל־הַמְּלָאכָה הַחִיצֹנָה
לְבֵית הָאֱלֹהִים מֵרָאשֵׁי הַלְוִיִּם:

17 Mattaniah son of *Micha* son of Zabdi son of *Asaf* was the head; at prayer, he would lead off with praise; and Bakbukiah, one of his brothers, was his second-in-command; and Abda son of Shammua son of Galal son of *Yedutun*.

וּמַתַּנְיָה בֶן־מִיכָה בֶּן־זַבְדִּי בֶּן־אָסָף
רֹאשׁ הַתְּחִלָּה יְהוֹדֶה לַתְּפִלָּה וּבַקְבֻּקְיָה
מִשְׁנֶה מֵאֶחָיו וְעַבְדָּא בֶּן־שַׁמּוּעַ בֶּן־גָּלָל
בֶּן־יְדִיתוּן [יְדוּתוּן]:

18 All the *Leviim* in the holy city – 284.

כָּל־הַלְוִיִּם בְּעִיר הַקֹּדֶשׁ מָאתַיִם
שְׁמֹנִים וְאַרְבָּעָה:

19 And the gatekeepers: Akkub, Talmon, and their brothers, who stood watch at the gates – 172.

וְהַשּׁוֹעֲרִים עַקּוּב טַלְמוֹן וַאֲחֵיהֶם
הַשֹּׁמְרִים בַּשְּׁעָרִים מֵאָה שִׁבְעִים
וּשְׁנָיִם:

20 And the rest of the Israelites, the *Kohanim*, and the *Leviim* in all the towns of *Yehuda* [lived] each on his estate.

וּשְׁאָר יִשְׂרָאֵל הַכֹּהֲנִים הַלְוִיִּם בְּכָל־עָרֵי
יְהוּדָה אִישׁ בְּנַחֲלָתוֹ:

21 The temple servants lived on the Ophel; Ziha and Gishpa were in charge of the temple servants.

וְהַנְּתִינִים יֹשְׁבִים בָּעֹפֶל וְצִיחָא וְגִשְׁפָּא
עַל־הַנְּתִינִים:

22 The overseer of the *Leviim* in *Yerushalayim* was Uzzi son of Bani son of Hashabiah son of Mattaniah son of *Micha*, of the Asaphite singers, over the work of the House of *Hashem*.

כב וּפְקִיד הַלְוִיִּם בִּירוּשָׁלַ͏ִם עֻזִּי בֶן־בָּנִי בֶּן־חֲשַׁבְיָה בֶּן־מַתַּנְיָה בֶּן־מִיכָא מִבְּנֵי אָסָף הַמְשֹׁרְרִים לְנֶגֶד מְלֶאכֶת בֵּית־הָאֱלֹהִים:

23 There was a royal order concerning them, a stipulation concerning the daily duties of the singers.

כג כִּי־מִצְוַת הַמֶּלֶךְ עֲלֵיהֶם וַאֲמָנָה עַל־הַמְשֹׁרְרִים דְּבַר־יוֹם בְּיוֹמוֹ:

24 Petahiah son of Meshezabel, of the sons of *Zerach* son of *Yehuda*, advised the king concerning all the affairs of the people.

כד וּפְתַחְיָה בֶן־מְשֵׁיזַבְאֵל מִבְּנֵי־זֶרַח בֶּן־יְהוּדָה לְיַד הַמֶּלֶךְ לְכָל־דָּבָר לָעָם:

25 As concerns the villages with their fields: Some of the Judahites lived in *Kiryat Arba* and its outlying hamlets, in Dibon and its outlying hamlets, and in Jekabzeel and its villages;

כה וְאֶל־הַחֲצֵרִים בִּשְׂדֹתָם מִבְּנֵי יְהוּדָה יָשְׁבוּ בְּקִרְיַת הָאַרְבַּע וּבְנֹתֶיהָ וּבְדִיבֹן וּבְנֹתֶיהָ וּבִיקַּבְצְאֵל וַחֲצֵרֶיהָ:

26 in *Yeshua*, in Moladah, and in Beth-pelet;

כו וּבְיֵשׁוּעַ וּבְמוֹלָדָה וּבְבֵית פָּלֶט:

27 in Hazar-shual, in *Be'er Sheva* and its outlying hamlets;

כז וּבַחֲצַר שׁוּעָל וּבִבְאֵר שֶׁבַע וּבְנֹתֶיהָ:

28 and in *Tziklag* and in Meconah and its outlying hamlets;

כח וּבְצִקְלַג וּבִמְכֹנָה וּבִבְנֹתֶיהָ:

29 in En-rimmon, in *Tzora* and in *Yarmut*;

כט וּבְעֵין רִמּוֹן וּבְצָרְעָה וּבְיַרְמוּת:

30 *Zanoach, Adulam*, and their villages; *Lachish* and its fields; *Azeika* and its outlying hamlets. They settled from *Be'er Sheva* to the Valley of Hinnom.

ל זָנֹחַ עֲדֻלָּם וְחַצְרֵיהֶם לָכִישׁ וּשְׂדֹתֶיהָ עֲזֵקָה וּבְנֹתֶיהָ וַיַּחֲנוּ מִבְּאֵר־שֶׁבַע עַד־גֵּיא־הִנֹּם:

31 The Benjaminites: from Geba, Michmash, Aija, and *Beit El* and its outlying hamlets;

לא וּבְנֵי בִנְיָמִן מִגֶּבַע מִכְמָשׂ וְעַיָּה וּבֵית־אֵל וּבְנֹתֶיהָ:

32 *Anatot, Nov*, Ananiah,

לב עֲנָתוֹת נֹב עֲנָנְיָה:

33 Hazor, *Rama*, Gittaim,

לג חָצוֹר רָמָה גִּתָּיִם:

34 Hadid, Zeboim, Neballat,

לד חָדִיד צְבֹעִים נְבַלָּט:

35 Lod, Ono, Ge-harashim.

לה לֹד וְאוֹנוֹ גֵּי הַחֲרָשִׁים:

36 Some of the Judahite divisions of *Leviim* were [shifted] to *Binyamin*.

לו וּמִן־הַלְוִיִּם מַחְלְקוֹת יְהוּדָה לְבִנְיָמִין:

12 1 These are the *Kohanim* and the *Leviim* who came up with *Zerubavel* son of *Shealtiel* and *Yeshua*: Seraya, *Yirmiyahu*, Ezra,

יב א וְאֵלֶּה הַכֹּהֲנִים וְהַלְוִיִּם אֲשֶׁר עָלוּ עִם־זְרֻבָּבֶל בֶּן־שְׁאַלְתִּיאֵל וְיֵשׁוּעַ שְׂרָיָה יִרְמְיָה עֶזְרָא:

2 Amariah, Malluch, Hattush,

ב אֲמַרְיָה מַלּוּךְ חַטּוּשׁ:

3 *Shechanya*, Rehum, Meramoth,

ג שְׁכַנְיָה רְחֻם מְרֵמֹת:

4 *Ido*, Ginnethoi, *Aviya*,

ד עִדּוֹא גִנְּתוֹי אֲבִיָּה:

5 Mijamin, Maadiah, Bilgah,

ה מִיָּמִין מַעַדְיָה בִּלְגָּה:

6 *Shemaya*, Joiarib, Jedaiah,

ו שְׁמַעְיָה וְיוֹיָרִיב יְדַעְיָה:

7 Sallu, Amok, *Chilkiyahu*, Jedaiah. These were the heads of the *Kohanim* and their brothers in the time of *Yeshua*.

ז סַלּוּ עָמוֹק חִלְקִיָּה יְדַעְיָה אֵלֶּה רָאשֵׁי הַכֹּהֲנִים וַאֲחֵיהֶם בִּימֵי יֵשׁוּעַ:

8 The *Leviim*: Yeshua, Binnui, *Kadmiel*, Sherebiah, Yehuda, and Mattaniah, in charge of thanksgiving songs, he and his brothers;

ח וְהַלְוִיִּם יֵשׁוּעַ בִּנּוּי קַדְמִיאֵל שֵׁרֵבְיָה יְהוּדָה מַתַּנְיָה עַל־הֻיְּדוֹת הוּא וְאֶחָיו:

9 and Bakbukiah and Unni [and] their brothers served opposite them by shifts.

ט וּבַקְבֻּקְיָה וענו [וְעֻנִּי] אֲחֵיהֶם לְנֶגְדָּם לְמִשְׁמָרוֹת:

10 *Yeshua* begot Joiakim; Joiakim begot *Elyashiv*; *Elyashiv* begot Joiada;

י וְיֵשׁוּעַ הוֹלִיד אֶת־יוֹיָקִים וְיוֹיָקִים הוֹלִיד אֶת־אֶלְיָשִׁיב וְאֶלְיָשִׁיב אֶת־יוֹיָדָע:

11 Joiada begot *Yonatan*; *Yonatan* begot Jaddua.

יא וְיוֹיָדָע הוֹלִיד אֶת־יוֹנָתָן וְיוֹנָתָן הוֹלִיד אֶת־יַדּוּעַ:

12 In the time of Joiakim, the heads of the priestly clans were: Meriaiah – of the *Seraya* clan; *Chananya* – of the *Yirmiyahu* clan;

יב וּבִימֵי יוֹיָקִים הָיוּ כֹהֲנִים רָאשֵׁי הָאָבוֹת לִשְׂרָיָה מְרָיָה לְיִרְמְיָה חֲנַנְיָה:

13 Meshullam – of the *Ezra* clan; *Yehochanan* – of the Amariah clan;

יג לְעֶזְרָא מְשֻׁלָּם לַאֲמַרְיָה יְהוֹחָנָן:

14 *Yonatan* – of the Melicu clan; *Yosef* – of the Shebaniah clan;

יד למלוכי [לִמְלִיכוּ] יוֹנָתָן לִשְׁבַנְיָה יוֹסֵף:

15 Adna – of the Harim clan; Helkai – of the Meraioth clan;

טו לְחָרִם עַדְנָא לִמְרָיוֹת חֶלְקָי:

16 *Zecharya* – of the *Ido* clan; Meshullam – of the Ginnethon clan;

טז לעדיא [לְעִדּוֹא] זְכַרְיָה לְגִנְּתוֹן מְשֻׁלָּם:

17 Zichri – of the *Aviya* clan...of the Miniamin clan; Piltai – of the Moadiah clan;

יז לַאֲבִיָּה זִכְרִי לְמִנְיָמִין לְמוֹעַדְיָה פִּלְטָי:

18 Shammua – of the Bilgah clan; Jehonathan – of the *Shemaya* clan;

יח לְבִלְגָּה שַׁמּוּעַ לִשְׁמַעְיָה יְהוֹנָתָן:

19 Mattenai – of the Joiarib clan; Uzzi – of the Jedaiah clan;

יט וּלְיוֹיָרִיב מַתְּנַי לִידַעְיָה עֻזִּי:

20 Kallai – of the Sallai clan; *Ever* – of the Amok clan;

כ לְסַלַּי קַלָּי לְעָמוֹק עֵבֶר:

21 Hashabiah – of the *Chilkiyahu* clan; Nethanel – of the Jedaiah clan.

כא לְחִלְקִיָּה חֲשַׁבְיָה לִידַעְיָה נְתַנְאֵל:

22 The *Leviim* and the *Kohanim* were listed by heads of clans in the days of *Elyashiv*, Joiada, *Yochanan*, and Jaddua, down to the reign of Darius the Persian.

כב הַלְוִיִּם בִּימֵי אֶלְיָשִׁיב יוֹיָדָע וְיוֹחָנָן וְיַדּוּעַ כְּתוּבִים רָאשֵׁי אָבוֹת וְהַכֹּהֲנִים עַל־מַלְכוּת דָּרְיָוֶשׁ הַפָּרְסִי:

23 But the Levite heads of clans are listed in the book of the chronicles to the time of *Yochanan* son of *Elyashiv*.

כג בְּנֵי לֵוִי רָאשֵׁי הָאָבוֹת כְּתוּבִים עַל־סֵפֶר דִּבְרֵי הַיָּמִים וְעַד־יְמֵי יוֹחָנָן בֶּן־אֶלְיָשִׁיב:

24 The heads of the *Leviim*: Hashabiah, Sherebiah, Yeshua son of *Kadmiel*, and their brothers served opposite them, singing praise and thanksgiving hymns by the ordinance of *David* the man of Hashem – served opposite them in shifts;

כד וְרָאשֵׁי הַלְוִיִּם חֲשַׁבְיָה שֵׁרֵבְיָה וְיֵשׁוּעַ בֶּן־קַדְמִיאֵל וַאֲחֵיהֶם לְנֶגְדָּם לְהַלֵּל לְהוֹדוֹת בְּמִצְוַת דָּוִיד אִישׁ־הָאֱלֹהִים מִשְׁמָר לְעֻמַּת מִשְׁמָר:

25 Mattaniah, Bakbukiah, *Ovadya*, Meshullam, Talmon, and Akkub, guarding as gatekeepers by shifts at the vestibules of the gates.

כה מַתַּנְיָה וּבַקְבֻּקְיָה עֹבַדְיָה מְשֻׁלָּם טַלְמוֹן עַקּוּב שֹׁמְרִים שׁוֹעֲרִים מִשְׁמָר בַּאֲסֻפֵּי הַשְּׁעָרִים:

26 These were in the time of Joiakim son of *Yeshua* son of *Yotzadak*, and in the time of *Nechemya* the governor, and of *Ezra* the *Kohen*, the scribe.

כו אֵלֶּה בִּימֵי יוֹיָקִים בֶּן־יֵשׁוּעַ בֶּן־יוֹצָדָק וּבִימֵי נְחֶמְיָה הַפֶּחָה וְעֶזְרָא הַכֹּהֵן הַסּוֹפֵר:

27 At the dedication of the wall of *Yerushalayim*, the *Leviim*, wherever they lived, were sought out and brought to *Yerushalayim* to celebrate a joyful dedication with thanksgiving and with song, accompanied by cymbals, harps, and lyres.

כז וּבַחֲנֻכַּת חוֹמַת יְרוּשָׁלַ͏ִם בִּקְשׁוּ אֶת־הַלְוִיִּם מִכָּל־מְקוֹמֹתָם לַהֲבִיאָם לִירוּשָׁלָ͏ִם לַעֲשֹׂת חֲנֻכָּה וְשִׂמְחָה וּבְתוֹדוֹת וּבְשִׁיר מְצִלְתַּיִם נְבָלִים וּבְכִנֹּרוֹת:

28 The companies of singers assembled from the [*Yarden*] plain, the environs of *Yerushalayim*, and from the Netophathite villages;

כח וַיֵּאָסְפוּ בְּנֵי הַמְשֹׁרְרִים וּמִן־הַכִּכָּר סְבִיבוֹת יְרוּשָׁלַ͏ִם וּמִן־חַצְרֵי נְטֹפָתִי:

29 from Beth-hagilgal, from the countryside of Geba and Azmaveth, for the singers built themselves villages in the environs of *Yerushalayim*.

כט וּמִבֵּית הַגִּלְגָּל וּמִשְּׂדוֹת גֶּבַע וְעַזְמָוֶת כִּי חֲצֵרִים בָּנוּ לָהֶם הַמְשֹׁרְרִים סְבִיבוֹת יְרוּשָׁלָ͏ִם:

30 The *Kohanim* and *Leviim* purified themselves; then they purified the people, and the gates, and the wall.

ל וַיִּטַּהֲרוּ הַכֹּהֲנִים וְהַלְוִיִּם וַיְטַהֲרוּ אֶת־הָעָם וְאֶת־הַשְּׁעָרִים וְאֶת־הַחוֹמָה:

31 I had the officers of *Yehuda* go up onto the wall, and I appointed two large thanksgiving [choirs] and processions. [One marched] south on the wall, to the Dung Gate;

לא וָאַעֲלֶה אֶת־שָׂרֵי יְהוּדָה מֵעַל לַחוֹמָה וָאַעֲמִידָה שְׁתֵּי תוֹדֹת גְּדוֹלֹת וְתַהֲלֻכֹת לַיָּמִין מֵעַל לַחוֹמָה לְשַׁעַר הָאַשְׁפֹּת:

32 behind them were Hoshaiah and half the officers of *Yehuda*,

לב וַיֵּלֶךְ אַחֲרֵיהֶם הוֹשַׁעְיָה וַחֲצִי שָׂרֵי יְהוּדָה:

33 and *Azarya, Ezra*, Meshullam,

לג וַעֲזַרְיָה עֶזְרָא וּמְשֻׁלָּם:

34 *Yehuda, Binyamin, Shemaya*, and *Yirmiyahu*,

לד יְהוּדָה וּבִנְיָמִן וּשְׁמַעְיָה וְיִרְמְיָה:

35 and some of the young *Kohanim*, with trumpets; *Zecharya* son of *Yonatan* son of *Shemaya* son of Mattaniah son of *Michaihu* son of Zaccur son of *Asaf*,

לה וּמִבְּנֵי הַכֹּהֲנִים בַּחֲצֹצְרוֹת זְכַרְיָה בֶן־יוֹנָתָן בֶּן־שְׁמַעְיָה בֶּן־מַתַּנְיָה בֶּן־מִיכָיָה בֶּן־זַכּוּר בֶּן־אָסָף:

36 and his brothers *Shemaya*, and Azarel, Milalai, Gilalai, Maai, Nethanel, *Yehuda*, and *Chanani*, with the musical instruments of *David*, the man of *Hashem*; and *Ezra* the scribe went ahead of them.

לו וְאֶחָיו שְׁמַעְיָה וַעֲזַרְאֵל מִלֲלַי גִּלֲלַי מָעַי נְתַנְאֵל וִיהוּדָה חֲנָנִי בִּכְלֵי־שִׁיר דָּוִיד אִישׁ הָאֱלֹהִים וְעֶזְרָא הַסּוֹפֵר לִפְנֵיהֶם:

37 From there to the Fountain Gate, where they ascended the steps of the City of *David* directly before them, by the ascent on the wall, above the house of *David*, [and onward] to the Water Gate on the east.

לז וְעַל שַׁעַר הָעַיִן וְנֶגְדָּם עָלוּ עַל־מַעֲלוֹת עִיר דָּוִיד בַּמַּעֲלֶה לַחוֹמָה מֵעַל לְבֵית דָּוִיד וְעַד שַׁעַר הַמַּיִם מִזְרָח:

38 The other thanksgiving [choir] marched on the wall in the opposite direction, with me and half the people behind it, above the Tower of Ovens to the Broad Wall;

לח וְהַתּוֹדָה הַשֵּׁנִית הַהוֹלֶכֶת לְמוֹאל וַאֲנִי אַחֲרֶיהָ וַחֲצִי הָעָם מֵעַל לְהַחוֹמָה מֵעַל לְמִגְדַּל הַתַּנּוּרִים וְעַד הַחוֹמָה הָרְחָבָה:

v'-ha-to-DAH ha-shay-NEET ha-ho-LE-khet l'-MOL va-a-NEE a-kha-RE-ha va-kha-TZEE ha-AM may-AL l'-ha-kho-MAH may-AL l'-mig-DAL ha-ta-nu-REEM v'-AD ha-kho-MAH ha-r'-kha-VAH

39 and above the Gate of *Efraim*, the Jeshanah Gate, the Fish Gate, the Tower of Hananel, the Tower of the Hundred, to the Sheep Gate; and they halted at the Gate of the Prison Compound.

לט וּמֵעַל לְשַׁעַר־אֶפְרַיִם וְעַל־שַׁעַר הַיְשָׁנָה וְעַל־שַׁעַר הַדָּגִים וּמִגְדַּל חֲנַנְאֵל וּמִגְדַּל הַמֵּאָה וְעַד שַׁעַר הַצֹּאן וְעָמְדוּ בְּשַׁעַר הַמַּטָּרָה:

40 Both thanksgiving choirs halted at the House of *Hashem*, and I and half the prefects with me,

מ וַתַּעֲמֹדְנָה שְׁתֵּי הַתּוֹדֹת בְּבֵית הָאֱלֹהִים וַאֲנִי וַחֲצִי הַסְּגָנִים עִמִּי:

41 and the *Kohanim* Eliakim, Maaseiah, Miniamin, *Michaihu*, Elioenai, *Zecharya*, *Chananya*, with trumpets,

מא וְהַכֹּהֲנִים אֶלְיָקִים מַעֲשֵׂיָה מִנְיָמִין מִיכָיָה אֶלְיוֹעֵינַי זְכַרְיָה חֲנַנְיָה בַּחֲצֹצְרוֹת:

42 and Maaseiah and *Shemaya*, *Elazar*, Uzzi, *Yehochanan*, Malchijah, Elam, and Ezer. Then the singers sounded forth, with Jezrahiah in charge.

מב וּמַעֲשֵׂיָה וּשְׁמַעְיָה וְאֶלְעָזָר וְעֻזִּי וִיהוֹחָנָן וּמַלְכִּיָּה וְעֵילָם וָעָזֶר וַיַּשְׁמִיעוּ הַמְשֹׁרְרִים וְיִזְרַחְיָה הַפָּקִיד:

43 On that day, they offered great sacrifices and rejoiced, for *Hashem* made them rejoice greatly; the women and children also rejoiced, and the rejoicing in *Yerushalayim* could be heard from afar.

מג וַיִּזְבְּחוּ בַיּוֹם־הַהוּא זְבָחִים גְּדוֹלִים וַיִּשְׂמָחוּ כִּי הָאֱלֹהִים שִׂמְּחָם שִׂמְחָה גְדוֹלָה וְגַם הַנָּשִׁים וְהַיְלָדִים שָׂמֵחוּ וַתִּשָּׁמַע שִׂמְחַת יְרוּשָׁלַם מֵרָחוֹק:

44 At that time men were appointed over the chambers that served as treasuries for the gifts, the first fruits, and the tithes, into which the portions prescribed by the Teaching for the *Kohanim* and *Leviim* were gathered from the fields of the towns; for the people of *Yehuda* were grateful to the *Kohanim* and *Leviim* who were in attendance,

מד וַיִּפָּקְדוּ בַיּוֹם הַהוּא אֲנָשִׁים עַל־ הַנְּשָׁכוֹת לָאוֹצָרוֹת לַתְּרוּמוֹת לָרֵאשִׁית וְלַמַּעַשְׂרוֹת לִכְנוֹס בָּהֶם לִשְׂדֵי הֶעָרִים מְנָאוֹת הַתּוֹרָה לַכֹּהֲנִים וְלַלְוִיִּם כִּי שִׂמְחַת יְהוּדָה עַל־הַכֹּהֲנִים וְעַל־הַלְוִיִּם הָעֹמְדִים:

12:38 The broad wall In recording the procession of the wall's dedication ceremony, *Nechemya* mentions the "broad wall." During the 1948 War of Independence, the entire Jewish quarter of Jerusalem's Old City was utterly destroyed. After the 1967 liberation, the quarter's returning residents wished to rebuild their homes, and in the process, many archeological excavations were carried out. One of the many incredible finds was Dr. Nahman Avigad's discovery of the seven-meter-wide "broad wall," mentioned in this verse as well as earlier in *Sefer Nehemiah* (3:8). It is thought to have been built during the reign of King *Chizkiyahu* in the late eighth century BCE, as a defensive structure against the expected invasion by King Sennacherib of Assyria. Today, modern apartments surround the ancient wall, enabling a harmonious existence between Jerusalem's rich past and blessed present.

The broad wall in Jerusalem

⁴⁵ who kept the charge of their God and the charge of purity, as well as to the singers and gatekeepers [serving] in accord with the ordinance of *David* and *Shlomo* his son –

מה וַיִּשְׁמְרוּ מִשְׁמֶרֶת אֱלֹהֵיהֶם וּמִשְׁמֶרֶת הַטׇּהֳרָה וְהַמְשֹׁרְרִים וְהַשֹּׁעֲרִים כְּמִצְוַת דָּוִיד שְׁלֹמֹה בְנוֹ:

⁴⁶ for the chiefs of the singers and songs of praise and thanksgiving to *Hashem* already existed in the time of *David* and *Asaf*.

מו כִּי־בִימֵי דָוִיד וְאָסָף מִקֶּדֶם רֹאשׁ [רָאשֵׁי] הַמְשֹׁרְרִים וְשִׁיר־תְּהִלָּה וְהֹדוֹת לֵאלֹהִים:

⁴⁷ And in the time of *Zerubavel*, and in the time of *Nechemya*, all *Yisrael* contributed the daily portions of the singers and the gatekeepers, and made sacred contributions for the *Leviim*, and the *Leviim* made sacred contributions for the Aaronites.

מז וְכׇל־יִשְׂרָאֵל בִּימֵי זְרֻבָּבֶל וּבִימֵי נְחֶמְיָה נֹתְנִים מְנָיוֹת הַמְשֹׁרְרִים וְהַשֹּׁעֲרִים דְּבַר־יוֹם בְּיוֹמוֹ וּמַקְדִּשִׁים לַלְוִיִּם וְהַלְוִיִּם מַקְדִּשִׁים לִבְנֵי אַהֲרֹן:

13 ¹ At that time they read to the people from the Book of *Moshe*, and it was found written that no Ammonite or Moabite might ever enter the congregation of *Hashem*,

יג א בַּיּוֹם הַהוּא נִקְרָא בְּסֵפֶר מֹשֶׁה בְּאׇזְנֵי הָעָם וְנִמְצָא כָּתוּב בּוֹ אֲשֶׁר לֹא־יָבוֹא עַמֹּנִי וּמֹאָבִי בִּקְהַל הָאֱלֹהִים עַד־עוֹלָם:

² since they did not meet *Yisrael* with bread and water, and hired Balaam against them to curse them; but our God turned the curse into a blessing.

ב כִּי לֹא קִדְּמוּ אֶת־בְּנֵי יִשְׂרָאֵל בַּלֶּחֶם וּבַמָּיִם וַיִּשְׂכֹּר עָלָיו אֶת־בִּלְעָם לְקַלְלוֹ וַיַּהֲפֹךְ אֱלֹהֵינוּ הַקְּלָלָה לִבְרָכָה:

³ When they heard the Teaching, they separated all the alien admixture from *Yisrael*.

ג וַיְהִי כְּשׇׁמְעָם אֶת־הַתּוֹרָה וַיַּבְדִּילוּ כׇל־עֵרֶב מִיִּשְׂרָאֵל:

⁴ Earlier, the *Kohen Elyashiv*, a relative of Tobiah, who had been appointed over the rooms in the House of our God,

ד וְלִפְנֵי מִזֶּה אֶלְיָשִׁיב הַכֹּהֵן נָתוּן בְּלִשְׁכַּת בֵּית־אֱלֹהֵינוּ קָרוֹב לְטוֹבִיָּה:

⁵ had assigned to him a large room where they used to store the meal offering, the frankincense, the equipment, the tithes of grain, wine, and oil, the dues of the *Leviim*, singers and gatekeepers, and the gifts for the *Kohanim*.

ה וַיַּעַשׂ לוֹ לִשְׁכָּה גְדוֹלָה וְשָׁם הָיוּ לְפָנִים נֹתְנִים אֶת־הַמִּנְחָה הַלְּבוֹנָה וְהַכֵּלִים וּמַעְשַׂר הַדָּגָן הַתִּירוֹשׁ וְהַיִּצְהָר מִצְוַת הַלְוִיִּם וְהַמְשֹׁרְרִים וְהַשֹּׁעֲרִים וּתְרוּמַת הַכֹּהֲנִים:

⁶ During all this time, I was not in *Yerushalayim*, for in the thirty-second year of King Artaxerxes of Babylon, I went to the king, and only after a while did I ask leave of the king [to return].

ו וּבְכׇל־זֶה לֹא הָיִיתִי בִּירוּשָׁלָ͏ִם כִּי בִּשְׁנַת שְׁלֹשִׁים וּשְׁתַּיִם לְאַרְתַּחְשַׁסְתְּא מֶלֶךְ־בָּבֶל בָּאתִי אֶל־הַמֶּלֶךְ וּלְקֵץ יָמִים נִשְׁאַלְתִּי מִן־הַמֶּלֶךְ:

⁷ When I arrived in *Yerushalayim*, I learned of the outrage perpetrated by *Elyashiv* on behalf of Tobiah in assigning him a room in the courts of the House of *Hashem*.

ז וָאָבוֹא לִירוּשָׁלָ͏ִם וָאָבִינָה בָרָעָה אֲשֶׁר עָשָׂה אֶלְיָשִׁיב לְטוֹבִיָּה לַעֲשׂוֹת לוֹ נִשְׁכָּה בְּחַצְרֵי בֵּית הָאֱלֹהִים:

⁸ I was greatly displeased, and had all the household gear of Tobiah thrown out of the room;

ח וַיֵּרַע לִי מְאֹד וָאַשְׁלִיכָה אֶת־כׇּל־כְּלֵי בֵית־טוֹבִיָּה הַחוּץ מִן־הַלִּשְׁכָּה:

9 I gave orders to purify the rooms, and had the equipment of the House of *Hashem* and the meal offering and the frankincense put back.

ט וָאֹמְרָה וַיְטַהֲרוּ הַלְּשָׁכוֹת וָאָשִׁיבָה שָׁם כְּלֵי בֵּית הָאֱלֹהִים אֶת־הַמִּנְחָה וְהַלְּבוֹנָה:

10 I then discovered that the portions of the *Leviim* had not been contributed, and that the *Leviim* and the singers who performed the [temple] service had made off, each to his fields.

י וָאֵדְעָה כִּי־מְנָיוֹת הַלְוִיִּם לֹא נִתָּנָה וַיִּבְרְחוּ אִישׁ־לְשָׂדֵהוּ הַלְוִיִּם וְהַמְשֹׁרְרִים עֹשֵׂי הַמְּלָאכָה:

11 I censured the prefects, saying, "How is it that the House of *Hashem* has been neglected?" Then I recalled [the *Leviim*] and installed them again in their posts;

יא וָאָרִיבָה אֶת־הַסְּגָנִים וָאֹמְרָה מַדּוּעַ נֶעֱזַב בֵּית־הָאֱלֹהִים וָאֶקְבְּצֵם וָאַעֲמִדֵם עַל־עָמְדָם:

12 and all *Yehuda* brought the tithes of grain, wine, and oil into the treasuries.

יב וְכָל־יְהוּדָה הֵבִיאוּ מַעְשַׂר הַדָּגָן וְהַתִּירוֹשׁ וְהַיִּצְהָר לָאוֹצָרוֹת:

13 I put the treasuries in the charge of the *Kohen* Shelemiah, the scribe *Tzadok*, and Pedaiah of the *Leviim*; and assisting them was Hanan son of Zaccur son of Mattaniah – for they were regarded as trustworthy persons, and it was their duty to distribute the portions to their brothers.

יג וָאוֹצְרָה עַל־אוֹצָרוֹת שֶׁלֶמְיָה הַכֹּהֵן וְצָדוֹק הַסּוֹפֵר וּפְדָיָה מִן־הַלְוִיִּם וְעַל־יָדָם חָנָן בֶּן־זַכּוּר בֶּן־מַתַּנְיָה כִּי נֶאֱמָנִים נֶחְשָׁבוּ וַעֲלֵיהֶם לַחֲלֹק לַאֲחֵיהֶם:

14 O my God, remember me favorably for this, and do not blot out the devotion I showed toward the House of my God and its attendants.

יד זָכְרָה־לִּי אֱלֹהַי עַל־זֹאת וְאַל־תֶּמַח חֲסָדַי אֲשֶׁר עָשִׂיתִי בְּבֵית אֱלֹהַי וּבְמִשְׁמָרָיו:

15 At that time I saw men in *Yehuda* treading winepresses on the *Shabbat*, and others bringing heaps of grain and loading them onto asses, also wine, grapes, figs, and all sorts of goods, and bringing them into *Yerushalayim* on the *Shabbat*. I admonished them there and then for selling provisions.

טו בַּיָּמִים הָהֵמָּה רָאִיתִי בִיהוּדָה דֹּרְכִים־גִּתּוֹת בַּשַּׁבָּת וּמְבִיאִים הָעֲרֵמוֹת וְעֹמְסִים עַל־הַחֲמֹרִים וְאַף־יַיִן עֲנָבִים וּתְאֵנִים וְכָל־מַשָּׂא וּמְבִיאִים יְרוּשָׁלַ͏ִם בְּיוֹם הַשַּׁבָּת וָאָעִיד בְּיוֹם מִכְרָם צָיִד:

16 Tyrians who lived there brought fish and all sorts of wares and sold them on the *Shabbat* to the Judahites in *Yerushalayim*.

טז וְהַצֹּרִים יָשְׁבוּ בָהּ מְבִיאִים דָּאג וְכָל־מֶכֶר וּמֹכְרִים בַּשַּׁבָּת לִבְנֵי יְהוּדָה וּבִירוּשָׁלָ͏ִם:

17 I censured the nobles of *Yehuda*, saying to them, "What evil thing is this that you are doing, profaning the *Shabbat* day!

יז וָאָרִיבָה אֵת חֹרֵי יְהוּדָה וָאֹמְרָה לָהֶם מָה־הַדָּבָר הָרָע הַזֶּה אֲשֶׁר אַתֶּם עֹשִׂים וּמְחַלְּלִים אֶת־יוֹם הַשַּׁבָּת:

18 This is just what your ancestors did, and for it *Hashem* brought all this misfortune on this city; and now you give cause for further wrath against *Yisrael* by profaning the *Shabbat*!"

יח הֲלוֹא כֹה עָשׂוּ אֲבֹתֵיכֶם וַיָּבֵא אֱלֹהֵינוּ עָלֵינוּ אֵת כָּל־הָרָעָה הַזֹּאת וְעַל הָעִיר הַזֹּאת וְאַתֶּם מוֹסִיפִים חָרוֹן עַל־יִשְׂרָאֵל לְחַלֵּל אֶת־הַשַּׁבָּת:

19 When shadows filled the gateways of *Yerushalayim* at the approach of the *Shabbat*, I gave orders that the doors be closed, and ordered them not to be opened until after the *Shabbat*. I stationed some of my servants at the gates, so that no goods should enter on the *Shabbat*.

ט וַיְהִי כַּאֲשֶׁר צָלְלוּ שַׁעֲרֵי יְרוּשָׁלַם לִפְנֵי הַשַּׁבָּת וָאֹמְרָה וַיִּסָּגְרוּ הַדְּלָתוֹת וָאֹמְרָה אֲשֶׁר לֹא יִפְתָּחוּם עַד אַחַר הַשַּׁבָּת וּמִנְּעָרַי הֶעֱמַדְתִּי עַל־הַשְּׁעָרִים לֹא־יָבוֹא מַשָּׂא בְּיוֹם הַשַּׁבָּת:

vai-HEE ka-a-SHER tza-l'-LU sha-a-RAY y'-ru-sha-LA-im lif-NAY ha-sha-BAT va-o-m'-RAH va-yi-sa-g'-RU ha-d'-la-TOT va-o-m'-RAH a-SHER LO yif-ta-KHUM AD a-KHAR ha-sha-BAT u-mi-n'-a-RAI he-e-MAD-tee al ha-sh'-a-REEM lo ya-VO ma-SA b'-YOM ha-sha-BAT

20 Once or twice the merchants and the vendors of all sorts of wares spent the night outside *Yerushalayim*,

כ וַיָּלִינוּ הָרֹכְלִים וּמֹכְרֵי כָל־מִמְכָּר מִחוּץ לִירוּשָׁלָם פַּעַם וּשְׁתָּיִם:

21 but I warned them, saying, "What do you mean by spending the night alongside the wall? If you do so again, I will lay hands upon you!" From then on they did not come on the *Shabbat*.

כא וָאָעִידָה בָהֶם וָאֹמְרָה אֲלֵיהֶם מַדּוּעַ אַתֶּם לֵנִים נֶגֶד הַחוֹמָה אִם־תִּשְׁנוּ יָד אֶשְׁלַח בָּכֶם מִן־הָעֵת הַהִיא לֹא־בָאוּ בַּשַּׁבָּת:

22 I gave orders to the *Leviim* to purify themselves and come and guard the gates, to preserve the sanctity of the *Shabbat*. This too, O my God, remember to my credit, and spare me in accord with your abundant faithfulness.

כב וָאֹמְרָה לַלְוִיִּם אֲשֶׁר יִהְיוּ מִטַּהֲרִים וּבָאִים שֹׁמְרִים הַשְּׁעָרִים לְקַדֵּשׁ אֶת־יוֹם הַשַּׁבָּת גַּם־זֹאת זָכְרָה־לִּי אֱלֹהַי וְחוּסָה עָלַי כְּרֹב חַסְדֶּךָ:

23 Also at that time, I saw that *Yehudim* had married Ashdodite, Ammonite, and Moabite women;

כג גַּם בַּיָּמִים הָהֵם רָאִיתִי אֶת־הַיְּהוּדִים הֹשִׁיבוּ נָשִׁים אשדודיות [אַשְׁדֳּדִיּוֹת] עמוניות [עַמֳּנִיּוֹת] מוֹאֲבִיּוֹת:

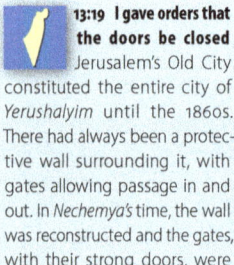

13:19 I gave orders that the doors be closed Jerusalem's Old City constituted the entire city of *Yerushalyim* until the 1860s. There had always been a protective wall surrounding it, with gates allowing passage in and out. In *Nechemya's* time, the wall was reconstructed and the gates, with their strong doors, were closed to bar passage from evildoers. When the Crusaders ruled over *Yerushalayim*, the walls surrounding the city had only four gates, but when Suleiman the Magnificent of the Ottoman Turkish Empire renovated the walls of *Yerushalyim* from 1538–42, he ensured that there were six functional gates. In 1887, the New Gate was added and the Tanners' Gate was discovered, and opened during

Gate of Mercy

excavations in the 1990s. Like *Nechemya's* gates, until 1887 the current Old City gates were closed each day before sunset and opened again at sunrise. Today, however, seven of the gates remain open all the time and have no doors. Only the Gate of Mercy on the eastern side of the Temple Mount wall remains sealed and, according to tradition, will be reopened in the days of the *Mashiach*. According to *Yechezkel*, in the future there will be twelve gates leading to the city of *Yerushalyim*, one for each of the twelve tribes of Israel (Ezekiel 48:31–34). No matter how many gates there are, "*Hashem* loves the gates of *Tzion*, more than all the dwellings of *Yaakov*" (Psalms 87:2), for they lead to his most precious city, *Yerushalayim*.

24 a good number of their children spoke the language of *Ashdod* and the language of those various peoples, and did not know how to speak Judean.

וּבְנֵיהֶם חֲצִי מְדַבֵּר אַשְׁדּוֹדִית וְאֵינָם מַכִּירִים לְדַבֵּר יְהוּדִית וְכִלְשׁוֹן עַם וָעָם:

*uv-nay-HEM kha-TZEE m'-da-BAYR ash-do-DEET v'-ay-NAM
ma-kee-REEM l'-da-BAYR y'-hu-DEET v'-khil-SHON am va-AM*

25 I censured them, cursed them, flogged them, tore out their hair, and adjured them by *Hashem*, saying, "You shall not give your daughters in marriage to their sons, or take any of their daughters for your sons or yourselves.

וָאָרִיב עִמָּם וָאֲקַלְלֵם וָאַכֶּה מֵהֶם אֲנָשִׁים וָאֶמְרְטֵם וָאַשְׁבִּיעֵם בֵּאלֹהִים אִם־תִּתְּנוּ בְנֹתֵיכֶם לִבְנֵיהֶם וְאִם־תִּשְׂאוּ מִבְּנֹתֵיהֶם לִבְנֵיכֶם וְלָכֶם:

26 It was just in such things that King *Shlomo* of *Yisrael* sinned! Among the many nations there was not a king like him, and so well loved was he by his God that *Hashem* made him king of all *Yisrael*, yet foreign wives caused even him to sin.

הֲלוֹא עַל־אֵלֶּה חָטָא־שְׁלֹמֹה מֶלֶךְ יִשְׂרָאֵל וּבַגּוֹיִם הָרַבִּים לֹא־הָיָה מֶלֶךְ כָּמֹהוּ וְאָהוּב לֵאלֹהָיו הָיָה וַיִּתְּנֵהוּ אֱלֹהִים מֶלֶךְ עַל־כָּל־יִשְׂרָאֵל גַּם־אוֹתוֹ הֶחֱטִיאוּ הַנָּשִׁים הַנָּכְרִיּוֹת:

27 How, then, can we acquiesce in your doing this great wrong, breaking faith with our God by marrying foreign women?"

וְלָכֶם הֲנִשְׁמַע לַעֲשֹׂת אֵת כָּל־הָרָעָה הַגְּדוֹלָה הַזֹּאת לִמְעֹל בֵּאלֹהֵינוּ לְהֹשִׁיב נָשִׁים נָכְרִיּוֹת:

28 One of the sons of Joiada son of the *Kohen Gadol Elyashiv* was a son-in-law of Sanballat the Horonite; I drove him away from me.

וּמִבְּנֵי יוֹיָדָע בֶּן־אֶלְיָשִׁיב הַכֹּהֵן הַגָּדוֹל חָתָן לְסַנְבַלַּט הַחֹרֹנִי וָאַבְרִיחֵהוּ מֵעָלָי:

29 Remember to their discredit, O my God, how they polluted the priesthood, the covenant of the *Kohanim* and *Leviim.*

זָכְרָה לָהֶם אֱלֹהָי עַל גָּאֳלֵי הַכְּהֻנָּה וּבְרִית הַכְּהֻנָּה וְהַלְוִיִּם:

30 I purged them of every foreign element, and arranged for the *Kohanim* and the *Leviim* to work each at his task by shifts,

וְטִהַרְתִּים מִכָּל־נֵכָר וָאַעֲמִידָה מִשְׁמָרוֹת לַכֹּהֲנִים וְלַלְוִיִּם אִישׁ בִּמְלַאכְתּוֹ:

31 and for the wood offering [to be brought] at fixed times and for the first fruits. O my God, remember it to my credit!

וּלְקֻרְבַּן הָעֵצִים בְּעִתִּים מְזֻמָּנוֹת וְלַבִּכּוּרִים זָכְרָה־לִּי אֱלֹהַי לְטוֹבָה:

Eliezer Ben-Yehuda
(1858–1922)

13:24 did not know how to speak Judean *Nechemya* bemoans the fact that in seventy years of exile the Jews of his generation forgot how to speak Hebrew. The situation was even worse in the modern era after 2,500 years of exile, when Hebrew was nearly extinct, reserved exclusively as the Jewish holy language for prayer and study. This all changed with the advent of the Zionist revival, thanks in large part to the efforts of one man, Eliezer Ben-Yehuda (1858–1922), who decided that "in order to have our own land and political life it is also necessary that we have a language to hold us together." Many scoffed at Ben-Yehuda's vision, but today Hebrew has been revived from the dustbin of history and is the official language of the State of Israel. Millions of Israeli Jews today converse in Hebrew, conduct their daily affairs in Hebrew, and can read the *Tanakh* in their original mother tongue as well. In the words of his biographer, "Before Ben-Yehuda people *could* speak Hebrew; after him, they *did.*"

List of Transliterated Words in *The Israel Bible*

The following is a list of nouns which have been transliterated into Hebrew in the English translation and commentary of *The Israel Bible*:

Hebrew Name	English Name	Pronunciation	Hebrew
Achan	Achan	a-KHAN	עָכָן
Achav	Ahab	akh-AV	אַחְאָב
Achaz	Ahaz	a-KHAZ	אָחָז
Achazyahu	Ahaziah	a-khaz-YA-hu	אֲחַזְיָהוּ
Achiezer	Ahiezer	a-khee-E-zer	אֲחִיעֶזֶר
Achihud	Ahihud	a-khee-HUD	אֲחִיהוּד
Achikam	Ahikam	a-khee-KAM	אֲחִיקָם
Achilud	Ahilud	a-khee-LUD	אֲחִילוּד
Achimelech	Ahimelech	a-khee-ME-lekh	אֲחִימֶלֶךְ
Achira	Ahira	a-khee-RA	אֲחִירַע
Achisamach	Ahisamach	a-khee-sa-MAKH	אֲחִיסָמָךְ
Achitofel	Ahithophel	a-khee-TO-fel	אֲחִיתֹפֶל
Achituv	Ahitub	a-khee-TUV	אֲחִיטוּב
Achiya	Ahijah	a-khi-YAH	אֲחִיָּה
Adam	Adam	a-DAM	אָדָם
Adar	Adar	a-DAR	אֲדָר
Adoniyahu	Adonijah	a-do-ni-YA-hu	אֲדֹנִיָּהוּ
Adulam	Adullam	a-du-LAM	עֲדֻלָּם
Agur	Agur	a-GUR	אָגוּר
Aharon	Aaron	a-ha-RON	אַהֲרֹן
Amasa	Amasa	a-ma-SA	עֲמָשָׂא
Amatzya	Amaziah	a-matz-YAH	אֲמַצְיָה
Amen	Amen	a-MAYN	אָמֵן
Amiel	Ammiel	a-mee-AYL	עַמִּיאֵל
Aminadav	Amminadab	a-mee-na-DAV	עַמִּינָדָב
Amitai	Amittai	a-mi-TAI	אֲמִתַּי
Amnon	Amnon	am-NON	אַמְנֹן

Hebrew Name	English Name	Pronunciation	Hebrew
Amon	Amon	a-MON	אָמוֹן
Amos	Amos	a-MOS	עָמוֹס
Amotz	Amoz	a-MOTZ	אָמוֹץ
Amram	Amram	am-RAM	עַמְרָם
Anatot	Anathoth	a-na-TOT	עֲנָתוֹת
Aron	Ark	a-RON	אָרוֹן
Aron HaBrit	Ark of the Covenant	a-RON ha-b'-REET	אָרוֹן הַבְּרִית
Arpachshad	Arpachshad	ar-pakh-SHAD	אַרְפַּכְשַׁד
Asa	Asa	a-SA	אָסָא
Asael	Asahel	a-sah-AYL	עֲשָׂהאֵל
Asaf	Asaph	a-SAF	אָסָף
Ashdod	Ashdod	ash-DOD	אַשְׁדּוֹד
Asher	Asher	a-SHAYR	אָשֵׁר
Ashkelon	Ashkelon	ash-k'-LON	אַשְׁקְלוֹן
Atalya	Athaliah	a-tal-YAH	עֲתַלְיָה
Avdon	Abdon	av-DON	עַבְדּוֹן
Avichayil	Abihail	a-vee-KHA-yil	אֲבִיחַיִל
Avidan	Abidan	a-vee-DAN	אֲבִידָן
Avigail	Abigail	a-vee-GA-yil	אֲבִיגַיִל
Avihu	Abihu	a-vee-HU	אֲבִיהוּא
Avimelech	Abimelech	a-vee-ME-lekh	אֲבִימָלֶךְ
Avinadav	Abinadab	a-vee-na-DAV	אֲבִינָדָב
Aviram	Abiram	a-vee-RAM	אֲבִירָם
Avishai	Abishai	a-vee-SHAI	אֲבִישַׁי
Aviya	Abijah	a-vi-YAH	אֲבִיָּה
Aviyam	Abijam	a-vi-YAM	אֲבִיָּם
Avner	Abner	av-NAYR	אַבְנֵר
Avraham	Abraham	av-ra-HAM	אַבְרָהָם
Avram	Abram	av-RAM	אַבְרָם
Avshalom	Absalom	av-sha-LOM	אַבְשָׁלוֹם
Azarya	Azariah	a-zar-YAH	עֲזַרְיָה
Azeika	Azekah	a-zay-KAH	עֲזֵקָה
Azza	Gaza	a-ZAH	עַזָּה

Hebrew Name	English Name	Pronunciation	Hebrew
B'nei Yisrael	The Children of Israel	b'-NAY yis-ra-AYL	בְּנֵי יִשְׂרָאֵל
Barak	Barak	ba-rakh-AYL	בָּרָק
Baruch	Baruch	ba-RUKH	בָּרוּךְ
Barzilai	Barzillai	bar-zi-LAI	בַּרְזִלַּי
Basha	Baasa	ba-SHA	בַּעְשָׁא
Batsheva	Bath-sheba	bat-SHE-va	בַּת־שֶׁבַע
Be'er Sheva	Beer-sheba	b'-AYR SHE-va	בְּאֵר שֶׁבַע
Be'eri	Beeri	b'-ay-REE	בְּאֵרִי
Beit Aven	Beth-aven	bayt A-ven	בֵּית אָוֶן
Beit El	Beth-el	bayt el	בֵּית אֵל
Beit Hamikdash	Temple	bayt ha-mik-DASH	בֵּית הַמִּקְדָּשׁ
Beit Lechem	Beth-lehem	bayt LE-khem	בֵּית לָחֶם
Beit Shean	Beth-shean	bayt sh'-AN	בֵּית שְׁאָן
Beit Shemesh	Beth-shemesh	bayt SHE-mesh	בֵּית שֶׁמֶשׁ
Berechya	Berechiah	be-rekh-YAH	בֶּרֶכְיָה
Betzalel	Bezalel	b'-tzal-AYL	בְּצַלְאֵל
Bilha	Bilhah	bil-HAH	בִּלְהָה
Binyamin	Benjamin	bin-ya-MIN	בִּנְיָמִין
Boaz	Boaz	BO-az	בֹּעַז
Buki	Bukki	bu-KEE	בֻּקִּי
Buzi	Buzi	bu-ZEE	בּוּזִי
Carmel	Carmel	kar-MEL	כַּרְמֶל
Chachalya	Hacaliah	kha-khal-YAH	חֲכַלְיָה
Chagai	Haggai	kha-GAI	חַגַּי
Chana	Hannah	kha-NAH	חַנָּה
Chanamel	Hanamel	kha-nam-AYL	חֲנַמְאֵל
Chanani	Hanani	kha-NA-nee	חֲנָנִי
Chananya	Hananiah	kha-nan-YAH	חֲנַנְיָה
Chaniel	Hanniel	kha-nee-AYL	חַנִּיאֵל
Chanoch	Enoch	kha-NOKH	חֲנוֹךְ
Chava	Eve	kha-VAH	חַוָּה
Chavakuk	Habakkuk	kha-va-KUK	חֲבַקּוּק
Chermon	Hermon	kher-MON	חֶרְמוֹן

Hebrew Name	English Name	Pronunciation	Hebrew
Chetzron	Hezron	khetz-RON	חֶצְרוֹן
Chever	Heber	KHE-ver	חֶבֶר
Chevron	Hebron	khev-RON	חֶבְרוֹן
Chilkiyahu	Hilkiah	khil-ki-YA-hu	חִלְקִיָּהוּ
Chizkiyahu	Hezekiah	khiz-ki-YA-hu	חִזְקִיָּהוּ
Chofni	Hophni	khof-NEE	חָפְנִי
Chogla	Hoglah	khog-LAH	חָגְלָה
Chulda	Hulda	khul-DAH	חֻלְדָּה
Chur	Hur	Khur	חוּר
Dan	Dan	Dan	דָּן
Daniel	Daniel	da-ni-YAYL	דָּנִיֵּאל
Datan	Dathan	da-TAN	דָּתָן
David	David	da-VID	דָּוִד
Devora	Deborah	d'-vo-RAH	דְּבוֹרָה
Dina	Dinah	DEE-nah	דִּינָה
Doeg Ha'adomi	Doeg the Edomite	do-AYG ha-a-do-MEE	דּוֹאֵג הָאֲדֹמִי
Efraim	Ephraim	ef-RA-yim	אֶפְרַיִם
Efrat	Ephrat	ef-RAT	אֶפְרָתָה
Efrat	Ephrathah	ef-RA-tah	אֶפְרָתָה
Ehud	Ehud	ay-HUD	אֵהוּד
Eila	Elah	AY-lah	אֵלָה
Eilon	Elon	ay-LON	אֵילוֹן
Ein Gedi	En-gedi	ayn GE-dee	עֵין גֶּדִי
Elazar	Eleazar	el-a-ZAR	אֶלְעָזָר
Elchanan	Elhanan	el-kha-NAN	אֶלְחָנָן
Eli	Eli	ay-LEE	עֵלִי
Eliav	Eliab	e-lee-AV	אֱלִיאָב
Elidad	Elidad	e-lee-DAD	אֱלִידָד
Eliezer	Eliezer	e-lee-E-zer	אֱלִיעֶזֶר
Elimelech	Elimelech	e-lee-ME-lekh	אֱלִימֶלֶךְ
Elisha	Elisha	e-lee-SHA	אֱלִישָׁע
Elishama	Elishama	e-lee-sha-MA	אֱלִישָׁמָע
Elisheva	Elisheba	e-lee-SHE-va	אֱלִישֶׁבַע

Hebrew Name	English Name	Pronunciation	Hebrew
Elitzafan	Eli-zaphan	e-lee-tza-FAN	אֱלִיצָפָן
Elitzur	Elizur	e-lee-TZUR	אֱלִיצוּר
Eliyahu	Elijah	ay-li-YA-hu	אֵלִיָּהוּ
Elkana	Elkanah	el-ka-NAH	אֶלְקָנָה
Elyasaf	Eliasaph	el-ya-SAF	אֶלְיָסָף
Elyashiv	Eliashib	el-ya-SHEEV	אֶלְיָשִׁיב
Enosh	Enosh	e-NOSH	אֱנוֹשׁ
Er	Er	ayr	עֵר
Eshtaol	Eshtaol	esh-ta-OL	אֶשְׁתָּאֹל
Esther	Esther	es-TAYR	אֶסְתֵּר
Eved Melech	Ebed-melech	E-ved ME-lekh	עֶבֶד־מֶלֶךְ
Even Ha-Ezer	Eben-Ezer	E-ven ha-E-zer	אֶבֶן הָעֶזֶר
Ever	Eber	AY-ver	עֵבֶר
Evyatar	Abiathar	ev-ya-TAR	אֶבְיָתָר
Ezra	Ezra	ez-RA	עֶזְרָא
Gad	Gad	gad	גָּד
Gadi	Gaddi	ga-DEE	גַּדִּי
Gadiel	Gaddiel	ga-dee-AYL	גַּדִּיאֵל
Gamliel	Gamaliel	gam-lee-AYL	גַּמְלִיאֵל
Gedalia	Gedaliah	g'-dal-YA (hu)	גְּדַלְיָהוּ
Gedera	Gederah	g'-day-RAH	גְּדֵרָה
Gershom	Gershom	gay-r'-SHOM	גֵּרְשֹׁום
Gershon	Gershon	gay-r'-SHON	גֵּרְשׁוֹן
Geshem	Geshem	GE-shem	גֶּשֶׁם
Geuel	Geuel	g'-u-AYL	גְּאוּאֵל
Gidon	Gideon	gid-ON	גִּדְעוֹן
Gilad	Gilead	gil-AD	גִּלְעָד
Gilgal	Gilgal	gil-GAL	גִּלְגָּל
Giva	Gibeah	giv-AH	גִּבְעָה
Givon	Gibeon	giv-ON	גִּבְעוֹן
Hadassa	Hadassah	ha-da-SAH	הֲדַסָּה
Har Eival	Mount Ebal	ay-VAL	הַר עֵיבָל
Har Gerizim	Mount Gerizim	g'-ri-ZEEM	הַר גְּרִזִים

Hebrew Name	English Name	Pronunciation	Hebrew
Har HaBayit	Temple Mount	har ha-BA-yit	הַר הַבַּיִת
Har HaZeitim	the Mount of Olives	har ha-zay-TEEM	הַר הַזֵּיתִים
Hashem	Lord/God		
Hayman	Heman	hay-MAN	הֵימָן
Hoshea	Hosea	ho-SHAY-a	הוֹשֵׁעַ
Ido	Iddo	i-DO	עִדּוֹ
Imanu-El	Immanuel	i-MA-nu ayl	עִמָּנוּ אֵל
Ish-boshet	Ish-bosheth	eesh BO-shet	אִישׁ־בֹּשֶׁת
Itamar	Ithamar	ee-ta-MAR	אִיתָמָר
Itiel	Ithiel	ee-tee-AYL	אִיתִיאֵל
Ivtzan	Ibzan	iv-TZAN	אִבְצָן
Iyov	Job	i-YOV	אִיּוֹב
Kadmiel	Kadmiel	kad-mee-AYL	קַדְמִיאֵל
Kalev	Caleb	ka-LAYV	כָּלֵב
Keesh	Kish	keesh	קִישׁ
Kehat	Kohath	k'-HAT	קְהָת
Keinan	Kenan	kay-NAN	קֵינָן
Kemuel	Kemuel	k'-mu-AYL	קְמוּאֵל
Keruvim	Cherubim	k'-ru-VEEM	כְּרוּבִים
Kilyon	Chilion	kil-YON	כִלְיוֹן
Kiryat Arba	Kiriath-arba	keer-YAT AR-bah	קִרְיַת אַרְבַּע
Kiryat Sefer	Kiriath-sepher	keer-YAT SAY-fer	קִרְיַת־סֵפֶר
Kiryat Ye'arim	Kiriath-jearim	keer-YAT y'-a-REEM	קִרְיַת יְעָרִים
Kislev	Chislev	kis-LAYV	כִּסְלֵו
Kohanim	Priests	ko-ha-NEEM	כֹּהֲנִים
Kohelet	Koheleth	ko-HE-let	קֹהֶלֶת
Kohen	Priest	ko-HAYN	כֹּהֵן
Kohen Gadol	High Priest	ko-HAYN ga-DOL	כֹּהֵן גָּדוֹל
Korach	Korah	KO-rakh	קֹרַח
Kushi	Cushi	ku-SHEE	כּוּשִׁי
Lachish	Lachish	la-KHEESH	לָכִישׁ
Leah	Leah	lay-AH	לֵאָה
Lemech	Lamech	LE-mekh	לֶמֶךְ

Hebrew Name	English Name	Pronunciation	Hebrew
Lemuel	Lemuel	l'-mu-AYL	לְמוֹאֵל
Levi	Levi	lay-VEE	לֵוִי
Leviim	Levites	l'-vee-IM	לְוִיִּם
Machla	Mahlah	makh-LAH	מַחְלָה
Machlon	Mahlon	makh-LON	מַחְלוֹן
Machseya	Mahseiah	makh-say-YAH	מַחְסֵיָה
Malachi	Malachi	mal-a-KHEE	מַלְאָכִי
Manoach	Manoah	ma-NO-akh	מָנוֹחַ
Mashiach	Messiah	ma-SHEE-akh	מָשִׁיחַ
Mefiboshet	Mephibosheth	m'-fee-VO-shet	מְפִיבֹשֶׁת
Mehalalel	Mahalalel	ma-ha-lal-AYL	מַהֲלַלְאֵל
Menachem	Menahem	m'-na-KHAYM	מְנַחֵם
Menashe	Menasseh	m'-na-SHEH	מְנַשֶּׁה
Menorah	Candlestick	m'-no-RAH	מְנֹרָה
Merari	Merari	m'-ra-REE	מְרָרִי
Metushelach	Methusaleh	m'-tu-SHE-lakh	מְתוּשָׁלַח
Micha	Micah	mee-KHAH	מִיכָה
Michael	Michael	mee-kha-AYL	מִיכָאֵל
Michaihu	Micaiah	mee-KHAI-hu	מִיכָיְהוּ
Michal	Michal	mee-KHAL	מִיכַל
Milka	Milcah	mil-KAH	מִלְכָּה
Miriam	Miriam	mir-YAM	מִרְיָם
Mishael	Mishael	mee-sha-AYL	מִישָׁאֵל
Mishkan	Tabernacle	mish-KAN	מִשְׁכָּן
Mitzpa	Mizpah	mitz-PAH	מִצְפָּה
Mizbayach	Altar	miz-BAY-akh	מִזְבֵּחַ
Mordechai	Mordecai	mor-d'-KHAI	מָרְדְּכַי
Moriah	Moriah	mo-ri-YAH	מוֹרִיָּה
Moshe	Moses	mo-SHEH	מֹשֶׁה
Nachbi	Nahbi	nakh-BEE	נַחְבִּי
Nachor	Nahor	na-KHOR	נָחוֹר
Nachshon	Nahshon	nakh-SHON	נַחְשׁוֹן
Nachum	Nahum	na-KHUM	נַחוּם

Hebrew Name	English Name	Pronunciation	Hebrew
Nadav	Nadab	na-DAV	נָדָב
Naftali	Naphtali	naf-ta-LEE	נַפְתָּלִי
Naomi	Naomi	na-o-MEE	נָעֳמִי
Natan	Nathan	na-TAN	נָתָן
Naval	Nabal	na-VAL	נָבָל
Navi	Prophet	na-VEE	נָבִיא
Navot	Naboth	na-VAL	נָבָל
Nechemya	Nehemiah	n'-khem-YAH	נְחֶמְיָה
Negev	Negeb	NE-gev	נֶגֶב
Nerya	Neriah	nay-ri-YAH	נֵרִיָּה
Netanel	Nethanel	n'-tan-AYL	נְתַנְאֵל
Neviah	Prophetess	n'-vee-AH	נְבִיאָה
Neviim	Prophets	n'-vee-EEM	נְבִיאִים
Nisan	Nisan	nee-SAN	נִיסָן
Noa	Noah	no-AH	נֹעָה
Noach	Noah	NO-akh	נֹחַ
Nov	Nob	nov	נֹב
Nun	Nun	nun	נוּן
Oded	Oded	o-DAYD	עוֹדֵד
Ohola	Oholah	a-ho-LAH	אָהֳלָה
Oholiav	Oholiab	o-ha-lee-AV	אָהֳלִיאָב
Oholiva	Oholibah	a-ho-lee-VAH	אָהֳלִיבָה
Omri	Omri	om-REE	עָמְרִי
Onan	Onan	o-NAN	אוֹנָן
Otniel	Othniel	ot-nee-AYL	עָתְנִיאֵל
Ovadya	Obadiah	o-vad-YAH	עֹבַדְיָה
Oved	Obed	o-VAYD	עוֹבֵד
Oved Edom	Obed Edom	o-VAYD e-DOM	עוֹבֵד אֱדוֹם
Pagiel	Pagiel	pag-ee-AYL	פַּגְעִיאֵל
Palti	Palti	pal-TEE	פַּלְטִי
Paltiel	Paltiel	pal-tee-AYL	פַּלְטִיאֵל
Pekach	Pekah	PE-kakh	פֶּקַח
Pedael	Pedahel	p'-da-AYL	פְּדַהְאֵל

Hebrew Name	English Name	Pronunciation	Hebrew
Pekachya	Pekahiah	p'-kakh-YAH	פְּקַחְיָה
Peleg	Peleg	PE-leg	פֶּלֶג
Penina	Peninnah	p'-ni-NAH	פְּנִנָּה
Peretz	Perez	PE-retz	פֶּרֶץ
Petuel	Pethuel	p'-tu-AYL	פְּתוּאֵל
Pinchas	Phinehas	peen-KHAS	פִּינְחָס
Rachel	Rachel	ra-KHAYL	רָחֵל
Ram	Ram	ram	רָם
Rama	Ramah	ra-MAH	רָמָה
Re'u	Reu	r'-U	רְעוּ
Rechovam	Rehoboam	r'-khav-AM	רְחַבְעָם
Reuven	Reuben	r'-u-VAYN	רְאוּבֵן
Rivka	Rebecca	riv-KAH	רִבְקָה
Rut	Ruth	rut	רוּת
Salma	Salmon/Salmah	sal-MAH	שַׂלְמָה
Salmon	Salmon	sal-MON	שַׂלְמוֹן
Sara	Sarah	sa-RAH	שָׂרָה
Sarai	Sarai	sa-RAI	שָׂרַי
Selah	Selah	SE-lah	סֶלָה
Seraya	Seraiah	s'-ra-YAH	שְׂרָיָה
Serug	Serug	s'-RUG	שְׂרוּג
Setur	Sethur	s'-TUR	סְתוּר
Shaarayim	Shaaraim	sha-a-RA-yim	שַׁעֲרַיִם
Shabbat	Sabbath	sha-BAT	שַׁבָּת
Shabbatot	Sabbaths	sha-ba-TOT	שַׁבָּתוֹת
Shafan	Shaphan	sha-FAN	שָׁפָן
Shafat	Shaphat	sha-FAT	שָׁפָט
Shalem	Salem	sha-LAYM	שָׁלֵם
Shalum	Shallum	sha-LUM	שַׁלּוּם
Shamgar	Shamgar	sham-GAR	שַׁמְגַּר
Shamua	Shammua	sha-MU-a	שַׁמּוּעַ
Shaul	Saul	sha-UL	שָׁאוּל
Shealtiel	Shealtiel	sh'-al-tee-AYL	שְׁאַלְתִּיאֵל

Hebrew Name	English Name	Pronunciation	Hebrew
Shear Yashuv	Shear-Jashub	sh'-AR ya-SHUV	שְׁאָר יָשׁוּב
Shechanya	Shecaniah	sh'-khan-YAH	שְׁכַנְיָה
Shechem	Shechem	sh'-KHEM	שְׁכֶם
Sheila	Shelah	shay-LAH	שֵׁלָה
Shelach	Shelah	SHE-lakh	שֶׁלַח
Shelumiel	Shelumiel	sh'-lu-mee-AYL	שְׁלֻמִיאֵל
Shem	Shem	Shaym	שֵׁם
Shemaya	Shemaiah	sh'-ma-YAH	שְׁמַעְיָה
Sheshbatzar	Sheshbazzar	shaysh-ba-TZAR	שֵׁשְׁבַּצַּר
Shet	Seth	Shayt	שֵׁת
Shevat	Shebat	sh'-VAT	שְׁבָט
Shilo	Shiloh	shi-LOH	שלה
Shim'i	Shimei	shim-EE	שִׁמְעִי
Shimon	Simeon	shim-ON	שִׁמְעוֹן
Shimshon	Samson	shim-SHON	שִׁמְשׁוֹן
Shlomo	Solomon	sh'-lo-MOH	שְׁלֹמֹה
Shmuel	Samuel	sh'-mu-AYL	שְׁמוּאֵל
Shofar	Horn	sho-FAR	שׁוֹפָר
Shofarot	Horns	sho-fa-ROT	שׁוֹפָרוֹת
Shomron	Samaria	sho-m'-RON	שֹׁמְרוֹן
Sivan	Sivan	see-VAN	סִיוָן
Tamar	Tamar	ta-MAR	תָּמָר
Tanakh	Hebrew Bible	ta-NAKH	תָּנַ"ךְ
Tapuach	Tappuah	ta-PU-akh	תַּפּוּחַ
Tavor	Tabor	ta-VOR	תָּבוֹר
Tekoa	Tekoa	t'-KO-a	תְּקוֹעַה
Terach	Terah	TE-rakh	תֶּרַח
Teveria	Tiberias	t'-ver-YAH	טְבֶרְיָה
Tevet	Tebeth	tay-VAYT	טֵבֵת
Tirtza	Tirzah	tir-TZAH	תִּרְצָה
Tola	Tola	to-LA	תּוֹלָע
Tzadok	Zadok	tza-DOK	צָדוֹק
Tzefanya	Zephaniah	tz'-fan-YAH	צְפַנְיָה

Hebrew Name	English Name	Pronunciation	Hebrew
Tzelofchad	Zelophehad	tz'-lo-f-KHAD	צְלָפְחָד
Tzeruya	Zeruiah	tz'-ru-YAH	צְרוּיָה
Tzfat	Safed	tz'-FAT	צְפַת
Tzidkiyahu	Zedekiah	tzid-ki-YA-hu	צִדְקִיָּהוּ
Tziklag	Ziklag	tzi-k'-LAG	צִקְלַג
Tzion	Zion	tzi-YON	צִיּוֹן
Tzipora	Zipporah	tzi-po-RAH	צִפֹּרָה
Tzora	Zorah	tzor-AH	צָרְעָה
Tzuriel	Zuriel	tzu-ree-AYL	צוּרִיאֵל
Ukal	Ucal	u-KAL	אֻכָל
Uri	Uri	u-REE	אוּרִי
Uriya	Uriah	u-ri-YAH	אוּרִיָה
Utz	Uz	Utz	עוּץ
Uzziyahu	Uzziah	u-zi-YA-hu	עֻזִּיָּהוּ
Yaakov	Jacob	ya-a-KOV	יַעֲקֹב
Yachaziel	Jahaziel	ya-kha-zee-AYL	יַחֲזִיאֵל
Yael	Jael	ya-AYL	יָעֵל
Yaffo	Joppa/Jaffa	ya-FO	יָפוֹ
Yair	Jair	ya-EER	יָאִיר
Yakeh	Jakeh	ya-KEH	יָקֶה
Yarden	Jordan	yar-DAYN	יַרְדֵּן
Yarmut	Jarmuth	yar-MUT	יַרְמוּת
Yechezkel	Ezekiel	y'-khez-KAYL	יְחֶזְקֵאל
Yechiel	Jehiel	y'-khee-AYL	יְחִיאֵל
Yechonya	Jeconiah	y'-khon-YAH	יְכָנְיָה
Yedutun	Jeduthun	y'-du-TUN	יְדוּתוּן
Yehoachaz	Jehoahaz	y'-ho-a-KHAZ	יְהוֹאָחָז
Yehoash	Jehoash	y'-ho-ASH	יְהוֹאָשׁ
Yehochanan	Jehohanan	y'-ho-kha-NAN	יְהוֹחָנָן
Yehonatan	Jonathan	y'-ho-na-TAN	יְהוֹנָתָן
Yehoram	Jehoram	y'-ho-RAM	יְהוֹרָם
Yehoshafat	Jehoshaphat	y'-ho-sha-FAT	יְהוֹשָׁפָט
Yehoshavat	Jehoshabeath	y'-ho-shav-AT	יְהוֹשַׁבְעַת

Hebrew Name	English Name	Pronunciation	Hebrew
Yehosheva	Jehosheba	y-ho-SHE-va	יְהוֹשֶׁבַע
Yehoshua	Joshua	y'-ho-SHU-a	יְהוֹשֻׁעַ
Yehotzadak	Jehozadak	y'-ho-tza-DAK	יְהוֹצָדָק
Yehoyachin	Jehoiachin	y'-ho-ya-KHEEN	יְהוֹיָכִין
Yehoyada	Jehoiada	y'-ho-ya-DA	יְהוֹיָדָע
Yehoyakim	Jehoiakim	y'-ho-ya-KEEM	יְהוֹיָקִים
Yehu	Jehu	yay-HU	יֵהוּא
Yehuda	Judah	y'-hu-DAH	יְהוּדָה
Yehudi	Jew	y'-hu-DEE	יְהוּדִי
Yehudim	Jews	y'-hu-DEEM	יְהוּדִים
Yered	Jared	YE-red	יֶרֶד
Yericho	Jericho	y'-ree-KHO	יְרִיחוֹ
Yerovam	Jeroboam	ya-rov-AM	יָרָבְעָם
Yerubaal	Jerubbaal	y'-ru-BA-al	יְרֻבַּעַל
Yerushalayim	Jerusalem	y'-ru-sha-LA-yim	יְרוּשָׁלַיִם
Yeshayahu	Isaiah	y'-sha-YA-hu	יְשַׁעְיָהוּ
Yeshua	Jeshua	yay-SHU-a	יֵשׁוּעַ
Yiftach	Jephthah	yif-TAKH	יִפְתָּח
Yigal	Igal	yig-AL	יִגְאָל
Yirmiyahu	Jeremiah	yir-m'-YA-hu	יִרְמְיָהוּ
Yishai	Jesse	yi-SHAI	יִשַׁי
Yisrael	Israel	yis-ra-AYL	יִשְׂרָאֵל
Yissachar	Issachar	yi-sa-KHAR	יִשָּׂשכָר
Yitzchak	Issac	yitz-KHAK	יִצְחָק
Yizrael	Jezreel	yiz-r'-EL	יִזְרְעֶאל
Yoash	Joash	yo-ASH	יוֹאָשׁ
Yoav	Joab	yo-AV	יוֹאָב
Yochanan	Johanan	yo-kha-NAN	יוֹחָנָן
Yocheved	Jochebed	yo-KHE-ved	יוֹכֶבֶד
Yoel	Joel	yo-AYL	יוֹאֵל
Yona	Jonah	yo-NAH	יוֹנָה
Yonadav	Jonadab	yo-na-DAV	יוֹנָדָב
Yonatan	Jonathan	yo-na-TAN	יוֹנָתָן

Hebrew Name	English Name	Pronunciation	Hebrew
Yoram	Joram	yo-RAM	יוֹרָם
Yosef	Joseph	yo-SAYF	יוֹסֵף
Yoshiyahu	Josiah	yo-shi-YA-hu	יֹאשִׁיָהוּ
Yotam	Jotham	yo-TAM	יוֹתָם
Yotzadak	Jozadak	yo-tza-DAK	יוֹצָדָק
Yozavad	Jozabad	yo-za-VAD	יוֹזָבָד
Zanoach	Zanoah	za-NO-akh	זָנוֹחַ
Zecharya	Zechariah	z'-khar-YAH	זְכַרְיָה
Zerach	Zerah	ZE-rakh	זֶרַח
Zerubavel	Zerubbabel	z'-ru-ba-VEL	זְרֻבָּבֶל
Zevulun	Zebulun	z'-vu-LUN	זְבוּלֻן
Zilpa	Zilpah	zil-PAH	זִלְפָּה
Zimri	Zimri	zim-REE	זִמְרִי

Jewish Holidays

Chanukah	Hanukkah	kha-nu-KAH	חֲנֻכָּה
Pesach	Passover	PE-sakh	פֶּסַח
Purim	Purim	pu-REEM	פּוּרִים
Rosh Hashana	Jewish New Year	rosh ha-sha-NAH	רֹאשׁ הַשָּׁנָה
Shavuot	Feast of Weeks	sha-vu-OT	שָׁבוּעוֹת
Shemini Atzeret	Eight Day of Assembly	sh'-mee-NEE a-TZE-ret	שְׁמִינִי עֲצֶרֶת
Sukkot	Feast of Tabernacles	su-KOT	סֻכּוֹת
Yom Kippur	Day of Atonement	yom kee-PUR	יוֹם כִּיפּוּר

Biblical Measurements

Amah	Cubit	a-MAH	אַמָה
Amot	Cubits	a-MOT	אַמוֹת
Bat	Bath	bat	בַּת
Batim	Baths	ba-TEEM	בָּתִּים
Beka	half-shekel	BE-ka	בָּקַע
Chomarim	Homers	kho-ma-REEM	חֳמָרִים
Chomer	Homer	KHO-mer	חֹמֶר
Efah	Ephah	ay-FAH	אֵיפָה
Geira	Gerah	gay-RAH	גֵּרָה

Hebrew Name	English Name	Pronunciation	Hebrew
Gomed	Gomed	GO- med	גֹּמֶד
Hin	Hin	heen	הִין
Kav	kab	kav	קַב
Kesita	kesitah	k'-see-TAH	קְשִׂיטָה
Kikar	talent	ki-KAR	כִּכָּר
Kikarim	talents	ki-ka-RIM	כִּכְּרִים
Kor	kor	kor	כֹּר
Letek	lethech	LE-tek	לֶתֶךְ
Log	Log	log	לֹג
Maneh	Mina	ma-NEH	מָנֶה
Manim	Minas	ma-NEEM	מָנִים
Omer	Omer	O-mer	עֹמֶר
Pim	Pim	peem	פִּים
Se'ah	Seah	say-AH	סְאָה
Se'eem	Seahs	s'-EEM	סְאִים
Shekalim	Shekels	sh'-ka-LEEM	שְׁקָלִים
Shekel	Shekel	SHE-kel	שֶׁקֶל
Tefach	Handbreadth	TE-fakh	טֶפַח
Zeret	Span	ZE-ret	זֶרֶת

Photo Credits

Ezra

1:11 SJ Travel Photo and Video/Shutterstock.com, **2:70** Moshe Milner, Government Press Office (Israel), **3:1** Yuri Yavnik/Shutterstock.com, **4:12** By https://www.flickr.com/people/45644610@N03 – https://www.flickr.com /photos/idfonline/6529877229/, CC BY-SA 3.0, https://commons.wikimedia .org/w/index.php?curid=34357516, **5:2** Konstantnin/Shutterstock.com, **6:14** Zoltan Kluger, Government Press Office (Israel), **7:9** By Tomer hu – Own work, CC BY-SA 4.0, https://commons.wikimedia.org/w/index.php?curid =43945537, **8:31** Teddy Brauner, Wikimedia Commons, **9:8** Moshe Milner, Government Press Office (Israel), **10:9** Moshe Milner, Government Press Office (Israel)

Nechemaya

1:9 SJ Travel Photo and Video/Shutterstock.com, **2:17** Aleksandra H. Kossowska/ Shutterstock.com, **3:15** Itamar Babai, Wikimedia Commons, **4:11** Moshe Milner, Government Press Office (Israel), **5:15** Great Siberia Studio/Shutterstock. com, **6:1** Eitan F, Wikimedia Commons, **7:4** volkova natalia/Shutterstock.com, **8:15** Ryan Rodrick Beiler/Shutterstock.com, **9:36** By Israel Defense Forces – IDF Medical Aid Team Performing Surgery in Haiti Field Hospital, CC BY 2.0, https://commons.wikimedia.org/w/index.php?curid=34362392, **10:34** mikhail/ Shutterstock.com, **11:1** StockStudio Aerials/Shutterstock.com, **12:38** Rachel Lyra Hospodar, Wikimedia Commons, **13:19** Wilson44691, Wikimedia Commons

Map of Modern-Day Israel and its Neighbors

The following is a map of modern-day Israel and the surrounding countries

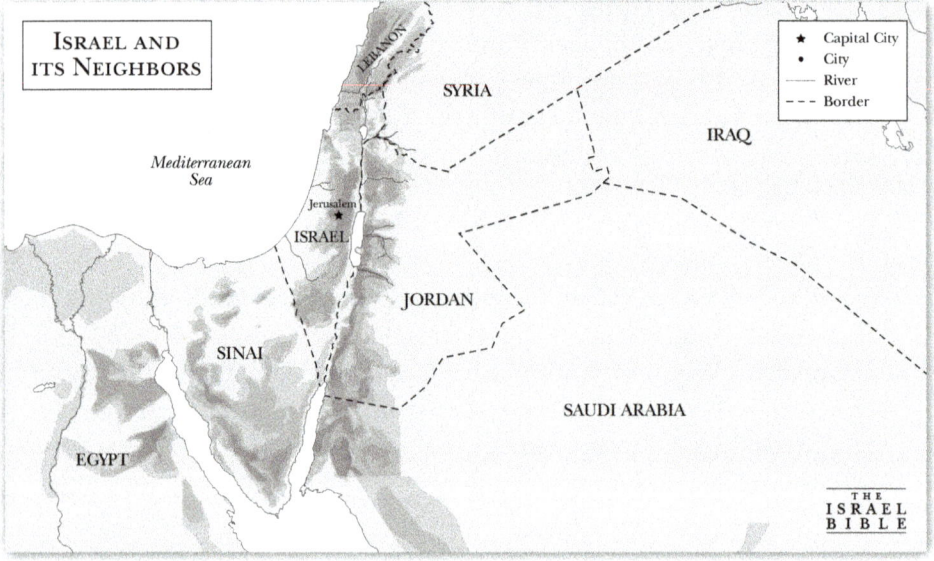

NOTES

NOTES

NOTES

NOTES

NOTES

For more inspiring commentary,
interactive maps, educational videos,
vivid photographs and more,
please visit our website

www.TheIsraelBible.com

THE
ISRAEL
BIBLE